Man Proposes, God Disposes

To Lawrence,
with warm greetings
from a fellow Albertan,

[signature]

Our Lives: Diary, Memoir, and Letters

SERIES EDITOR: JANICE DICKIN

Today's students, living in a world of blogs, understand that there is much to be learned from the everyday lives of everyday people. Our Lives seeks to make available previously unheard voices from the past and present. Social history in general contests the construction of history as the story of elites, and the act of making available the lives of everyday people — of remarking on the unremarkable — further subverts the traditional assumptions of historiography. It also reinforces the mission of Athabasca University, which, as Canada's open university, seeks to include rather than exclude. At the same time, Our Lives aims to make available books that make good reading, books that those who wrote them would enjoy themselves.

Series Titles

A Very Capable Life: The Autobiography of Zarah Petri
John Leigh Walters

Letters from the Lost: A Memoir of Discovery
Helen Waldstein Wilkes

A Woman of Valour: The Biography of Marie-Louise Bouchard Labelle
Claire Trépanier

Man Proposes, God Disposes: Recollections of a French Pioneer
Pierre Maturié, translated by Vivien Bosley

Man Proposes, God Disposes

Recollections of a French Pioneer

PIERRE MATURIÉ

A translation of
Athabasca, Terre de ma jeunesse
by Vivien Bosley

With an introduction
by Robert Wardhaugh

AU PRESS

First published in France as *Athabasca, Terre de ma jeunesse* (Paris: La Pensée universelle, 1972).
English translation copyright © 2013 Vivien Bosley.
Introduction copyright © 2013 Robert Wardhaugh.

Published by AU Press, Athabasca University
1200, 10011 – 109 Street, Edmonton, AB T5J 3S8

ISBN 978-1-926836-55-3 (print) 978-1-926836-56-0 (PDF) 978-1-926836-57-7 (epub)

A volume in Our Lives series
ISSN 1921-6653 (print) 1921-6661 (electronic)

Cover and interior design by Natalie Olsen, Kisscut Design.
Cover photograph © kavram / Shutterstock.com
Printed and bound in Canada by Marquis Book Printers.

Library and Archives Canada Cataloguing in Publication
Maturié, Pierre
Man proposes, God disposes : recollections of a French pioneer / by Pierre Maturié ;
translation by Vivien Bosley ; with an introduction by Robert Wardhaugh.

(Our lives: diary, memoir, and letters, ISSN 1921-6653)
Translation of: Athabasca, terre de ma jeunesse.
Also issued in electronic format.
ISBN 978-1-926836-55-3

1. Maturié, Pierre. 2. Canadians, French-speaking — Alberta — Athabasca
River Region — Biography. 3. Frontier and pioneer life — Alberta — Athabasca
River Region. 4. Pioneers — Alberta — Athabasca River Region — Biography.
5. Athabasca River Region (Alta.) — Biography. I. Bosley, Vivien Elizabeth
II. Title. III. Series: Our lives: diary, memoir, and letters

FC3695.A85Z4913 2013   971.23'202092   C2011-906693-9

We acknowledge the financial support of the Government of Canada through the
Canada Book Fund (CBF) for our publishing activities.

Canada Council   Conseil des Arts
for the Arts   du Canada

Assistance provided by the Government of Alberta, Alberta Multimedia Development Fund.

**Government
of Alberta** ■

CONTENTS

PREFACE

Man Proposes, God Disposes takes us back to the small Alberta town of Athabasca in the years immediately prior to the First World War. Pierre Maturié arrived in Athabasca in December 1910 in the company of his two brothers-in-law, Armand and Jean Brunie, all three of them very young men. Born in 1890, Maturié had begun studying law in his native town of Brive, in south-central France, as had Jean Brunie. It was Armand Brunie, employed at the time as an insurance inspector in Paris, who had the idea of going to Canada. His wife, Marguerite, who was Maturié's sister, would follow in October 1911, leaving the couple's infant son at home, in the care of her parents. Pierre and the Brunie brothers remained in Athabasca until 1914, when, one after the other, they returned to France and became caught up in the war.

In *Man Proposes, God Disposes* we see a society full of energy, where hopes were high. An atmosphere of openness and generosity seemed to pervade the community, which was known as the gateway to the Canadian Northwest. Most of what we read about early Athabasca, however, whether in contemporary newspapers or subsequent histories, is the account of anglophone settlers, and it is they whose names are most frequently mentioned in the society columns and in the minutes of meetings. Quite apart from its intrinsic interest as an adventure story, Maturié's memoir thus offers valuable insight into a francophone society that has been drowned out by English voices and serves a useful corrective to our impression of the ethnic mix of the town.

Although the French government was, at the time, attempting to discourage emigration, there were other ways to attract French settlers to Canada. On 2 December 1910, just as Maturié and his brothers-in-law were arriving in Athabasca, an article appeared in *Le Courrier de l'Ouest,* the main French-language newspaper of the Canadian Northwest. It quoted from a piece written by a recent visitor to Alberta, Édouard Brunet, for his hometown newspaper, *Le Havre-Éclair:*

> We can't say to all French people "Go to Canada," but to those who are willing to leave their homeland and are seeking a rich, hospitable land, we would urge reflection about the choice of a country where there is absolute freedom, where there are thousands of French Canadians who would welcome them without asking them to abandon their nationality, their language, and their faith, and where . . . after a few years of work, they can find a comfortable life of independence.

It is evident from Maturié's account that some of the French speakers he knew had succeeded spectacularly in achieving "a comfortable life of independence." Isaïe Gagnon was the wealthiest man in Athabasca Landing and one of the great success stories of the province; another Frenchman, Dr. Joseph Olivier, was mayor of the town. Members of the Lessard family were political and commercial leaders, well known throughout the province, and at the time Révillon Frères was the largest furrier business in the world. The Catholic faith was also well established in the area. Father Beaudry, of Athabasca's St. Gabriel's Church, is typical of the many Roman Catholic clergy who came from France to minister to the needs of local francophones and the Métis. The French bishops whom Maturié mentions have left traces of their influence in many place names throughout western Canada.

And so, when Maturié's horses skittered out of control down the hill into Athabasca Landing, he soon found that his lack of English did not isolate him from the town completely: there were enough French-speaking residents to allow him to function comfortably.

Maturié's arrival in Athabasca coincided with an economic boom — brought about in part by the impending arrival of the railroad — that had made the town a major provincial centre. An aggressive campaign was underway to attract settlers from Europe and the United States to the Canadian Northwest, but an item in the *Northern News* of 25 March 1911 makes it clear that people from even farther afield were aware of the opportunities: "Mr. Chin You of Canton, China, arrived in the Landing the latter part of last week and will be associated with Hoy Kee in conducting the well-known Hoy Kee restaurant. Mr. You says he was induced to come to the Landing by reading the *Northern News,* copies of which were furnished him by Hoy Kee from time to time." Settlers were indeed pouring in from many parts of the world, and many other immigrants passed through on their way farther north. Writing of the northern pioneers, Emily Murphy commented, "All of these people are topful of enthusiasm, being of wise and gallant mind. Indeed the whole country seems surcharged with it . . . and the settlers will tell you the only 'knocker' here is Opportunity." [1] Not all of these settlers remained, of course. The land was the great magnet, but the regulations governing land claims were quite stringent. In his history of the area, David Gregory estimates that "rather less than half the pioneers who homesteaded in the Athabasca region before the First World War succeeded in winning full title to their chosen quarter sections." [2]

Although small and still relatively remote, Athabasca was by no means a social and cultural desert. The advent of newcomers was duly noted in the local paper, which reported on 17 January 1911: "The three French gentlemen who recently arrived from Paris have been busily engaged erecting necessary building to fulfill their homestead duties. It is said that upon completion a house-warming will take place and Mr. Jos. Tobaty will be major-domo of the event." Maturié refers to the brawls that sometimes broke out among the rougher elements in town, but at the other end of the social spectrum there was no dearth of entertaining diversions. He mentions the lively Christmas dinners served at the Grand Union Hotel and the impromptu parties he and his brothers-in-law gave or attended, at which French was the lingua franca. In genteel anglophone society, there were tea parties and at-homes, and young ladies flirted with young men on riding and hunting expeditions.

We can also find reports of the events at "Social" and "Literary" evenings, which included debates on timely topics and musical and dramatic renderings by local residents. The *Northern News* of 25 February 1911 contains an account of a recent debate on women's suffrage. The negatives won, but during the debate mention was made of the women in Wyoming, Utah, and other American states, who had recently won the right to vote. Just before and during Maturié's stay, the paper also featured pieces about such diverse cultural subjects as a performance of Richard Strauss's new opera, *Salomé,* at Covent Garden in London and the Canadian actress Margaret Anglin, who was about to play the role of Antigone in the theatre at the University of California at Berkeley.

Nor was the spiritual aspect of pioneer life ignored. The three churches — Catholic, Anglican, and Methodist — ministered to the community's religious needs and were led by distinguished clerics. For the Christmas Eve mass that Maturié attended as soon as he arrived the choir of St. Gabriel's was "practicing Lambillotte's mass in C" and was said to have a reputation "that might surprise visitors from the East." [3] The church itself had been elaborately renovated, making it quite an architectural showpiece, and the installation of "a new, modern improvement . . . the illumination system which consists of gasoline pumped through wire tube by air pressure" must have made it a sight to behold. Its priest, Father Desmarais, impressed his congregation by preaching in Cree, as well as French and English. In this, he was an exception to the unspoken rule among most of the townspeople to the effect that the Aboriginal population (including the Métis) should be ignored. Emily Murphy is another honourable exception: she writes eloquently of her visit to several Cree families in their tents. In recording his contacts with characters like Limping Jo, Maturié is similarly exceptional. It seems he was much more accepting of the Aboriginal population than most of the Euro-Canadians in the area.

All the intense activity in the region did not come without cost, of course — though the cost proved a windfall for some. Maturié half bemoans the fact that he lacks the business acumen required to make a killing in the real estate boom, but he is in the same moral camp as the editor of the *Northern News*. "The Evil of Unscrupulous Booming" read the paper's headline on 10 May 1911, and the lead article went on to castigate those who sought to profit from the local bonanza from afar: "There are numerous instances throughout the West of towns that have been victimized by unprincipled land sharks who care nothing how they get their money . . . and town lots have been sold by misrepresentation which in many instances are of no more value as town lots than they are as gold mines." One cost of progress was the persistent danger of fire in a community built more or less entirely of wood — a cost that Maturié himself incurred when his house burned down. A large part of Athabasca Landing was destroyed by a devastating fire in 1913. "There is no direct proof," writes David Gregory, "that the attempt to pipe natural gas into town for lighting and heating purposes was the cause of the rash of fires that afflicted the Landing between 1912 and 1914, but it is difficult to believe that the two things were entirely coincidental." [4] Another kind of cost is mentioned by Emily Murphy in *Seeds of Pine:* "To build even one of our railways, a hundred forests are sacrificed, and, in the uncanny gloom of the dead country which lies at the heart of the earth, thousands of bowed, grim workers toil, Vulcan-like, for the iron to make spikes and rails." [5]

Maturié — who, on the one hand, sang hymns of praise to the pristine beauty of his adoptive home and, on the other, spoke of the satisfaction of making virgin land productive — was caught in this dilemma, between love of the wilderness and a desire to tame unruly nature in the service of progress. For him, the solution ultimately lay in the prism of memory. His musings under his catalpa tree in France took place sixty years after the events he described. There, he could dream of his years in Athabasca Landing in terms reminiscent of those the *Northern News* used to describe St. Gabriel's Church:

> One would travel far and wide to find a more picturesque land-scape than that seen from the site of the church. The magnificent surroundings of this village, in winter with a surface of white, in summer with a border of green and the beautiful stream of the Athabasca flowing slowly by to say nothing of the river traffic and steam boats, all this, as viewed from the church front would make a splendid object for a landscape painter.

Maturié has painted with words; *Man Proposes, God Disposes* is that portrait.

Gilles Cadrin and Vivien Bosley

TRANSLATOR'S ACKNOWLEDGEMENTS

My first debt of deep gratitude is to Gilles Cadrin, without whom the story of Pierre Maturié would remain unknown. It was through Professor Cadrin's acquaintance with Madame G. de la Rochefoucault, of the Société France-Canada in Paris, that Maturié's *Athabasca, Terre de ma jeunesse* came to light. He went on to meet Bernard Brunie and his wife, Catherine, the executors of the author's literary estate, and was able to discuss the prospect of a new edition of the French text as well as a translation into English with their son Sébastien. They have all been enthusiastic supporters of the project, and the new French edition is now available from the Institut pour le patrimoine de la francophonie de l'Ouest canadien, Campus Saint-Jean, University of Alberta.

It is also thanks to Professor Cadrin's generosity that we are able to reproduce photos of Pierre Maturié and of his house in Athabasca. Thanks also to the very knowledgeable Marilyn Mol, of the Athabasca Archives, who answered all queries promptly and insightfully and was responsible for pointing me to the photo archive.

Vivien Bosley

INTRODUCTION

The France of twenty-year-old Pierre Maturié was a vibrant place. It was 1910, only four years before the world would be turned upside down by the horrors of the "Great War." At the beginning and again at the end of the year, the Seine flooded Paris through its sewers and subway tunnels after months of heavy rain. In March, a production of Oscar Strauss's operetta *A Waltz Dream* opened in Paris, while a meeting of the learned societies declared in favor of women's suffrage. In the May legislative elections, the Republican, Radical and Radical-Socialist Party emerged victorious, with a governing coalition. It was an age of transition, and the forces of modernity were visible everywhere. Electric streetcars carried thousands of passengers through busy, well-lit streets; high overhead the first commercial air flights were taking place. The Paris Prefect of Police published an ordinance regulating automobile traffic, while time signals were transmitted from the Eiffel Tower as regular service for the first time. In Rome, the Vatican responded by ordering that all Catholic priests take an oath against this "modernism."

But the modernity of urban, cosmopolitan France would not be as evident where the young Pierre Maturié and his brothers-in-law, Armand and Jean, were headed. In many ways, Maturié was an ideal candidate for a pioneer to the Canadian West. Like so many young boys, he had grown up on the adventure stories of the American frontier: "I was twenty years old, at the age of wild dreams; I was fit and athletic and full of the spirit of adventure that had informed my early reading." And he was the perfect fit for what the Canadian High Commission in Paris was seeking to "populate and cultivate" the "sparsely inhabited" Prairie West.

The High Commission, however, was having little success in Paris, or throughout France for that matter, in "trying to nudge possible applicants towards Catholic and French-Canadian settlements." Despite promotional literature that, as Maturié informs us, "painted a rosy picture of vast, open spaces full of the promise of riches, of free land, of the expansive, independent life of the settler who was master of his own destiny," the efforts largely failed. But they found a receptive audience in Pierre Maturié and his compatriots.

Other than romanticized adventure stories, however, Maturié knew little of Canada, the Prairie West, or the rugged Athabasca country in which he would soon find himself. He had no idea that he was headed for a land "on the margins," a "Gateway to the North" that possessed a rich history. The Athabasca region had long been a borderland, positioned between the south and the far north, between Prairie and Shield. Prior to the immigration boom that began in the mid-1890s, the Canadian Northwest was home to First Nations, the Métis, and a scattering of white settlers. The Métis — the mixed-blood population created by the union of European fur traders with Aboriginal women — became the "people in-between" and formed a substantial presence in Red River, in the Qu'Appelle Valley, along the banks of the North Saskatchewan River around Prince Albert, and in the regions north of Edmonton in the Athabasca country and beyond. When the Catholic Church in Québec sent out its Oblate missionaries and priests, they found a largely French-speaking, Catholic population scattered throughout the Northwest.

The Athabasca and the Peace River countries were important areas during the fur trade era, and they became one of the most violent battlegrounds during the "fur trade wars" between the North West Company (the "Nor'westers") and the Hudson's Bay Company (HBC), which lasted from the 1770s to 1821. In addition, these vast areas needed to be crossed, as explorers and fur traders continued the search for the Northwest Passage and the route to the Pacific coast. Rivers were the main means of transportation, and a relatively short portage supply trail connected two massive systems of waterways, linking Fort Edmonton, on the North Saskatchewan River, and the entire Nelson River drainage basin, which empties into Hudson Bay, with the Mackenzie watershed and the northerly flowing Athabasca River leading to the Arctic Ocean.

The Nor'westers, led by Peter Pond, reached the Methye Portage between the Churchill and Athabasca rivers in 1777–78 and crossed into "the land of Lake Athabasca, the Eldorado of the trade as it came to be known."[1] Here, beyond the reach of the HBC monopoly, the North West Company controlled the trade. Within a decade, Alexander Mackenzie was dispatched to the Athabasca country to work with Pond, and in 1789 he continued the search for the western sea. Instead, he found the Arctic. (In 1793, Mackenzie's persistence paid off, and he reached the Pacific.) The Hudson's Bay Company initially had difficulty rivalling the better organized Nor'westers, and it was only in 1802 that the first HBC post was built on Lake Athabasca. The first decades of the nineteenth century were marked by intense rivalry between the two, during which fortunes shifted, and the HBC finally gained the upper hand. In 1821, the fur trade wars ended when the North West Company was merged into the Hudson's Bay Company.

By the 1870s, the HBC was searching for an alternate route to move its goods northwest from Fort Edmonton to Fort Assiniboine, on the lower Athabasca River. In 1874, the company surveyed the area from Fort Edmonton to the southern loop of the Athabasca, and in the summer of 1876 the hundred-mile "Landing Trail" (the Athabasca Trail) was cleared for transportation. Goods were moved by cart in the summer and by sleigh in the winter. But the trail wound through such difficult country — marred by mud holes in the spring and autumn and by mosquitos and black flies in the summer months — that its passing was arduous, to say the least. As one traveller attested: "The flies bothered us greatly; the large bulldogs, looking like a cross between a bee and a blue-bottle, drove the horses almost to madness, and after our midday halt it was no easy matter to put the harness on; fortunately we had netting, or the poor beasts would have fared much worse: as it was the blood was streaming from their flanks during the heat of the day. The mosquitoes appeared towards evening, but as the nights were usually chilly they annoyed us only for a few hours." [2]

Athabasca Landing was established as a supply point by the Hudson's Bay Company in 1877. Each spring, local Métis were hired to construct a fleet of boats to move supplies northwest to Lesser Slave Lake and posts beyond. This became known as the "Athabasca Brigade." Boat building became a primary industry at the Landing and remained so for years to come. Each spring, feverish construction occurred while the river thawed. The boat builders, mainly Métis, stayed at Athabasca Landing for only a few weeks, living on the east hill in a work camp of tents or rough lean-tos made from logs, brushwood, and mud. The most common boat was the scow. Constructed of rough lumber, it resembled a long, narrow raft with wooden walls and a flat bottom; most were broken up and used as building timber when they reached their destination. Each scow carried a crew of five or six men and held about eight tons of freight. By the end of 1880, Athabasca Landing had become the main transfer point for all furs being moved along the Athabasca, Peace, and Mackenzie river systems and the central distribution point for all goods being shipped to the North. By the 1880s, the HBC had abandoned its old routes, such as the Methye Portage, and began shipping trade goods and furs via steamboat.

No people lived the year round at Athabasca Landing until 1884, when the Hudson's Bay Company warehouse was upgraded into a trading post and Leslie Wood became the first permanent resident. The company constructed new buildings, and in the summer of 1888 a steamboat was built, the S.S. *Athabasca*, to ply the central section of the Athabasca River between Mirror Landing (near Lesser Slave Lake) and Pelican Portage, further north.

Roman Catholic, Anglican, and Methodist missionaries soon followed the fur traders. The Catholic Oblates "held the upper hand in the Athabasca–Great Slave Lake regions because of their ability to muster support for larger, more self-sufficient missions than the Anglicans could realize. They also had over a decade of northern experience before the first Anglican missionaries arrived." [3] But the Anglicans came to the Landing first. By 1893, the North-West Mounted Police had also arrived, and in 1897 an outpost was established to introduce "a little law and order into the north land." [4] The Athabasca Trail was improved in 1885 and again in the 1890s. After homesteading began in 1886, journeys along the trail became so routine that a stagecoach service between Edmonton and Athabasca Landing was started by J. H. Kennedy in 1898. The Edmonton and Athabasca Stage Company sent coaches from Edmonton every Tuesday morning at 7:30, arriving at the Landing on Thursday. The trail was surveyed in 1898 and became a public road. [5]

The Prairie region, meanwhile, was transformed by the immigration boom of 1896 to 1913. With the land cleared for settlement by the Canadian government through the signing of the seven numbered treaties with the First Nations, followed by the building of the transcontinental railroad (completed in 1885), all that was needed to finish building the West was people. During the first decade of the twentieth century, immigrants poured in from Britain, the United States, and central Europe, but only a tiny fraction came from France. The numbers coming to the West from Québec were also disappointing.

The numerical importance of the French Catholics in the Northwest had long been reflected in the Hudson's Bay Company's administration of the region. The Roman Catholic bishop of St. Boniface, in Manitoba, was a de facto member of the Council of Assiniboia. The council officially sanctioned the use of French in court cases involving francophones, and French-speaking magistrates were appointed. In the 1850s, the council made grants to both Protestant and Catholic churches for the support of schools. "The French and Catholic fact," Arthur Silver points out, "had, thus, considerable institutional basis in Rupert's Land." [6] After the Red River Resistance and Manitoba's entry into Confederation in 1870, a flood of immigrants came west from Ontario. But few came from Québec, even though Catholic missionaries in the West pressured the federal government in Ottawa as well as the provincial government in Québec to send settlers. The problem was that Québec had its own frontier, once the areas north of the St. Lawrence were opened for settlement, and it was this area that was promoted by church colonization societies in Québec. There was also the problem of emigration. Québec nationalists were already bemoaning the low birth rate in the province and the loss of population through migration to the New England states. In the 1870s and 1880s, efforts to attract French-Catholic immigrants to the West fell to the Church under Archbishop Alexandre Taché of St. Boniface. The plan was to create a bloc settlement to the west of Red River. When this scheme failed, the Church turned to the idea of "a chain of parishes across the west from the Red River to the Rockies"— and yet, by 1891, the French element in the Northwest had decreased to between 4 and 5 percent.[7]

It was only natural that Wilfrid Laurier, the first French-Canadian prime minister, elected in 1896, also wished to see large numbers of francophone immigrants to the West. This bicultural attitude was not, however, shared by most of the English Canadians in his government. The minister of the interior, Clifford Sifton, was in charge of western immigration. Sifton was an energetic lawyer from Portage la Prairie, Manitoba, and he was an anglophile. His "hierarchy of immigration" clearly separated the desirable immigrants from the undesirables. Americans and British were at the top of the list, while blacks, Asians, and Jews were at the bottom. Immigrants from France were desirable for racial, religious, and cultural reasons, but very few came, regardless. France had its own colonies for settlement, particularly in northern Africa. In addition, as in Québec, the birth rate in France was dropping, so emigration was discouraged.

Yet despite the problems attracting French settlers to the West, there was still a significant francophone presence, largely as a result of the Métis population. This presence was influential enough that in 1877 the North-West Territories made French an official language and instituted denominational (Catholic) schooling rights. When Alberta and Saskatchewan became provinces in 1905, and Prime Minister Laurier attempted to extend these rights, Clifford Sifton feared the situation that had developed in Manitoba and the ensuing Schools Question. He resigned from cabinet. Laurier backed down, and the new provinces followed the Ontario model of non-sectarian, English-language public schools.[8] Sifton's replacement, Frank Oliver, from Edmonton, was even more of an anglophile. The West was perceived as an Anglo-Protestant society and not particularly welcoming to French Catholics. As Gerald Friesen points out, "fainter hearts would be deterred from western migration by Quebec newspaper attacks on 'Ontario fanaticism' which allegedly resulted in assaults on French rights."[9] Arthur Silver goes one step further: "French Canadian culture itself was inimical to adventure. . . . Quebecois were less likely to try their luck in an unknown land, preferring instead the familiar ambiance of their province or the niche already created for them by their compatriots in the eastern United States. The prairies were just too far away and too strange for Quebecois."[10] Even the presence of a significant Métis population did not encourage immigration from Québec. As Robert Painchaud observes: "If French Quebeckers did not look on Rupert's Land as part of their country, neither did they look on the French-Catholic Métis as part of their own nationality."[11]

By 1901, there were only 23,000 French speakers in the Northwest. According to Friesen, such a small base discouraged "chain migration — the links that encouraged residents of a community to join friends in a new land." When combined with the dismantling of French language and Catholic schooling rights that continued over the next several decades, "the result was that Canada's newest regional community did not provide the bilingual compromises of Canada's federal government, and did not appear to be a congenial destination to French-speaking immigrants in the years of prairie growth after 1900."[12] Yet despite the problems with French immigration to the Prairie West, there were pockets of settlement, and Pierre Maturié discovered one of them.

Meanwhile, with the immigration boom underway, Edmonton had become a major centre by the 1890s. The old fur trade economy was superseded by developments in agriculture and mining, and the population increased significantly. The railroad arrived in 1891, and Edmonton served as a departure point for travellers heading to the Athabasca country and points further north.

But while the seven numbered treaties had extinguished Aboriginal title to most of the Prairie West, none of them dealt with the North. Although a treaty was anticipated, there was no sense of urgency to negotiate for the area that included Lake Athabasca and the surrounding territory. The situation changed in 1896, however, when gold was discovered in the Klondike. Edmonton became the staging point for two overland routes, one by way of Lesser Slave Lake and Peace River and the other following the traditional fur trade river route from Athabasca Landing.[13] "Gold Fever" gripped the population of the Landing when news arrived of successful strikes on the Klondike, a full two months before news reached the rest of the country. In the summer of 1897, John Segers, captain of the S.S. *Athabasca,* declined to renew his contract with the HBC and began making preparations to lead a ten-man party of prospectors to Dawson City, in the Yukon. The all-Canadian water route to the Yukon was half the length of the American route, and 775 prospectors attempted the 2,000-mile trek northward. Most stayed at the Landing only long enough to get supplies and build a scow. Realizing the potential of the Landing, however, some of these would-be prospectors decided to stay.

The Klondike gold rush, and the increased chances of conflict between whites and Natives that accompanied it, pressured the Canadian government into negotiating Treaty Eight in 1899 with the Cree, Beaver, and Chipewyan First Nations of the area that is now northern Alberta, northeastern British Columbia, and the southernmost portion of the Northwest Territories. Half-breed scrip was issued at the same time to deal with Métis land claims and hopefully to avoid the troubles that had occurred earlier, with Louis Riel's Red River Resistance in 1870 and the Northwest Rebellion in 1885. These joint processes extended federal, provincial, and territorial structures into the North. According to the *Edmonton Bulletin,* the northern lands were "now open to the enterprise of civilization, under the full legal administration of the government of Canada." [14]

It would take approximately two decades for the weight of Canada's administrative powers to reach the Athabasca region and for it to become fully integrated into the province and nation. The fur trade was declining, as was evident from the HBC monopoly falling under attack not only from free traders but also from rival fur trading companies such as Révillion Frères, as well as a rival transportation firm, the Northern Transportation Company, which arrived at the Landing in 1903.

In 1905, the same year that Alberta became a province, Athabasca Landing was incorporated as a village. By 1908, it had been transformed from an HBC outpost into a transportation hub and then into a thriving northern frontier town. "Here we have a large establishment of the Hudson's Bay Company," the writer and educator Agnes Deans Cameron observed, "an Anglican and a Roman Mission, a little public school, a barracks of the Northwest Mounted Police, a post office, a dozen stores, a reading-room, two hotels, and a blacksmith shop, and for population a few whites leavening a host of Cree-Scots half-breeds." [15]

Between 1906 and 1911, the population of Alberta doubled. In 1912 and 1913, the province received nearly 13 percent of all the immigrants arriving in Canada. By 1906, however, there was still very little agriculture occurring around Athabasca Landing. The area had been surveyed into quarter sections according to the dictates of the Dominion Lands Act, but it was not attracting settlers.

In 1910, the Athabasca Landing Board of Trade published its own optimistic brochure promoting the area for homesteading and investment.[16] Finally, between 1909 and 1914, the area was claimed by homesteaders. Between these years, some 1,500 settler families (a population of perhaps 5,000) moved into the area.[17] Among the newcomers were Pierre Maturié and his two brothers-in-law.

In 1910, at the time of Maturié's arrival, Athabasca Landing was little more than a village, inhabited by just a few hundred people. By August 1913, when "Landing" was officially dropped from the town's name, the population was close to 2,000.[18] It was a bustling place, with a constant movement of people. On 17 January 1911, an amusing advertisement appeared in the local paper, the *Northern News:* "WANTED in Athabasca Landing before May 1st 100 carpenters, 2 brickmakers, 10 bricklayers, 2 tinsmiths, 2 shoemakers, 20 sawmill hands, 2 dressmakers, 1 milliner, 1 taylor, 500 men to buy town lots." The path of settlement in the West usually preceded the coming of the railroad. Speculators bought and sold sections of land on the strength of the assumption that the railroad would soon arrive and the price of land would increase sharply. As Maturié's memoir makes clear, speculation fever was running rampant. The poet Robert Service, visiting the Landing in 1911, wrote in his book *Ploughman of the Moon:*

> The Landing was abustle with spring activity and the Company was the centre of all movement. I went into the office where two men were standing over a blueprint. It was a plan of the newly conceived townsite.
>
> "There you are," said one, "a chance to make your fortune. There's a corner lot you can have for three hundred dollars. In time it will be worth three thousand." If he had said "thirty thousand" he might have been nearer the mark. At that time I think I had enough money to buy up the whole townsite; but I am glad I did not, for then I might have become a multimillionaire, and such a fate I would not wish anyone.[19]

False-front buildings stood along the muddy streets, lined by wooden boardwalks. The small town boasted the Grand Union Hotel, which rose to three storeys and featured balconies and an elegant entryway, three churches (Catholic, Anglican, and Methodist), and three banks (Royal, Imperial, and Commerce). The Hudson's Bay Company and Révillon Frères, rivals in the fur trade, each built impressive headquarters. Other structures included a Dominion Lands Office, a Government Telegraph Office, a surveying firm (Côté and Smith), a Massey-Harris farm implements dealer, and a public schoolhouse.

Maturié comments on the excitement and energy of the place but also on the sense of impermanence. In fact, very few settlers were able to put their quarter sections under cultivation within the required three years. Most needed at least an extra year, and, if wooded areas had to be cleared, the process could take as long as six years. Over half — roughly 56 percent, according to one estimate — of the would-be homesteaders gave up owing to the difficulty of preparing the land.[20] Maturié happened to arrive during a period when summers were usually hot and relatively dry, which inspired confidence that the Athabasca region could become a northern breadbasket. It soon became apparent, however, that the growing season in the north was typically too short to enable wheat farmers to compete with the harvests of the southern prairies. Farmers were thus obliged to diversify, and mixed farming became the norm.[21]

In 1911, the Alberta government decided that a demonstration farm was to be opened near Athabasca Landing. Located on the east hill, about a mile and a half outside of town, the farm was put into operation between 1912 and 1914. Such farms undertook experiments with cultivation methods, animal breeding, and new varieties of crops. In addition, the Athabasca demonstration farm offered local homesteaders practical advice on how to cultivate their land more productively. The hope was that the ready availability of such advice would make the area more attractive to homesteaders — that it would translate into "better yields, more settlers, and higher land values."[22]

It was to the Athabasca country of western Canada that Pierre Maturié decided in 1910 to journey with his brothers-in-law, Armand and Jean Brunie, abandoning his law studies in his native town of Brive. Unlike most immigrant stories, Maturié's account pays little attention to the journey by ship across the Atlantic. Upon arriving in Nova Scotia, however, he provides a revealing glimpse of Canada in 1910, from the "gloomy, mournful aspect" of Halifax's docks to Montréal, "the historic city dear to the heart of French people, who cannot but feel a sense of repossession." As he travels across Ontario by rail, the impact of the Canadian landscape upon a metropolitan European becomes evident:

> For me, the trip was like a nature film: the train traversed mile upon mile of forest, forests that sometimes allowed us to glimpse, beneath their blanket of snow, a lake, a little log cabin with a plume of smoke rising from the chimney, the home of a settler trying to clear the land. . . . But at each moment, the image vanished to make way for a different scene, like an old-fashioned magic lantern show.

In Winnipeg, "the impressive capital of Manitoba," Maturié's attention is drawn by the presence of all three national railways and by the imposing Fort Garry Hotel. Then it's on to "the wheat-growing region of Manitoba, then Saskatchewan, vast stretches of treeless land, the great Prairie, where herds of countless bison had left their mark."

Finally, Maturié reaches Edmonton. Only a few years before "a major fur trading centre on the banks of the North Saskatchewan River," by 1910 the Alberta capital had become a busy, commercial centre with approximately fifty thousand people. Edmonton was an exciting place in 1910. Despite the onset of an economic recession in Canada, the western boom was still in full swing, "a phenomenon," Maturié writes, "that attracted to this expanding and dynamic Canadian north a continual influx of settlers and farmers." Edmonton was also "the wide-open door to the vast

North." The land was divided into building lots, "which were subject to wild speculation, with fortunes being made every day."

Edmonton's saloons are filled with a changing sea of faces, but it is the "old-timers" who convince Maturié and his brothers-in-law to go on to Athabasca Landing, 110 miles north of the city. The Landing was only a small town, but it was the supply centre for the North, and when the railway arrived there, a boom was expected. In the meantime, it could only be reached by wagon in the summer and sled in the winter. The most important feature of the town was the bend of the Athabasca River, the "Highway to the North."

If the numbers of francophone immigrants coming to the West were disappointing, Maturié was not aware of it. He discovers a strong French presence in the area. "Athabasca Landing is part of the British Empire," Agnes Deans Cameron commented in 1908. "But English is at a discount here; Cree and French and a mixture of these are spoken on all sides." [23] The French character of the town becomes immediately clear in Maturié's account, as he makes contacts wherever he goes. When the three men depart Edmonton in the middle of winter for the Athabasca, equipped with their sled and provisions, they are advised by an Oblate Father to spend the night with a French family who are "always happy for a visit from new settlers from the old country." These ethnic webs provide important support for incoming settlers, as well as a comforting sense of contact with the "old country" and home. Upon arrival in Athabasca, Maturié learns that the manager of the hotel, and the wealthiest man in town, is a French Canadian, Isaïe Gagnon. The barkeeper, the local physician, and the owner of the general store are also French, from either France or Québec. When Maturié's party needs a guide to help them select their homestead, they are put in contact with "a Métis named Sidore Lafleur, half Cree and half French Canadian, who had always lived in the region and knew it like the back of his hand." Heading out to stake their claim, "about two miles from the village we were scheduled to stop at the house of a Frenchman, Jo Tobaty, who had been one of the first immigrants to settle in the area." To help them build their house, they hire two French Canadians who were "typical of real *coureurs des bois*, descended from the race that had created Québec City and Montréal." Even their nearest neighbour, Menut, is "a former miner from northern France who'd come two years earlier with his entire family and two sons-in-law to try their luck in the New World."

With a knack for description, Maturié populates his story with a cast of colourful characters straight from the pages of a western adventure story. Indeed, one of the most delightful aspects of this memoir is Maturié's writing. Even in translation, the author's stylistic flair and skill as a storyteller come through in his evocative images of the landscape, the people, and the conditions:

> After two or three hours we were awakened by an unexpected concert. In the still night, beneath a superb moon that had risen over the forest giving enough light to read by, we heard howling and baying in the distance, coming nearer then moving away again, with a din that was fairly impressive to ears that were still conditioned to human sounds of the city. . . . It wasn't long since we'd left Brive and France, yet here everything was so different: men, nature, climate. We had to revise all the ideas of life we'd had up to then to get in tune with the demands of life in vast, rugged Canada.

The richly detailed narrative provides revealing insights into the challenges facing pioneers attempting to settle the Athabasca country, but it also captures the frontier experience in all its human immediacy.

Maturié's memoir fits into what historians call the "myth of the pioneer." As Friesen points out, "pioneers were the heroes of the prairie agricultural epic." The frontier is depicted as a land of opportunity and hard work. It is populated by a cast of rough-and-tumble characters who are at the same time egalitarian and neighbourly. A keen sense of the sublime pervades Maturié's descriptions of the climate and landscape. Not surprisingly, the winters leave the deepest impression:

It's a far cry from the poets' sonnets about the great white silence, the jewels and beads that delicately festoon the branches of the pine trees, the immaculate carpet of snow, to a temperature of forty to fifty degrees below zero; an apparently benevolent sun that does nothing to warm; the insidious numbness that suddenly penetrates your limbs and sends to you sleep to kill you more effectively; the frigid air that freezes your lungs; the snow-blindness from the expanses of white. Everything presents a danger for the presumptuous amateur.

We can also detect a strong element of the utopian in Maturié's descriptions of "his" Athabasca. In many ways, his memoir reminds us the popular novels of Ralph Connor, which "told the stories of western missionaries, doctors, and Mounted Policemen — good-hearted and manly men — who confronted the rough life of bush camps and mine towns. . . . It was a society close to nature, not urban; it was young, not old; it was free, not bound by convention." [24]

No doubt the fact that, in its final form, Maturié's memoir was written in the 1970s, near the end of his life, contributes to its romanticism. While it remains a vivid and personal account of his experiences, it is inevitably coloured by nostalgia and the passing of years. As Neil Sutherland points out, such reminiscences offer a way for people to "take stock" and "look back over a whole existence in order to justify themselves, to make the self-edited sum of their lives to have been worth living." [25] Maturié writes from the perspective of an older man looking back on his younger and more adventurous days, and his memoir supports the traditional portrayal of the frontier as a "young man's country."

But Maturié offers us more than just an account of the Athabasca country. Once his homestead is built and the land cultivated, he takes on other forms of work outside the immediate area — from delivering mail by sled in the dead of winter, to working in a railway camp in the Rockies, to prospecting for gold, to bringing in the harvest in the wheat fields of Saskatchewan. Such experiences were in fact common for pioneering men: "Many thousands of prairie farmers in the pre-war years had been, of necessity, part-time labourers. They sustained their homestead gamble — as the economists would say, their 'undercapitalized' business — by working on larger neighbouring farms as hired hands, by joining itinerant threshing crews, and by heading out for a road or rail construction site, logging camp, or mine town." [26] This need to make financial ends meet contributed in turn to the sense that Prairie society was marked by a crossing of social boundaries. "We had the impression," Maturié writes after arriving at the rail camp, "despite all our experience with bars and saloons with their roughneck customers of all stripes, that we'd landed among a band of convicts." But, of course, with the rougher elements came the heroic and mythic Mounties, the red-coated symbol of law and order, "splendid examples of manhood in their scouts' hats, red tunics, blue trousers with the yellow stripe, and leather boots. As soon as a criminal turned up, he was hunted down like game, as far as the shores of the Arctic if necessary, and it was a rare man who escaped the Mounties."

In the spring of 1913, Maturié travels with his friend Marius Clément into the Rockies to prospect for gold. They stay with the Métis "Old Joe." Like those of the environment, Maturié's descriptions of First Nations are couched in romantic terms, based around the longing for a lost world of nature: "We listened to him with religious attention, for in that night that was both calm and wild, near the glowing fire, his words seemed to come from the far distance of his origins." Old Joe becomes the stereotypical "Indian," caught between two worlds. "He let it be known that the elders of his tribe knew the places where the Great Manitou had hidden the 'gold metal,' but if the Whites knew, it would be the end of their race." Unlike the fevered prospectors, Old Joe has no care for wealth; he lives alone in his cabin, still maimed from a grizzly attack, content to be surrounded by his animals and the bounty of nature: "No passion in him, but rather an immense serenity in harmony with the beauty of the night. . . . His existence lay in the heart of nature, in which he relived the history of his people and the heady scent of liberty. Rather than the violent, artificial light of the city, with its endless noise, he preferred the gentle splendour of the starry nights and the peace of the great forest amid the rustling of the leaves and the babbling of the waters."

After three years, Maturié looks upon the Athabasca country as home: "When I trod again the wooden sidewalks of my Athabasca, I had the pleasant impression of feeling enveloped in the loving atmosphere of home. Indeed, the former Tawatinaw was dear to me, the place I had known in its earliest days and that, over the past three years, had changed its appearance completely." The railway had come, and with more accessible transportation, the place lost some of its isolated character: "In short, beneath the skies of the Great North, man had made an indelible mark." While Maturié appreciates the lures of "civilization," he is critical of the darker sides of the northern frontier:

> Although the coin had a fine, brilliant side, the other side was not so attractive: saloons and sleazy bars had sprung up like poisonous mushrooms; hotels all had bars, and whisky flowed when the end of the harsh winter months saw the arrival of trappers with their rich furs, loggers and camp workers with their hard-earned dollars, boys from the ranches around Baptiste Lake, and all the prospectors who were impatient for the big thaw to descend the Athabasca with the scows and paddle boats towards the unexplored lands on the Big Lakes and the Mackenzie. So the Mounted Police needed reinforcements.

But, as he is quick to point out, "this evolution in Athabasca wasn't necessarily an evil inherent in the country, nor in our own life. As long as man evolves in the heart of unsullied nature, he remains pure despite all its harshness and danger."

If there is a moral to most pioneering tales, it is perseverance. By choosing a quarter section and filing a claim with the government's land office, a pioneer promised to break 30 acres of land, to construct a house worth at least $300, and to reside on the land for half of each year for three years. If these conditions were fulfilled, 160 acres, valued at perhaps ten or fifteen dollars an acre on the open market, would be his at the end of the three-year period. Labouring against the odds, Maturié manages to fulfill the requirements and eventually gain title to his homestead. And yet, despite all the hard work and sacrifices, and despite the optimistic tone of his memoir, the homestead experiment ultimately fails. His house burns down, and his farm, after some initial successes, fails to produce the expected bounties.

By 1914, the adventure is largely complete, and Maturié's brothers-in-law are looking to return to France. Pierre has to decide whether he will stay or return himself. His original plan was to remain for three or four more years and then sell the homestead for a profit after the area had developed further. Instead, the fortunes of Athabasca Landing began a steady decline. In May of 1912, when the railroad reached Athabasca, the entire community came out, "all waiting for the big celebration when the locomotive would appear on the horizon." But, as with other "northern gateways," the result was disappointment. Hope was that Athabasca would become "the junction point on a line leading northwest to the Peace River country, and northeast to Fort McMurray. This optimism began to fade, however, following the Great Fire of 1913 when over one-half of the downtown area was destroyed. Only a few owners would rebuild, many others deciding to call it quits after the fire, especially as the writing was on the wall that new railway lines to Peace River would bypass Athabasca." [27] The homesteading boom in the Northwest was over, and by 1914 the major railway companies were in dire economic straits.

Maturié returns to France, where he spends the "golden summer of 1914." Late in June, word arrives from Jean, who has not yet left for France, that the three of them have won title to their lands in Athabasca, having fulfilled the homestead requirements. Pierre longs for the natural surroundings of his Athabasca and plans a quick return: "As I went about my business in Paris — which hadn't yet become the tentacular city of today — I pitied all those people who came rushing out of their places of work with their heads down, like a herd of cows in the ranches of the West, the only difference being that the horizons of the former were limited to blocks of apartments that were often in pockmarked and foul-smelling streets, whereas the latter looked out onto the vast open spaces of the Prairies, with the perfume of pine forests wafting from the Rockies, and the white salt pans where in ancient times the buffalo had come to drink."

But the Great War intervenes. "Man proposes, God disposes," Maturié writes. "The projects of human beings, however well structured and carefully planned, are as fragile as soap bubbles that burst at the slightest breath of wind." War is declared on 3 August, and although, as a naturalized Canadian citizen, Pierre Maturié is exempt from military service, he decides to sign on as a volunteer. His plans to return are therefore put on hold. Although he claims to have no regrets and feels that he is fighting for a just cause, there are echoes of lost opportunity, particularly amidst the horrors of war:

Everything I had experienced, and also those radiant memories, so recent, but which seemed to rise up from a distant past, seemed to me now like mere dreams in the night, which are chased away like the mist by the light of day. I was a soldier; I no longer belonged to myself; I was a tiny entity in a mass of men who had been gathered from everywhere with all their weaknesses, but also their heroism, and were destined for the next hecatomb.

While he is away at war, Maturié asks the "blond girl" of his childhood, who has dominated his romantic aspirations, for her hand. They are married in April 1919, after the war's end. But she has lost her brother to the carnage, and Pierre has lost both Jean and his dear friend Max Gaspéri, both of whom survived the war only to die in the devastating Spanish flu epidemic.

In May 1919, Pierre Maturié finally returns to Athabasca. But in the intervening time, while he was off fighting in Europe, he has become one of the many who lost their homesteads. His beloved "Bellevue" is gone, and so he purchases a ranch in the Peace River district.

In the years that followed the Great War, the "myth" of the pioneer and the "utopianism" of Prairie society proved to be just that. The war highlighted ethnic cleavages and nativism. The social equality and mobility evidenced by the atmosphere of neighbourly cooperation gave way to social divisions. As Friesen points out, "this was a time of testing for agriculture when, as the novels of Robert Stead suggested, the agrarian myth could no longer be accepted as a prevailing truth." [28] The subject of his "second stay" Maturié planned to keep for a "second book." Unfortunately, it was never written, and his impressions are lost to us.

In the end, his second stay proves to be brief. His wife's parents are ill, and she pushes for the family's return to France so that she can be close to them. As a result, the rest of Pierre's life is spent in France. As he looks back upon his life, his failure to return permanently to Canada emerges as his main source of regret:

> Now, just as evening brings shadows to the light of the finest day, the sadness of things past descends on my declining years. And when, on nostalgic autumn evenings, my heart sometimes feels too heavy, I see again in my mind's eye the splendour of the Canadian forests and the sweetness of the lakes surrounded by a fringe of leaves, and creeks babbling at the bottom of coulees. But where, now, after half a century, are the trails through the bush and the paths I made? . . . Where do you all sleep, dear friends of my youth?"

His questions will remain unanswered. But he has left us a memorable tale.

Robert Wardhaugh

Man Proposes,
God Disposes

This book, *Athabasca,* was written for my children and family, but also for all the young people who are wandering aimlessly through life, trying to find their way through our century of mud and iron. I hope these few pages, written without flourish from my notes and memory, and with no pretension to great literature, will provide a window wide open to a world that still exists for eager minds — even in an age of flights to the moon and Mars — and that they will serve as a guide in moments of doubt and temptation.

Departure from Brive

How did we decide to leave and why?

There was a concatenation of circumstances, and neither the initial idea nor the first move came from me. I won't elaborate; suffice it to give a brief résumé.

It was in October 1910. My sister Marguerite had recently married Armand, who was reasonably well off and could amply support a family content with a comfortable, if not luxurious, life.

At that time the Canadian High Commission in Paris was making a great push to attract fresh immigrants to this new, sparsely inhabited country so that they would populate and cultivate it. In addition to the most alluring pamphlets, there were talks by representatives of the Canadian government and by the Oblate Fathers, among whom was Father Giroux, who were trying to nudge possible applicants towards Catholic and French-Canadian settlements.[1] They painted a rosy picture of vast, open spaces full of the promise of riches, of free land, of the expansive, independent life of the settler who was master of his own destiny, and of the enthusiasm of creating something with one's own hands.

Armand, who knew the Canadian High Commissioner in Paris, Sir Philippe Roy, and had talked to him at various meetings during visits to the capital, allowed himself to be persuaded and decided to follow the siren call of the unknown.[2] He had a perfect command of the language of Shakespeare, having visited England several times after his studies. His father had already recognized that mastery of the language that was understood in most countries would be a valuable asset for the rest of his life.

In addition, he was a great reader of books like those of Baron Mandat-Grancy — *Fleur de Lys,* for instance — that told tales of French officers whose names he recognized and who had gone into exile for political reasons.[3] And, finally, he loved horses, having served in the 21st Cavalry and often taken part in races for his regiment, so that one way or another, he was perfectly equipped for an "uprooting," as Philippe Roy, in his splendid apartment on the Boulevard des Capucines, jokingly called our departure.

When Armand spoke of his plans to escape, he naturally found an eager listener in me. I was twenty years old, at the age of wild dreams; I was fit and athletic and full of the spirit of adventure that had informed my early reading. I had embarked on the study of law very unenthusiastically, and I couldn't imagine feeling either regret or guilt if I gave up all its definitions and jargon. And I knew I was fully capable of forging my own destiny outside the well-beaten paths of our old France.

The trails followed by trappers and Indians seemed to me like luminous avenues leading to days of exultation, where all that was needed was a willing heart and brawny arms.

For Jean, Armand's brother, who had also begun to study law, and who had an indolent, easygoing temperament, the departure seemed more like an amusing interlude, a vacation in a foreign country, than a leap into a new life rooted in the soil of the New World. He knew perfectly well that whatever happened, his share of the family inheritance spread out in the Limousin and locked away in his father's safe would offer him, with perhaps the added advantage of a good marriage, unimpeded entrée into a successful bourgeois life in France.

Naturally, Armand would be travelling by himself, leaving my sister to join us later. The age of their son, Christian, didn't allow her to leave him, but it was agreed that she would join her husband as soon as we were more or less ready to receive her.

Our plan was to settle in northern Alberta, the last province before the Rockies and the Pacific, somewhere near Lac La Biche, which had been mentioned in Canadian propaganda.

I spare the reader the details of the preparations for departure. As usual, we were tempted to take great quantities of things that seemed essential but in the event were superfluous. And I still remember our last evening in Paris when, as we sat on the terrace of the Café de la Paix, my good friend Maxime Gaspéri came looking for me to hand over, with an air of mystery, his revolver.

Our fortune consisted of about 16,000 or 18,000 francs (I forget the exact amount) and our passage came to between 350 and 400 francs. It was the time of "oil lamps and sailing ships," when a pair of oxen cost about 500 or 600 francs.

The exchange on the dollar was 5.25 francs, so we had about $3,400 to get us there and to get settled. When we'd used up this capital, we would have to provide for all the necessities of our new life strictly though our own labour, our bare arms, and our initiative.

We made the crossing on the *Victorian,* a ship of the Allan Line, and the voyage went without a hitch. The ship was no greyhound of the seas, so it took twelve days — all in bad weather that gave some indication of what awaited us on the New Continent. In fact, we were almost immobilized by thick fog at one point, and the foghorn sounded most lugubrious, especially during the night. Despite a bit of pitching and tossing during a storm — which had little effect on us — the days, with their constant novelty and unexpected incident, passed pleasantly and we pictured ourselves as sons of the ancient Argonauts, setting off on a quest for the Golden Fleece.

PIERRE MATURIÉ

Arrival in Canada

The St. Lawrence estuary was already jammed with ice, so all maritime traffic went through the ports of New Brunswick or Nova Scotia — Saint John or Halifax. We disembarked in Halifax, of which my only memory is of the gloomy, mournful aspect of its docks blanketed by a heavy snowfall that had been dirtied by trucks and transport. We were to travel overnight to Montréal on a special train, which gave us a foretaste of the comfort of Canadian trains, and in the morning we set foot in Montréal, the historic city dear to the heart of French people, who cannot but feel a sense of repossession. As our stay there was to be brief — we'd get supplies at the end of the journey in Edmonton — we stayed in a big, grand hotel, the Windsor, and I still have a vivid memory of its vestibule with its onyx and green marble bar.

The following day we began the long journey across the Canadian continent, since from the Atlantic and the province of Québec we were travelling to the Rockies and the province of Alberta, the last one before British Columbia and the Pacific. So we had to cross not only Québec, but also Ontario, Manitoba, and Saskatchewan, a journey of five days and five nights, with stops at stations where there were double passing tracks. In fact, for almost the whole distance, there was only single track at that time, so these stations were passing points where two trains were signalled on the same stretch.

But Canadian trains were well equipped for these long journeys and even in tourist class, which corresponds to our third class, were genuinely comfortable. The coaches were divided down the middle by an open corridor, on each side of which were four seats, facing each other two by two. At night the black porter in each coach lowered the top panel of the compartment and pushed the seats together, which made them into comfortable couchettes with mattresses and blankets, given privacy with thick curtains and lit by bedside lamps. In addition, at the end of each coach were two toilet compartments: "Gentlemen" and "Ladies," with towels and seats, nothing like our toilets, which are like telephone booths. Here five or six people at a time could comfortably wash, shave or apply makeup. There was even, to our great astonishment, a small kitchen, where one could prepare meals. We bachelors went to the dining car, which didn't put too great a strain on our budget.

For me, the trip was like a nature film: the train traversed mile upon mile of forest, forests that sometimes allowed us to glimpse, beneath their blanket of snow, a lake, a little log cabin with a plume of smoke rising from the chimney, the home of a settler trying to clear the land. That was the typical rustic dwelling of the immigrant, with its modest stable, also built of unstripped logs, with a flat roof covered with sod; bales of hay harvested last summer probably in a small clearing beside a nearby lake and a pile of firewood beside the door. But at each moment, the image vanished to make way for a different scene, like an old-fashioned magic lantern show; we passed timber yards where brawny lumberjacks in heavy woollen checked shirts were sawing railroad ties; small isolated stations with wooden platforms, with sometimes a few more prosperous farms around them; rivers sleeping the sleep of winter beneath the snow.

Night didn't extinguish our curiosity, and I often took my time in lowering the blind; for in the clear, lovely, boreal moonlight those vast, snowy expanses took on an unreal, almost ghostly appearance. On the second night there was an alert; the chief engineer on the train, a very lofty personage, came through each coach to take the men aside to warn them, without alarming the ladies, that they'd had word of a plot to stop and attack the train. We were delighted, and tales of Fenimore Cooper, Mayne Reid, and Buffalo Bill flooded into our minds.[4] But after we'd spent the night sleeping with one eye open, day dawned without the slightest sign of bandits.

PIERRE MATURIÉ

We stopped for several hours in Winnipeg, already the impressive capital of Manitoba. We took advantage of the stop to stretch our legs on the streets and sidewalks of the city. Just a few years previously, this had been a mere Hudson's Bay Company post called Fort Garry. These centres were all called "Fort" something-or-other, because they were not only commercial centres, but also garrisons for the troops or for the police in charge of keeping order in the region.

The three main railroad companies — the Grand Trunk Pacific, the Canadian Pacific Railway, and the Canadian National Railway — had all realized the future importance of this city, and the Grand Trunk Pacific had built a splendid hotel there, the Fort Garry, as they had done in other provincial capitals: the Château Frontenac in Québec, the Château Laurier in Montréal, the Macdonald in Edmonton, and I believe, a superb hotel in Banff in the Rockies as well.

As I wandered round the town gazing into shop windows, I had an amusing adventure. I went to get a shave in a barber shop and found myself unable to keep up my end of the conversation. All I could do was to say "yes" to all the questions the barber asked, so that after he'd exhausted all his topics, I had to pay three dollars, which was a considerable sum in those days. The train continued imperturbably on its way on rails nailed to the sleepers that had cost so much labour and so many deaths a few years earlier. For this was old Indian territory, their great hunting grounds, and the local tribes had not looked with indulgence upon the intrusion by the Palefaces. There had been ambushes and skirmishes, with warriors swooping down on the workmen and riding off moments later leaving bloody bodies and scalped heads scattered around the campsite. It had taken all the authority and loyalty of Father Lacombe, Oblate missionary to the West, to impose the idea of peace between the Indians and the white pioneers.[5] A treaty was signed between them, a treaty that was often disputed by the Canadian government, or rather by its subordinates, officers, soldiers, or representatives.

The scene changed, for now we were passing through the wheat-growing region of Manitoba, then Saskatchewan, vast stretches of treeless land, the great Prairie, where herds of countless bison had left their mark on the ground on trails that led to the salt flats they loved. These can still be seen wherever the plough has not passed. And an old prairie dweller told us that it's not rare to find carcasses and horns of these mighty creatures now on the verge of extinction. Indeed, the Indians first, and then the whites, with their more accurate guns, heedlessly slaughtered these beasts by the thousand, using only their woolly coats, their hump, and their tongue, the preferred morsels, and leaving on the ground vast heaps of meat on which the coyotes feasted.[6] The herds that remain are either in national parks or roaming wild in the extreme north of Alberta, where there are two fairly large herds, one belonging to a Métis. It is now absolutely forbidden to kill them except in cases of extreme necessity.

The rails ran on straight towards the west, revealing more cultivated lands clustered along the tracks, villages that seemed prosperous because of their proximity to the means of transportation, magnificent stretches of wheat that grow with no need of fertilizer or rotation. At each little station, the grain elevators rose like towers, testifying to the richness of the soil. There was scarcely any sign of the land having been recently cleared, because those who had been fortunate enough to settle first in this region, right behind the railroad, had not had to face the hard labour of clearing forests. But there, as everywhere else, there was the other side of the coin. In various places there was a shortage of potable water: it was brackish and horrible-tasting. No trees, often for miles and miles, and the only shadows were cast either by one's own body or by the telegraph poles. Obviously, man had tamed nature and wise settlers had managed to create around their dwellings areas of greenery, like oases, and with improved technology, they understood how to get water from deep wells.

As the train ate up inexorably the miles through Saskatchewan,

PIERRE MATURIÉ

the scenery changed; gradually, undulations appeared in the land to form gentle valleys with small clumps of trees and little rivers. After the previous uniformity, it came as a relief. Finally, after passing through the fairly large towns of Brandon and Regina and seeing on the platforms of some small stations Indians, who had doubtless come in from nearby reserves, selling trinkets (moccasins, glass necklaces), and after passing through several time zones, since we'd moved from Eastern Time to Central Time to Mountain Time, we reached Edmonton.

Arrival in Edmonton

Edmonton, the former Fort-des-Prairies, our last stop before the Great North. It was early in December 1910. Edmonton had been, until a mere few years before, a major fur trading centre on the banks of the North Saskatchewan River. Then emigration, pushing westwards with the thrust that characterizes migration and settlement, and with pioneers setting their sights towards the lands of the North, fierce guardians of the riches that had filled their imagination (precious metals, furs), they needed a starting point whence their dreams could take off and become reality. Which is why Edmonton became the wide-open door to the vast North and a supply point that had become so prosperous that by the time we got there, it had nearly fifty thousand inhabitants. In addition, the surrounding land for a radius of about twenty to twenty-five miles had turned out to be fertile and easy to cultivate, and the arrival of settlers who raised grain and livestock, and who were also, of course, consumers, had contributed to its development. The city, sparkling new, was spread out on a grid, with streets and avenues intersecting at right angles. The avenues, with Jasper the main one, ran east-west and the roads north-south.

The city had every amenity, like the towns on the old continent, but with greater comfort: large, splendid hotels, shops, big banks, administrative offices, cinemas. The land was divided into building lots, which were subject to wild speculation, with fortunes being made every day.

We had no idea where to stay in this unknown town. A Canadian we met on the platform noticed our hesitation and kindly gave us the names of several hotels, with a special recommendation for the one where he stayed himself: the Cecil Hotel, which had moderate rates and would not make too big a dent in our funds, which we were trying to hang on to. So we headed for the Cecil, built, naturally, of wood, and near Jasper Avenue beside the boardwalk like in a Western film: huge entrance hall, with a big reception desk, leather armchairs, and brass spittoons, and the inevitable bar, long enough to accommodate fifty thirsty clients. Price one piastre fifty per day, "piastre" being the word used by the Native people for the Canadian dollar, which was divided into a half (fifty) and a quarter. The price was reasonable and the manager, realizing we'd come from "the Old Country," gave us a small reduction and a round of drinks at the bar.

At that time, newcomers were an object of curiosity for the locals, and especially when they learnt they came from "over there," that they were, in fact, "green," as people liked to call them, and easily taken in. Newspaper reporters, always with their ear to the ground, used to come to the hotels to find out the names of the latest arrivals and to interview them if they were foreigners like us. They used to ask all kinds of questions about plans and intentions and embroidered the stories shamelessly. The following day, therefore, we were visited by land agents and salesmen with offers of building plots and even farms in the surrounding area. Maybe we would have done well to invest a few hundred dollars in these lots, which often saw a huge increase in value from one month to the next. But it was speculation in a country completely unknown to us, and we thought of it as snake oil. However, as events proved, this was not at all the case, since the plots we could have bought for $200 or $250 were resold after various transactions, for a final price of $2,000 to $4,000. It was the boom, a phenomenon that attracted to this expanding and dynamic Canadian north a continual influx of settlers and farmers.

From various conversations, with Armand always acting as interpreter when we weren't speaking to French Canadians, we began to get some idea of the next stage of our journey. Several "old-timers" — the expression used to designate all those — trappers, prospectors or farmers — who had been living in the North for a long time (some had even been in the Klondike gold rush) — urged us most strongly to abandon the idea of Lac La Biche, a dead end with no future, and to go on to Athabasca Landing, 110 miles north of Edmonton. At the time it was a very small settlement on the great river from which it took its name, the Athabasca. The railroad didn't yet go that far North, so it had to be reached by one's own means, namely on a simple trail by horse and wagon in summer and by sledge in winter. But they all told us that it was already the distribution centre for supplies for the area to the north, and that as soon as the railroad was in, there would be a remarkable boom.

For us, Lac La Biche, Athabasca, they were all the same, a window to the unknown, especially as we'd heard nothing in particular in favour of Lac La Biche, whereas the arguments put forward by our unsolicited advisors seemed perfectly valid.[7] It was that decision, therefore, that put us on the road to Athabasca.

Two days later, we began making a list of all the things we'd need for the actual trip; anything else needed to get settled could be purchased when we got there. The advice we got from our new friends was invaluable, since they'd all come down from the North in order to live it up for a few days in town and to get supplies for the winter months. One of them was going back to Fort McMurray, where he worked as a trapper in winter and hired himself out on the boats that crossed Lake Athabasca in summer; another was working in a logging camp in the forest and, with the return of summer, was going back to his concession, where he'd cleared 30 acres.

Naturally, all these conversations and the advice that went with them were accompanied by several rounds at the bar, where a good deal of whisky was drunk — by them, at least; we, out of nervousness, but also from lack of habit, went easy on this novel drink.

We needed to kit ourselves out; our biggest purchase, which was the most important, since it would be responsible for the success of the whole journey, was a team of horses and a vehicle. Armand, who had served in a cavalry regiment and had even raced when he was a sub-lieutenant in the army, was our authority when it came to horse buying. We went to several stables that rented or sold all kinds of horses, for the horse was king at that time, like cars and garages today. After visiting several of them, he decided upon a team of geldings — a bit light, in my view — bays named Gay Boy and Colonel. His army training was obviously an influence on him.

As for the sled, that was easy: we got a second-hand "democrat" in good condition, with a single seat in front and all the back part for the goods we were going to take with us.[8] These were mainly items or perishables we'd need either on the road or as soon as we arrived. First, a camping mattress and blankets, our luggage from France, a case of provisions (bacon, pork and beans, sugar, tea, coffee, condensed milk, a pail of lard, jam, biscuits, a few preserves), a storm lantern, a can of gasoline, an axe, a spade, horse blankets, a bale of hay, and a bag of oats. We'd brought with us from France two guns, one, a twelve-bore belonging to Jean, the other my grandfather Soulacroix's .16-calibre. And we'd finally bought a second-hand Winchester .32 and a little .22 for small game like partridge or rabbit.

The road — to give the trail a name it hardly deserved — was very difficult in parts, according to our information, so we couldn't expect to do more than twenty-five miles — or forty kilometres — a day.

We planned to camp at night in wayside hostels, called "stopping places," where there was shelter for beasts and men in a cabin that was warm and, of course, built of logs, since the logs were free. People did their own cooking — such as it was — and laid their mattresses and blankets on the floor. For the animals, there was a stable with a roof covered in earth and straw, so fairly warm. Hay was supposed to be provided by the "innkeeper," and water was available, if not from a tap, at least from a well, which was usually beside a small creek. One way or another, in another day and age, it would have been "lodging for man and beast" in the time of oil lamps and sailing ships.

Departure for Athabasca and Visit with the Le Galls

So, having bought all the necessary equipment and made an inventory of it in our log book, we stowed it all on our democrat and on the morning of our sixth day, we set out at about eleven in the morning. We weren't heading directly for Athabasca because an Oblate Father had told us about a French family who'd been living for several years northwest of Edmonton towards Morinville and who were always happy for a visit from new settlers from the old country. We had warned them of our arrival and of the priest's recommendation. For us it was a simple outing, a sort of dry run to give us and the horses some experience, since the road we were to take was relatively well worn through government business. It was an area that had been cleared and settled and was in full expansion.

We had about twenty miles to cover, which wasn't excessive, even with a stop for a rest and a meal. It was a perfect northern winter day; the sun was shining on the immaculate snow-covered fields and countryside beneath a sky that was a deeper blue than we ever saw in the Limousin. The cold was quite bitter, about fifteen or eighteen degrees below zero. But we were dressed like Canadians: fleece-lined jackets, trousers tucked into thick woollen socks and high moccasins of boiled leather, because it was impossible to travel, even to make a visit, in city clothes.

The trip was uneventful, but gave us the opportunity to get to know our horses, which seemed very amenable. They trotted at a steady pace to the accompaniment of the bells that were the only sound in the great silence, together with the squeaking of the skis on the sledge on the tracks left by previous vehicles. We sometimes rode and sometimes walked beside the sledge, chatting about our new life and smoking a pipe or a cigarette. When we arrived at the Le Galls' farm, it was already dark.

The reception we were given was truly astonishing. Even if it's the custom in foreign, far-flung countries to give a warm welcome to visitors, especially if they come from the same country of origin, we could never have imagined such kindness. The family, which was originally from Brittany, consisted of two parents, two sons of sixteen and twenty, and a daughter of eighteen, Madeleine. When we stopped in the yard, at the sound of our bells the doors were flung open and everyone stepped outside, despite the biting cold, and there were exclamations of delight as if we were expected with eager anticipation. We hadn't had a moment to say who we were before we were dragged indoors, the eldest son making it clear that he would take care of the horses.

The interior was a revelation of how settlers could look after themselves: an attractive kitchen, a simple but comfortable living-room with mahogany furniture, no doubt from Eaton's catalogue, and the inevitable rocking chairs. The house was warmly heated by a stove and an impressive heater that managed to heat even the upstairs thanks to some pipes that wound up the stairs. It was built of wood, naturally, as were all the houses in the country, but it had several layers with air space between them; the roof was covered in shakes, a kind of tile of red pine or cedar.

When we'd been shown our room — a big double bed and a mattress on the floor, and the son had returned from the stable after unhitching the horses and tending to them — we were introduced to the table.

It certainly wasn't every day that they put on such a reception. At the sight of the dishes on the table and the splendid table cloth that covered it, we realized the honour our hosts wanted to do us and the joy and emotion our visit brought them.

Naturally the meal was very lively, and we were bombarded with questions about the old country. And when the table was cleared and Jean appeared with one of our bottles of Bisquit Dubouché VSOP that Armand had been given by his neighbour in Champanatier, Monsieur Vayle, who was proprietor of the brand, excitement reached the point of delirium. The evening continued till very late, with the gramophone playing *La Marseillaise* and other French songs and dances in which Jean partnered the young and pretty Madeleine, who seemed most appreciative of his gallantry.

The following day was spent on a tour of inspection of the property, which must have been over 200 acres. They lived a comfortable life and planned to expand to accommodate marriages, and they had a healthy bank account, whereas in France they would have remained smallholders or tenant farmers.

But all good things come to an end. Yet I still have fond memories of that visit, since they still warm my heart fifty years later. Despite their insistence that we prolong our stay, we had to break the spell and think about leaving. We thought that any delay would be harmful to us and there wouldn't be any good land left in Athabasca by the time we arrived.

We had to get back onto the trail for Athabasca via a cut in the forest that followed, for the most part, the breaks cut to define the township boundaries. As we were leaving, the Le Galls gave us detailed directions, but as the markers were already vague, we had to keep our wits about us. If someone says, for example, "After six or seven miles, you'll see a big pine tree ahead of you, and you have to take a sharp left," you have, first of all, to estimate the distance, and then there are a lot of pine trees. Then, "five or six miles further on, there's a fork in the trail, and you have to follow the one where several trees have had their branches cut to about seven feet." You have to have eyes like an Indian to find all that, and anyway the branches could have been torn off by the wind or snapped off by other travellers since the time when they were a sign. The cut was frequently crossed by trails made haphazardly by settlers looking for good trees with which to build their houses and stables, and as traffic was not frequent in these parts, the trails had been covered with fresh snow. Thus the horses had to pull hard all the time, and our progress suffered accordingly. So, what with stops so that the horses, who were giving their all, could catch their breath, breaks for meals, detours we had to take to avoid hidden and dangerous stumps, and sometimes the removal of a tree that had fallen in a storm, we couldn't do more than three miles an hour.

But the weather continued fine, with the same sunshine and constant cold, which was made more bearable by the cover of the trees. We took turns at driving, with the others walking behind, both to keep warm and to lighten the load. The day passed without incident; there were many new things to see: spruce grouse like little pheasant chicks, with the males sometimes spreading their tails, ran away into the thicket; prairie chickens, another kind of grouse, perched like little balls of feathers at the tops of the poplars; white rabbits watching us go by, sometimes no farther away than a whip length, with only their coal-black eyes visible in the surrounding whiteness as they stood stock still.

Night fell after a mere four hours, rapidly, almost like a veil descending, when we had hoped to come to the Athabasca trail, already pleased that the day had passed without incident; for we knew that as soon as we hit the trail, there'd be a stopping place a mere three miles further along. The twilight allowed the team to carry on, and it was then, without warning, that an unexpected accident occurred to mock our best intentions.

Suddenly, without any warning jolt, without any sign of danger on the trail, we felt the sled rise up on the right and tip over to the left, hurling the load and the driver into a deep snowbank. The horses, surprised at feeling the whole equipage swerving onto their croups, sidestepped and tried to run away. But Jean, who was driving at that moment, hung onto the reins and, getting up quickly, soon had them under control. After a few soothing words and some stroking of their necks they calmed down completely.

After unhitching the horses and tying them up, we had to take stock of the disaster. The first thing was to right the sled, which was not too hard a job. But its contents were woefully scattered in snow that was about three feet deep, so there was no question of looking for them in the dark. Since our petrol lamp had also disappeared, we couldn't even follow Soubise's example when he was searching for his army.⁹ The best thing was to try to find the items we'd need for a night's camping: blankets, food supplies, the bale of hay, and the oats. That also was easy, given the size of those objects. For the rest, it was best not to trample around, for fear that everything would be buried deeper in the snow.

We put into operation our basic training and the first test of the tricks we'd been taught by our friends at the Hotel Cecil. First order of business: get a fire going; the rest can wait. The axe and shovel were strapped on to the front of the sled, thus immediately to hand, so after we'd made a clearing near a tall pine, we soon had a fine blaze going — not some modest little fire that would barely warm the bottom of a pot, but a real bonfire. In the warm light it shed over the surrounding forest, we began to think of food for men and beasts. The horses, tied up to the box on the sled that was their manger, got their rations of hay and oats, and the protection of their blankets over their backs. For us, cans of pork and beans heated in a pan, boiling hot tea, a sip of whisky with a pipe or a cigarette — a meal we would have thought barely fit for a tramp in Paris, but which we consumed with an appetite made keener by our little adventure.

All in all, there was nothing catastrophic about our situation. We looked upon it philosophically and even with a certain pride. Wasn't it, after all, baptism by fire? And we thought that although we were complete novices, we hadn't managed too badly.

We decided to take it in turns to keep watch, tend the fire, and look after the horses. We had to prepare our beds and gather enough firewood. The last task was easy, as the forest had been exploited by settlers for their building needs, and the remains of their felling lay all around in the form of big branches and tops of trees. You don't need sheets and a chambermaid to make up a bed; our friends in the hotel had given us good advice: first clear away the snow around the fire; cut a few fresh pine branches and spread them out on the cleared space, taking careful note of the wind direction. With a tarpaulin or canvas hung behind the mattress of branches, and blankets wrapped around you, you can withstand very cold temperatures, since the screen reflects the heat of the fire onto you.

The first watch began. After two or three hours we were awakened by an unexpected concert. In the still night, beneath a superb moon that had risen over the forest giving enough light to read by, we heard howling and baying in the distance, coming nearer then moving away again, with a din that was fairly impressive to ears that were still conditioned to human sounds of the city. It came from packs of coyotes that were on a rabbit hunt through the forest, like a pack of hunting dogs. As soon as we realized what it was, our anxiety subsided, since we'd discovered, in those interesting conversations that had been like a manual for life in the North, that coyotes don't attack people, unlike the big timber wolves, which are truly dangerous animals but which are found only in the far North, way beyond Athabasca. After this interlude of local colour, we went back to sleep, and for Armand and me, it brought back memories of a night we'd spent on the roadside in the Lorian the year before, when our car had broken down. We'd been awakened at dawn by the magnificent music of the finely tuned voices of a pack of hounds running a hare in the valleys.

Daybreak came gradually like the slow awakening of a beautiful girl; little by little the forest emerged from the darkness, the trees stood out despite their mantle of snow, and near the fire that was still burning bright, the kettle was singing.

We took care of the horses, ate breakfast, and started to search for our lost possessions. Daylight made it easy for us to find every-thing and reload it, checking it off in the list in our notebook, which, we realized, was extremely useful. The accident was soon repaired and there were no serious consequences to bemoan. What we discovered was that in the darkness the right ski on the sled had run over a big tree stump hidden under the snow, and that had caused the load to become unbalanced. Finally, we made a reconnaissance of the trail ahead and discovered that there was a dead end a hundred yards ahead of us in a clearing that must have been a source of logs for some settler or other, and probably still was, since there were many fine, straight trees there.

We turned around and got back onto the trail a few hundred yards further on, and we knew now that the Athabasca Trail couldn't be too far away.[10] The day's stage would of course have to be a bit longer since we would have to catch up on the miles between our night's camp and the stopping place where we should have spent the night. But the prospect didn't bother us, since as soon as we got to the northern trail, the route would be more clearly defined, lessening the risk of getting lost and therefore one less source of worry. After an extra stop to rest our horses, which were making heroic efforts, we arrived at the second stop-ping place just after nightfall. It was a well-built hostel made of logs. It wasn't exactly three-star, but the common room was vast and clean and comfortably heated, which was the most important thing in this climate. It was comforting indeed for people who had spent a day in biting cold to relax in this atmosphere, which was like a haven of rest — though the furnishings were fairly basic: a table of roughly sawn wood, same for the benches, and a big zinc basin for toilet needs. The toilets in the stables, with the warmth from the horses, had explicit instructions to pitch the produce of intestinal evacuations outside, onto the manure heap.

Other travellers were camping with us, since the transportation of all merchandise passed along this route from Edmonton to Athabasca, where it was then redirected according to the needs of various destinations, overland in winter and by water in summer, towards Lesser Slave Lake and Peace River in the west, or Fort McMurray for the larger lakes in the North. With these rough but interesting men, the evening was a source of information to us. We needed to learn everything, and without having to ask questions, but by keeping our ears open — with Armand always as interpreter — we got valuable information for the next day's stage, which was giving rise to heated discussion among the men. They had been in the business for several years and knew all the pitfalls and all the good places: log bridges in a poor state of repair, steep slopes, rough drops to the side, etc., for there was no such thing as a Public Works Department in this part of the world.

For another three days we made slow but steady progress towards the North that was a blank on maps, like unknown lands. It wasn't long since we'd left Brive and France, yet here everything was so different: men, nature, climate. We had to revise all the ideas of life we'd had up to then to get in tune with the demands of life in vast, rugged Canada. But each day, sometimes a hard taskmaster, gave us the best possible practical lessons. No other accident befell us, despite some difficult patches like crossing creeks where the trail was like a roller coaster and the horses thundered down in order to gallop up the other side. But we soon got the hang of it, and quickly took it in our stride. We saw our first ermine one day streaking ahead of us with its little black tuft erect at the end of its tail. I tried to catch it by running after it — like a greenhorn — but it ran lightly over the snow, whereas I sank up to my knees. This was a magnificent spectacle for us, since it represented to our eyes the best possible fur that decorated royal robes or capes of elegant rich women leaving a ball.

One day we had a snow flurry that only lasted for part of the morning, but was enough to make the terrain more difficult for the horses. Then the weather cleared up again and went back to being cold, and it was with a bright sun shining in the northern blue sky that we arrived that afternoon within sight of Athabasca.

Arrival in Athabasca

From the plateau where thick woods had given way for some miles to a few patches of bush among which were clearings with their settlers' cabins, we emerged suddenly into the valley of the Athabasca River, which unfurled the meanderings of its white ribbon before our astonished eyes. We were expecting something like the ones at home, but instead there appeared a mighty river several hundred feet wide. The village was spread out along its banks with its streets laid out on a grid and little wooden houses and bungalows lining Main Street. The trail descended a steep slope towards the street as if travellers, eager to reach the end of their journey, had no time to make any detours.

After stopping for a moment to admire the impressive panorama of the land that was to become our own, we began the descent down the hill, which didn't seem to us to present any particular difficulties. The first few yards were easy. The horses, with the brake on, kept their footing well. But little by little, as the slope became steeper and they slipped on their hind legs, the back part of the sled began to slip out and then, swerving round completely, got caught on the front ski. And before long, we were hurtling down helter-skelter with the horses sliding on their backsides, the sledge crosswise on the trail, the drivers hanging on to the load, and the whole slithering down the hill with a din of bells to come to a skidding halt in the middle of Main Street.

Every arrival in these northern communities, remote from the outside world — and especially in such circumstances — constitutes an event. So before long there was a small crowd of curious bystanders on the wooden boardwalk, which we could just as well have done without. In front of the Grand Union Hotel — the only hotel in town — the usual seasonal clients — prospectors, trappers, settlers, and idlers of all kinds — were laughing heartily and slapping their thighs. But with great goodwill, they also came to help us put things to rights. In fact, there was no damage, either to the horses, which had merely grazed their behinds, or to the sled, which hadn't tipped over. The only thing broken was a strap on the brake, and that was easy to repair.

Given the general hilarity, all we could do was to take it all in good part. It was the best strategy to adopt with these good folk who were cut off from all amusements and saw a chance to have a laugh at our expense, when the occasions for doing so were very rare. One of them — a stable boy who subsequently became a good friend — undertook to look after the horses and the reloading, and Armand announced a round of drinks for everyone, which meant that we immediately became one of them and were adopted by them straight away. And as we drank, we learnt the secret of the descent down the hill: the only way to brake a sled is to wrap around one of the rear skis a heavy logging chain with its end fixed to the crossbar of the sled. What we had done was to simply come straight down on ordinary skis, hence the wonderful result. But when all was said and done, we couldn't have made a better entrance, and from the moment people learnt that we were Frenchmen from the old country, they named us, with the greatest of goodwill, the Frenchies. And later on they quite often reminded us laughingly of our unceremonious arrival in Athabasca.

Athabasca (which the Indians had originally called Tawatinaw) was situated on the river of the same name, which, as I mentioned earlier, was the size of France's biggest rivers. It rises in the Rockies, in Lake Brown in Jasper National Park, then, after flowing through the town of Athabasca, goes almost straight north to reach, after almost seventy miles of dangerous rapids, the village of Fort McMurray, and goes on to flow into Lake Athabasca.

For quite some time — ever since the railroad had approached Edmonton — the Hudson's Bay Company had abandoned the prairie route via the La Loche River, La Biche Lake, and McMurray that it had used as a highway to its trading posts in the North, and instead used one that connected Edmonton along a trail via the nearest bend in the Athabasca River, to create a new jumping-off point to the Mackenzie basin. And from that time to our arrival in Athabasca, that's where all the boats coming from and going to the North tied up. Now a ferry, mounted on a cable and pulley, plied across the river to the north shore, beyond which stretched what was still considered Indian territory.

The village, which had two hundred and fifty inhabitants, boasted several general stores, among them Révillon and the Hudson's Bay,[11] two banks, a post office, a livery barn, the Lands Office, two restaurants independent of the hotel, barber shops, a bakery, a real estate office, two Protestant churches, a Catholic church, and a hospital, the Sacred Heart. These were the essentials for a small community that had as yet few external roots, since the arrival of settlers ready to clear land was only just beginning.

For us, getting settled in the Grand Hotel, which had about twenty rooms at that time, was a great relief. Although we had adapted to life on the trail, it was very pleasant to sleep in beds and especially to get undressed. Naturally the furnishing was very basic: iron and leather bed, a table, a chair, a dressing table. But the temperature was acceptable since the building was heated by huge wood-burning furnaces and heating vents. The windows were double-glazed, and when the thermometer registered twenty or twenty-five below zero, it was positively luxurious to snuggle into the armchairs in the lounge.

We had a great and pleasant surprise when we checked in: the manager of the hotel (which was owned at that time by a French Canadian, Isaïe Gagnon) was a Frenchman from France called Servestre.[12] We got to know each other straight away, of course, and he became a good friend. Another Frenchman of about sixty, "Old Goyet," served as barman — a position he exploited to the full, unfortunately. He was rumoured to be a former banker, who had ended up there after who knows what misfortunes. It was obvious from his conversation that he was well educated, but he didn't talk much about his early life. His face, framed by an almost white beard, had an air of mischievous intelligence. But this country often held surprises like that, for there was such a mix of races, origins, and social class that the initial surprise soon wore off. Work, of whatever kind, was a noble enterprise and diminished no one. We were able to verify this through our own experience in the months that followed. So it was normal to see the stable boy take off his overalls and sit down in the restaurant beside the doctor or a lawyer with no breach of etiquette.

The following day we met some other people, either in the hotel lobby, which had become our headquarters, or through introductions by friends. And all these connections contributed to our complete integration into the community, which at that time was a mere settlement of immigrants. The local mayor, the "Major," was an energetic young French-Canadian physician, Dr. Olivier;[13] one of the important tradesmen, owner of a general store, was called Lessard, and was also a French Canadian, brother of P.-E. Lessard, a minister in the legislature in Edmonton.[14] I mentioned that the hotel was owned by Isaïe Gagnon, a French Canadian and one of the first people to live in the area.[15] Very wealthy, he'd made most of his fortune in land speculation, buying up property at the very beginning for ridiculously low prices and dividing it into lots. In addition to the Grand Hotel, he owned several apartment buildings in the village and had interests all around. From a financial point of view, he was number one in the area and had the reputation of being an astute driver of hard bargains. He gave us no cause for complaint later on, for he always treated us with consideration. For most of the residents, we represented a young, open element from the old country who had arrived among them, not running away from past errors, but seeking adventure and an independent life.

They soon realized this, since we did not act like most of the immigrants, who were largely uncultivated people destined to remain anonymous. We, on the other hand, thought it would be useful to make the social round, so we called on our priest, Father Desmarais,[16] Dr. Olivier, the Mounted Police sergeant, the postmaster, the director of the Dominion Lands Office — in fact, on everyone we hadn't already met in the hotel or the bar. And in four days all our new friends were calling us by our first names, and vice versa.

The Search for Land

But we hadn't come to wallow in a garden of earthly delights. We were impatient to go off in search of the land we were to colonize, which seemed to us like the Promised Land. And starting the search was even more urgent, since we weren't the only ones who had arrived in Athabasca, and the Bureau of Land Claims was registering new entries every day.

What we needed was a guide, someone trustworthy who knew the area and who would show us places where we might settle. Servestre put us in touch with a Métis named Sidore Lafleur, half Cree and half French Canadian, who had always lived in the region and knew it like the back of his hand.[17] We didn't want to be too far, both so that we could enjoy the amenities of the village, and also to make the most of the boom that might take place in a few months' time when the railroad arrived.

We easily came to terms with the Métis and agreed to a salary of $3 per day, with food thrown in — and also tobacco. And as an added incentive, we had promised, if we found something satisfactory through his efforts, a bonus of $6, which whetted his appetite. We gave him carte blanche to organize our little expedition. We needed horses: we already had our two and Lafleur had his cayuse. So from the stable he needed to get three others, one to be saddled and the others to haul our paraphernalia (blankets, oats, tent, etc.). This presented no difficulty, since the horse, together with sled dogs, was the only method of locomotion at that time of year.

We had decided to make four sorties, one in each of the cardinal directions, so that we could get an overview of the topography of the area around Athabasca and have some basis for making our choice.

Our first trip was towards the west, following the course of the Athabasca for a few miles, then making an oblique arc back towards the village. We had with us, besides Lafleur's large-bore shotgun, our little .22 in the hope of killing a few rabbits or partridges to offer as our contribution to whoever would give us lodging for the night. The first two days of prospecting were not very satisfactory, for the lands we visited were either too heavily wooded or, if they seemed to be cleared, were too marshy, according to our guide. We had to be cautious at this time of year, for the cold and frost gave consistency to areas that, with the spring thaw, would be revealed as wet and spongy, or muskeg as they were called. To trained eyes, the appearance of trees, thickets, or the vegetation in general could gave valuable information. In addition, if we came upon land that looked promising, we would take a little sample with the help of our pick and shovel to assess its quality and composition.

The survey maps provided by the Lands Office and the markers left by the surveyors in the centre of each section gave the approximate distance of the section from the village. It was, therefore, a methodical task that we undertook, but one that was extremely interesting in this absolutely new wilderness: towards the west, the region stretched towards Baptiste Lake, about twenty miles from Athabasca.[18] A rudimentary trail, practicable by wagon for six or seven miles, left the village, and along this path homesteads had already been registered by settlers, and at certain points there were signs of the beginnings of settlement: houses or cabins and barns under construction, trees cut down, land cleared ready for ploughing next spring.

About two miles from the village, we were scheduled to stop at the house of a Frenchman, Jo Tobaty, who had been one of the first immigrants to settle in the area.[19] Servestre had told us about him and had strongly advised us to pay him a visit, which we would have done anyway, as we were anxious to get to know the whole French colony.

After a while, we saw a house built of wooden boards typical of the West, and Lafleur confirmed that was our first stop. Jo was at home finishing his breakfast, and he gave us a most cordial welcome. Although he was of an equable disposition, one might even say reserved, it was easy to see that he was happy to welcome compatriots newly arrived from the country he had left many years before, and he put himself at our entire disposal to advise us about our plans. Part of his land had already been planted, and he lived a solitary bachelor existence there like a real philosopher. He had two good horses to keep him company, and with an apparently well-padded bank account, he had created a happy, peaceful existence. He, too, was counting on a boom when the trains arrived, and his land and the lots he had bought in town would certainly increase in value when they did. But he told us all this perfectly calmly, without a trace of excitement, and it was obvious that his life wouldn't change when all that happened. During our conversation over cups of steaming hot coffee, he suggested, in case we were interested, that if we didn't find anything suitable on Baptiste Lake, he knew of some land towards the northwest, overlooking the river, that might be what we needed for three sections. As it was still early in the morning and we had plenty of time, we decided to go ahead towards Baptiste Lake so that we wouldn't kick ourselves later on for not looking it over, and to come back via the route that would allow us to see the land he'd mentioned. Jo and Lafleur knew the area equally well, so Lafleur had no trouble in locating the land, just before the confluence of Baptiste Creek and the Athabasca River.

We left Tobaty, pleased with the useful information he'd so generously given us. The weather was cold and very clear, and the sun made the frost on the branches sparkle like garlands of silver paper. We were full of confidence and enthusiasm, for the words of Tobaty, coming from such a calm, reasonable man, seemed full of promise.

When we got near Baptiste Lake, we had to leave the trail to ride through woods and thickets to get to the lands Lafleur knew. It was fairly flat land, with vast clearings here and there made by ancient forest fires. When we took samples, the soil looked suitable for cultivation. Unfortunately, when we followed the surveyors' lines that marked out the three sections we were allowed, we were disappointed to discover, on the survey maps we'd been given in the Lands Office, that two of the sections had already been taken. The ones that were left were, therefore, separated, and it would be impossible to make a single big lot out of our property.

But our disappointment was tempered by the hope that Tobaty's directions had aroused in us, and we were anxious to examine the value of the property, its situation, and the advantages it might have to offer. In any case, there was already an important point in its favour: it was relatively close to town, a mere five or six miles.

We had to hurry, for we had a long way to go. Lafleur, who travelled through this country like a fish in an aquarium (he'd hunted and fished here since he was a boy), decided to cut across towards Baptiste Creek, and then to follow it along a trail that reached the Athabasca. We observed in astonishment the ease with which Sidore Lafleur found his bearings and moved through those woods that presented not only the difficulty of their density, but also that of obstacles like fallen trees hidden under the snow. He found, either by some special sense or instinct or atavism, a path that he'd travelled months, or even years, previously when he was trapping or hunting moose. To us, everything looked the same in this tangle of bushes and thickets buried under a thick layer of snow; to him, every little hump or each turn of a stream had a particular significance. He'd told us that we'd find, near a clearing, a former beaver dam, and indeed, after a while, we did cross such a dyke, after which it was child's play to follow the course of the creek, which had broadened out. And at about one o'clock, we saw spread out before us the vast, frozen, white stretch of the mighty Athabasca.

For us it was almost like entering the Promised Land. To the left of the confluence, forests of great pine trees, tamaracks, and spruce descended the steep slope almost down to the river; but to our right, the banks rose up to the plateau by a series of steps, like a great staircase. There the forest, probably burnt down over the course of centuries, gave way to thin clumps of undergrowth and widely spaced thickets. Near the mouth, and just as we had been told, an ancient trappers' cabin still stood, with a path that was just visible through the undergrowth leading up from it. We decided to climb this path straight away and to eat a hasty lunch on the plateau, for we were eager to see what lay in store for us. But following Lafleur's advice, we took care to let the horses drink through a hole we made in the ice, and to fill our kettle with chunks of ice, since it takes a vast amount of both snow and time to get the same result, and we were in a hurry.

The climb was only about five or six hundred metres and presented no great difficulty. So a few minutes later we reached the plateau and there a revelation awaited us. This was the place where we'd pitch our tent.

After a quick bite gobbled down in haste, we made an initial inspection of the property. A plateau stretched along the banks we'd just climbed for about 40 or 50 acres; it would be easy to clear for it was covered by brush and stands of young trees that would be easily cleared by a couple of fires. On the northern edge, the land fell away to the river over five or six hundred metres in a series of valleys that we'd seen when we'd stopped at the mouth of the creek. Towards the south the land undulated gently, as it did towards the east, where a small lake drained the water from the forest to flow into a creek through a coulee towards the Athabasca.

From the edge of the plateau there was a splendid view: the Athabasca, flowing from the east, made a great curve in front of us and carried on towards the village. In winter, the river was the main transportation route for the hundreds of sleds that left the town to supply all the lands to the northwest, via Lesser Slave Lake and, about three hundred miles farther on, Peace River and Grande Prairie.

At the moment we stopped, we could see lines of ten or fifteen sleds gliding on the trail made in the ice on the river. The view was so panoramic both to our right and our left, and also over the undulations descending towards the bank, that we took the decision right there and then to plant our flag on the spot, like explorers in an unknown land, and to build our house there.

It was too late to find and mark the boundaries of the three sections we wanted to claim. But the survey sheets didn't show any indication that an option had been taken out on this property. The only receipt indicating that new settlers had arrived was far to the southwest, and the Lands Office told us that they were French people. What we had to do, urgently, was to find one of the section markers to let the Lands Office know the numbers on the homesteads we were hoping to lay claim to. It didn't take Lafleur long to make out, along the survey line, the little mound and the iron post with all the essential information engraved on it. And we deduced from this information, and from orientation on the survey maps, that this land was four and a half miles as the crow flies from the city limits.

It was beginning to get dark but we couldn't bring ourselves to leave. We had to tear ourselves away from our contemplation, however, so we decided to return early the following morning to officially mark the boundaries of our three sections and to have them registered in the government offices. Next day, it was scarcely light before we were already in the saddle heading towards "our" land. And as soon as we got there, we started the serious business of surveying and listing the marks and dimensions inscribed on the survey markers.

I digress a moment here to explain the conditions of staking a claim. Almost the whole of northern Canada from the border with the United States had been surveyed and staked out by special crews of surveyors; the result is a checkerboard of townships, sections, and quarter sections, or land claims known as homesteads. The townships are bounded by north–south and east–west cuts laid out in straight lines like avenues across the landscape, crossing forests, waterways, marshes. These townships are made up of six-mile squares and are aligned in north–south groups known as ranges. Each township contains six sections, numbered from one to thirty-six from the lower right corner to the upper right corner, each measuring a mile square. Each section, in turn, contains four quarter sections a half-mile square, or 800 metres. At the centre of each section four holes have been dug; the dirt from these holes forms a mound into which is planted a solid iron post, engraved with the number of the section, its orientation, the number of the township and the range.

Thus, when one has found a suitable property, one has to find this mound and take note of the information engraved on the marker. This information has to be checked against a survey map, so that the precise position of the property can be established.

After four hours of really hard work — it entailed tramping in all directions through thick snow, stumbling over hidden roots and branches in search of the snow-covered mounds — we finally found all the necessary information. The first two concessions were easy to calculate, since they were in the same section. The third was more troublesome, since it was in another section that abutted the others at a corner. It wasn't the only completely adjacent property, but it would be easy to negotiate later on by some kind of arrangement with the owner of the neighbouring lot if it should find a buyer. This was not at all certain, for this quarter section lay largely either at the bottom of the coulee coming from the little lake or on the banks sloping down to the river. We were hoping to have this piece classified as uncultivable and good for grazing land, and to be able to rent it for five cents per acre. It was understood that the three pieces would form an inseparable whole and could not be sold without the consent of all three parties, each one of us keeping right of veto. These clarifications were necessary because the house was to be built on Jean's lot, which thus became the headquarters with appropriate dependencies.

During the afternoon, after a festive picnic on "our" plateau, we could go back to Athabasca and present ourselves at the Lands Office to register our lands for the very reasonable price of $10 each. The formalities had been reduced to a minimum and we began to appreciate the administrative simplicity for which our dear France had not prepared us. It was December 20, 1910. Lafleur received his daily salary of $3 as we had agreed, and as we had nothing but praise for his behaviour, as well as for his knowledge, we added the $6 bonus, although it was actually on Jo Tobaty's recommendation that we'd found the property. He was delighted and broadcast to all and sundry the Frenchies' fair play. I suspect we were in part responsible for the drinking binge he went on to celebrate. So now we were true settlers and considered as fellow citizens by the people of Athabasca. The community had adopted us completely, and everyone, from the Mounties to the local Métis, knew us and hailed us as we passed in the street. Along with the rights to the land concession, we also had responsibilities towards the government to obtain final and legal ownership. The owner of a homestead was obligated to build or have built a house worth at least $300, to clear and put under cultivation ten acres per year for three years, and to be resident for at least six months of the year, the rest being spent, at the discretion of the settler, either on his property or elsewhere to earn money. After this period of three years, there was an inspection of the land, and if everything was in order, the title of the property was given, with all rights of cession, by sale or by testament.

As we weren't there as tourists, we had to think of getting down to work, despite the harshness of the climate, and first of all to build a barn. We didn't want to wait in the hotel for spring to arrive before starting to build. It would have been just possible, but hardly advisable, since our little fortune would have been badly depleted (as it was already), and we needed to hang on to what we had. The local people thought that since we were greenhorns newly arrived from the old country, we'd let ourselves be seduced by the pleasant life in the hotel. So they were astonished when we said that we were going to start on the building right away. But since it was so close to Christmas, we decided to put off the house building till after the festivities. In any case, we had to get our equipment together and to find one or two experienced workmen — real lumberjacks, as we were using logs for building. We'd have to cut down the trees, measure the logs to set up the frame, calculate the openings, put on a roof and so on, all of which were tasks for which we were completely unqualified. Through Servestre, who was an invaluable intermediary, we were put in touch with two French Canadians who had left their camp laying railroad sleepers, and were thinking of going south towards Edmonton or Calgary if they couldn't find work on the spot. We offered them employment for the period it took to build, at the rate of $4 per day with food included, a salary they accepted.

But there was one big hitch in our plans: every day we had to go back and forth to the village, which took a heavy toll on men and beasts. They suggested, therefore, that we live in a tent, a suggestion we wouldn't have dared make, since it seemed to us that the rigours of the season would have made it impossible for such a long time. But they quickly disabused us of that idea, declaring that it would be nothing new for them. As for us, we'd have to weigh our physical possibilities before deciding, since we were immediately intrigued by the idea. And as we were full of self-confidence and wanted to keep up the reputation of the French, we accepted.

The two French Canadians were typical of real *coureurs de bois*, descended from the race that had created Québec City and Montréal. One of them, Daigneau, was between forty-five and fifty with a calm, reflective temperament and very skilled in carpentry.[20] He seemed an ideal foreman. Originally from Québec, he had for many years been moving from place to place around the North-West. The other, Lamothe, was about thirty and was also from the East, though with a homestead in North Battleford, Saskatchewan. Both were geniuses with the axe, like all trimmers of railroad ties. As this is piecework, to make any money at it, you can't afford to be either lazy or clumsy. Events proved that we'd made the right choice. If possible, we hoped not to have to purchase a tent that would be of no use to us afterwards. When we spoke to Dr. Olivier, he introduced us to the manager of the Hudson's Bay Company in Edmonton, who was a frequent visitor to the posts in the North and especially to Athabasca, and who happened to be in town at that moment. He very kindly allowed the local manager to rent to us, for a very modest sum, one of the large tents that were used less and less frequently and only on rare occasions, for temporary storage of supplies. It was a fairly capacious tent with three mica windows and could hold all five of us. Now we would have to set it up so that we could begin to work in earnest the very day that we went up to our property. Following Daigneau's advice, we bought a number of planks to make a floor and metre-high walls, which would allow a buildup of snow to conserve warmth. We should also plan for a small stable, just big enough to shelter the two horses that were absolutely necessary to haul the sawn and trimmed logs. Planks would be necessary for that, too, but as we weren't cutting them, they could be used later for the house or the new stable.

To transport all this gear to our property, our democrat was no longer sufficient. We had to get a sturdy sled that could carry heavy weight. But as this country was a place of trading as well as of credit, we managed to trade our vehicle for a proper farm sled in very good shape. As soon as we'd taken care of that problem, we had to bend our minds to another: that of our horses. Several of the locals, including Jo Tobaty, had delivered an opinion about them: they were good trotting horses, mainly meant for a spin in the country, for swift buggy rides on good roads. It was quite a different matter to drag trees from the forest, or to haul heavy loads on unpaved roads. We were so persuaded by these arguments that we decided to put them to the test right away with a load of planks for the tent and the temporary stable and various tools. It wasn't a particularly heavy load, but just out of Athabasca, there were several slopes on the trail to the plateau. In addition, in the Canadiens' gear, there was a big hauling chain that we were intending to use in a trial run at dragging three or four good tree trunks out of the forest. The attempt was, unfortunately, proof of our friends' opinion. On the slopes our horses were brave and willing, but too impetuous, thrusting too hard at their collars rather than applying an even force, with the result that they became needlessly fatigued. In the woods, where calm and regular pulling is needed, they strained at the least resistance instead of waiting for the master's commands and pulling the load easily. Obviously, with time and habit, we could have got them to work more consistently and efficiently. But we couldn't afford that because we'd need a team that was used to hauling as soon as the first tree was felled. So there was only one alternative: we had to sell them directly to someone who needed them, or trade them in at the leasing stable with which we'd been doing business since we'd arrived. We easily came to an arrangement with Fitzgibbon, the stable owner, to trade them for a team of brown bays that we'd already been looking at.

Tom and Chief were a pair of handsome, well-trained six-year-olds that looked like Breton post-horses. They were as well adapted for roads as for heavy hauling. Well versed as we were in the trading practices of peasants from the Quercy or the Limousin, we were soon convinced that they had nothing on those of the Canadians. Finally, after some time, we concluded the deal leaning on the bar of the Grand Union Hotel: $100 rebate on the team and $10 for the harness; but the stable owner, after two or three rounds of whisky, threw in the stabling of the horses as well.

After we'd pitched the tent in the shelter of a slight mound quite near the plot we'd staked out for the house, we came back to spend the day of Christmas Eve on our "ranch" to build the stable. It took no time at all for the two lumberjack/carpenters to build the frame of the little structure, which, although it was primitive, was sufficient to protect our horses from snow and blizzard. Covered and lined with tarpaper, with a thick layer of straw on the roof and a snow barrier piled up around three sides, it even offered them a certain level of "comfort." It wasn't a meticulous piece of work; the boards, which hadn't been cut to size, stuck out at the back, but that meant they could be used later for other purposes. Still, we'd finished by evening and it was already dark by the time we left for the village. So everything was ready and we felt free to abandon ourselves to the spirit of Christmas. And when we went back up there, we'd be able to get down to the serious business of building.

This festive season, spent thousands of kilometres from our native land, from our family and loved ones, was, despite everything, tinged with a hint of melancholy. We all did our best to look cheerful, but in the depths of our hearts, we cherished memories of past Christmases. All the same, there was plenty of good cheer everywhere — in the streets, saloons, houses, and Indian cabins; for in these remote lands in the icy solitudes of the North, it was still Christmas. Métis, Indians, Canadiens, settlers from far and near, all the adventurers descending like a migrating flock: trappers, lumberjacks, prospectors, all had braved severe fatigue, exhausting treks in the frigid cold and often real danger, to get to this Athabasca sparkling with all its lights and all its shop-windows, like shepherds following the Star. But the Star wasn't necessarily the one on the church for everyone; for most of them it shone on the brightly lit hotel and its roaring bar, on restaurants that felt comfortably warm, and on the shops that offered many, many nice things to satisfy their desires.

We went to midnight mass and to our great astonishment found that the church was almost too small to hold the large congregation. Settlers, villagers, Métis, and Indians wearing Native costume and brightly coloured scarves filled the nave, which had been prettily decorated with pine branches and coloured paper flowers by the Grey Nuns from the hospital.[21] Father Desmarais preached a sermon in three languages, French, English, and Cree, and beneath a magnificent moon shining in the boreal night, everyone hurried off to the warmth of their houses and their groaning tables.

We had arranged to spend this extraordinary evening with our two Canadiens and had also invited Tobaty and the two Frenchmen from the hotel, Servestre and Old Goyet, to dinner. The midnight feast was perfectly acceptable, even for stomachs that still retained memories of France: oatmeal soup, roast turkey, moose liver grilled on a spit, applesauce, two or three kinds of pie (apple, raisin, and strawberry), pudding, and, on each table, big bowls of flaming punch. And to help the customary tea or coffee go down, we'd asked the barman to bring a bottle of claret — from California!

In the euphoria of the moment, in that atmosphere of deafening laughter, song, and music, in that overheated room where the upper crust of local society rubbed shoulders with the orphans of the Great North, we let ourselves drift off into dreaming Christmas dreams of what the baby Jesus would put in our stockings to give success to our enterprise. Dr. Olivier, as the town's mayor, made a speech — and a very good speech it was — singing the praises of the future of the region, announcing the imminent arrival of the railroad, and wishing everyone — in particular the Frenchies — the best of luck, and then, with great sensitivity, he had put on the phonograph the only two French songs the establishment possessed. He really was an extremely nice man, and was to prove himself so later on in dramatic circumstances. And in the big hotel lobby, the evening ended, naturally, with dancing, jigs or polkas which are brought back to me by the Western films I so enjoy watching, the costumes less fancy perhaps, but the same gaiety and the same joie de vivre of big children starved for joy in their daily lives.

The Promised Land: Living in the Tent and Building the House

At dawn on the 26th, we left Athabasca and the hotel for good to settle on our own land. We took with us our luggage and a few necessary provisions, for since we were so close to town, we didn't want to further clutter our tent, which was already pretty crowded with our five mattresses — though they did make useful extra seats when we rolled them up in the morning. These beds, as you can imagine, were hardly four-posters, but a simple envelope of firm canvas stuffed with the mane and hair of moose; this was saved by the Indians when they'd scraped the hide, which they subsequently tanned in thick smoke from fires made of green branches and leaves.

As soon as we'd arrived and unpacked, we set to work straight away. It was agreed that Jean, who didn't mind cooking, would be our resident chef. He would be responsible for the fire, meals, hot drinks, etc. Armand and I would help the Canadiens drag out the logs with a chain and bring them to the spot where the house would be built. The first morning was spent looking for the right trees to cut down. For a house of the dimensions we envisioned, we'd need at least a hundred pretty good-sized ones for the frame, floorboards, ceilings, roof struts, etc. We wanted to build a fairly large, comfortable house right away, as we were thinking in particular of the projected arrival of my sister. Close to the camp, there were already about thirty good-sized pine trees, very tall and straight as an arrow. We had no qualms about using them, as they were on land that we planned to clear anyway. As for the rest, we'd have to get them from the other side of the plateau, outside our property in the woods that sloped down towards Baptiste Creek. It didn't look as if these would be so easy to drag out, to our eyes at least, but the Canadiens didn't seem too worried about it, and obviously we lacked experience. So by the end of the morning, we had taken stock of our possibilities and were reassured that there would be no lack of our main raw material. That was a stroke of luck, since sometimes people had to go miles to find suitable trees, which meant a big loss of time, extra work, and additional fatigue for the horses.

The first axe blow fell in the early afternoon after a meal where Jean first showed his colours, earning congratulations all round. This was actually no challenge, since we had ferocious appetites: we were at that age, but also the biting cold air was a great stimulant. Right from the first axe blow, we learnt exactly what it means to be a lumberjack worthy of the name. When one of them had assessed the height of a tree, its shape, and the volume of the branches, he selected the fall point and invariably the victim fell on that precise spot. Our role was to saw off the branches and to cut it to the required length with our big two-handed saw. The prepared trunks were pulled out of the woods by chain, loaded onto the sled, and brought to the site of the new house. This was the part of the work that made us appreciate our heavy horses; they knew how to get the collar into the right position, pulling the reins taut and moving off with ease, with a firm but unhurried pace. So we had the team we needed. After such a busy day, we returned eagerly to our tent, which was already looking like "home." There we found warmth — relative to the cold outside, of course — and we also found, beneath the dim light of two storm lamps, the table that master chef Jean had laid on two packing cases that fitted into each other during the day, all part of our strategy of making the most of what we had. Every evening, one of us would put out a noose, and in the morning, almost invariably, we'd find near the tent one or two rabbits to supplement our menu. We had the same luck with the prairie chickens or partridges that were added to our diet, for we always had our .22 shotgun with us, on the road or on the work site. So our meals were varied and got us away from the pork and beans, corned beef, etc., that were a last resort. In addition, thanks to Lafleur, we had a haunch of moose from which Jean cut splendid steaks. But we needed to get another as well as a stock of frozen fish, for with all of us eating, stocks were rapidly depleted. And to satisfy my ambition, I bought a dozen medium-sized traps for mink and set them on the trail that led to our tree felling. The day after I'd set them, I was pleased to find in the jaws of one of them a superb mink that had frozen to death. Lamothe showed me how to skin it, which wasn't any more difficult than catching it. It hardly represented a future fortune, since at that time skins were worth only about fifty or sixty cents apiece.

We went on with the felling for about a week, interrupted by the 1st of January, which was a holiday for us. We were invited by Jo Tobaty to his little house and spent several pleasant hours with him; apart from being French, he was full of wise advice, so we were able to take advantage of his lengthy experience in the country.

The following day we were visited in our camp by a near neighbour, a former miner from northern France who'd come two years earlier with his entire family and two sons-in-law to try their luck in the New World. His name was Menut, and from that very moment we always called him "Old Menut" because he was getting on — nearly sixty — and it showed. Altogether they owned three concessions to the southwest of our property about two kilometres away, but because of straitened circumstances, they'd taken some time to make a start and hadn't made much progress. They were kind, helpful neighbours to us, and later on we were able to return all their favours by being of service to them. With very few exceptions, mutual help was not an empty concept in this new country where nature is fierce and man is often in need of man.

After we'd felled and hauled the trees and aligned them near the site we'd chosen, we all four set about the task of stripping the bark, since mould and rot can set in if the bark is left on. Jean came periodically throughout the afternoon to lend a hand. At last, when a good selection of logs was ready, Daigneau and Lamothe began the actual construction work, leaving us to finish the planing of the trees they'd numbered according to their appearance and shape.

We'd really been lucky to find these men and be able to hire them. They were perfect workers, completely competent with an axe and with the maneuvring of the heavy pieces of wood. They used their tools like virtuosos, with the blade landing on exactly the right spot, the chips flying, the cuts widening before our very eyes and the trunk falling right beside the previous one as precisely as if a machine were doing it. And in addition they were happy, cheerful companions, easy to get along with.

Little by little the frame began to take shape, but how many attempts did it take to swivel every log before we got a perfect fit along the whole length! Even though each one was fully mature, there were always a few irregularities, bumps, excrescences, knots of branches, etc., which had to be eliminated gradually to get a perfect fit with the log below. In the places where the doors and windows were to go, it was useful to prepare the spot where an opening would be sawn out. And there were masses of other details that would complicate the work if they were skipped over at this stage.

January went by with alternating periods of intense cold and snowstorms. Sometimes we had to halt the work for two or three days. In our tent, the fire roared non-stop and life was bearable. However, towards the end of the month, the thermometer dropped to fifty-five degrees below zero. The air was clear as crystal, the smoke rose pure white in the sky and straight as a die; you could hear the trees cracking with the cold, and as their wood cracked, it made a sound like a gunshot. When we were outside, we had to be careful not to touch a piece of iron with our bare hands, or the skin stuck to it and suppurated like a burn. A bottle of brandy was half frozen. The fire burnt us in front but our backs stayed frozen. To water the horses from our little lake, we had to cut through the ice with an axe, and the ice kept reforming, and fingers, even wrapped in mittens, had a hard job holding on to the handle. All animal life seemed suspended in the forest, and beasts huddled in the crook of branches that were buried in snow. Luckily there was plenty of dead wood outside our tent, and like careful ants, we'd laid in a good stock. But in spite of all this, in spite of the inhuman temperature that turned the landscape into an unknown planet, good humour never flagged under our fragile canvas, and all of us took turns at telling stories as we smoked a pipe or cigarettes. Daigneau and Lamothe, like the prudent men they were, sharpened or repaired their tools for the work to come.

Finally, one night, the weather "broke," as the Canadiens say, and the sky clouded over. It was the prelude to another snowfall. This was a matter of serious concern for us, as the fodder for the horses was sadly diminished and we would soon run out. We decided to go down to Athabasca the next day to get six or eight bales of compressed hay and to replenish our supplies.

When Jean and I set out the following morning, a few snow-flakes had already fallen during the night, but the cold had let up and it couldn't have been much more than fifteen to eighteen degrees below zero. It was lucky for us, as we had to go to the village anyway, for the sake of the horses at least, as with the work they were doing in the bitter cold and in their rudimentary stable, they were eating a lot more than usual. This was the best way of warming them up — a kind of central heating. We imagined we'd be back in time for the noon meal, for as soon as we'd completed our purchases, there was nothing to keep us in Athabasca.

We were in sight of the village when the snow started up again. We thought it would be a mere few flakes like the previous night, but as we were doing our errands, it developed into a blizzard, so that when we set out again for our property, the tracks on the trail were completely filled in. As far as Jo Tobaty's place, the horses were more or less all right. Jo tried to persuade us to stay and have lunch with him in the hope that the storm would pass as we were eating. Finally, we accepted, mainly for the sake of the horses, who could rest as they were munching some good fodder, before undertaking the last part of the trip, which would probably be the most challenging.

But the snow continued to fall and it looked as if night would come early. Jo would gladly have kept us for the night, but we didn't want to leave our companions alone, which would have doubled their watches and fire duty. So as soon as the meal was over, we set off on the last few miles that would take us to the tent we were so anxious to see.

The snow was now being driven by a blizzard and whipped the horses' eyes and heads, which were soon hooded in white. At one point, in places less sheltered by the woods, the snow had been blown into drifts, barring the path of the sled, so that we had to dig with big snow shovels. And in other places, we had to unhitch the horses and go back and forth for about a hundred metres to create a double track to help the sled get through.

When we arrived at the fork leading to our camp, it was already getting dark, and we were afraid we wouldn't be able to find our way in the cotton-wool landscape where all tracks had been erased since we'd driven through that morning. Luckily, partly as a joke and partly as a kind of intuition, I'd nailed to a tree trunk where the path diverged, a plank on which I'd painted, in black letters, the name that we'd already decided on for our property: "Bellevue."

It was with great delight and happy appreciation of this initiative that we saw this landmark, as from there we only had another mile to go, and although it would be no easier than the others, having been only recently created, like the horses we could smell the barn and shelter. The storm began to die down, and the sturdy beasts found their way in the darkness better than we could have done ourselves. We'd covered a few hundred metres when we saw a flickering light coming towards us. It was one of our trusty Canadiens who, armed with a storm lamp, was on a reconnaissance trip to the main trail to make sure we hadn't taken a wrong turn at the fork. A quarter of an hour later, we were in camp, at home; and you cannot possibly understand what this "at home" meant to us, even if it was only a tent in the woods, for in the northern night, everything is hostile and icy and everything seems inhuman; but under the simple, fragile canvas rampart, we knew that we'd find gentle warmth, the friendly light of the lamp, the good smell of pork and beans or ham and eggs, and the presence of men.

Our first task was to tend to the horses, who so richly deserved our attention. Lamothe did that whilst we unloaded the provisions. And then, after a meal that seemed to us like a royal repast, with a pipe in our mouths and a glass in our hand, came the time to recount the story of the day. This little epic in the storm was our passport into the good books of the roughnecks who made up the larger part of the population of Athabasca. Indeed, several of them had watched us setting out when the blizzard was at its height, and with Jo Tobaty adding his grain of salt, we'd gone up several notches in their estimation, and it was generally agreed that even if we were green, we were no slouches.

The beginning of February saw the completion of the frame of the building. We'd decided on a porch all around, so we needed a set of shorter logs to support the floor; as for the roof, it was quite splendid and had taken really very skilled workmen to execute something that was so out of the ordinary in that part of the world. At the risk of blowing my own trumpet, I have to confess that it was my design. As far as we knew and could tell from reports of friends, ours was the only house like it in the whole of the North-West at the time.

We'd decided to finish only one room for the time being; it would serve as kitchen and bedroom until my sister came to join us. She wasn't due to arrive until the return of milder weather; for what might be all right for men would hardly be all right for a woman used to every comfort who would see her whole life turned upside down.

The roof, which was waterproofed with a layer of planks covered by a sheet of tarred, sanded felt, allowed us to work sheltered from the elements if the weather was too harsh for outside work. There was plenty of this, with the construction of a stable, which was as necessary for the animals as the house was for humans. Our presence wasn't as useful to the Canadiens as it had been when they were preparing the logs, so we were able to haul wood for the floors and the ceilings as well as for the doors and windows, which then had to be installed. Following Daigneau's advice, we used these trips to take into Athabasca loads of firewood, which we soon sold.

So, little by little and day by day, everything took shape; buildings rose in the midst of this still-wild nature, which became tamed by their very presence. The large panes of the windows shone in the sunshine, and when we arrived, we looked for smoke curling up from the galvanized chimney made by the village tinsmith. But our men were already starting to talk about leaving, since the agreement was that they'd be free to go around March 15th. So they made sure they did the jobs that we couldn't do ourselves, like the stable and the excavation of a little cellar under the living-room. The stable didn't require the same finesse as the house, neither for the frame nor for the number or size of the openings. As for the roof, a mere two sloping beams over the building, with the loft to be added later in between them.

The days went by, still cold, but perfectly bearable, with the clear sky of those harsh winters, which allowed us to work unhampered, for the body in motion warms up by itself. By now we'd been broken into this life under canvas and were proud of ourselves.

Our diet had been fairly varied, with the addition of all the game that yielded delicious meals, together with another delivery of elk meat brought by Lafleur, along with at least fifty whitefish, delicious fleshy fish as big as fine French carp. Our refrigerator worked well: it was huge, since it was the whole of the outdoors. It was also simple: a rope and hook for meat and a bag for fish. Very economical.

So on March 16th, Daigneau and Lamothe left us as we had agreed, with each side perfectly satisfied with the other. Their behaviour and their work had been irreproachable, and we'd been really fortunate that they'd been free at the precise moment when we'd needed them so urgently. From then on, we were left to our own devices, and despite the difficulties we were bound to encounter on the way, we embarked confidently and without trepidation upon the next chapter of our lives. The work accomplished by our two Canadiens was really enormous: the biggest part was already done. The house was up, roofed, enclosed and most of the cellar dug and panelled. The struts for the interior wall that was going to enclose our personal "apartment" (one of the five rooms we'd planned) were in place, as were the ceiling panels. It was left to us to nail the wall panels and the flooring, all work that we could manage, without being exactly master carpenters. As long as you could wield a hammer . . . In the stable, the frame was completely finished, as was the roof, still simple, awaiting a real hayloft.

We still had to make the mangers for hay and grains, for which we'd kept all the pieces left over from the roof timbers.

This is why we stayed on in the tent for another few days, especially for the finishing of the house. We also had to buy and transport whatever furniture was absolutely necessary: bedding, kitchen stove, table, a few chairs. We did our accounts after paying for hired men and the building materials. Dollars had melted away: out of our initial funds, there remained only $1,313, from which we'd have to take expenses for furniture and provisions for men and beasts for the next few months.

For a few days, Armand, following Servestre's advice, had been in touch with the hotel owner about a position as receptionist and assistant bookkeeper. He spoke English well and found working in a frock coat more to his taste than the hard work on the land. He came to an agreement with them and would go to live in the Grand Union Hotel as soon as we could move into our fine house. He would be fed and housed with a monthly salary that, if it wasn't enormous, was still more than adequate. He was to subtract a certain amount from his salary to contribute to his share of the value of the property and to our upkeep.

We bought two iron and brass beds and sufficient bedding, a few household linens, an ordinary stove, which we got on sale, and the three or four chairs we'd need. If some day we had more visitors than that, well, there were still the stools from the tent.

Home at Last: The Move into the Big House

We moved into the big house as soon as we'd finished installing the wall and the floors. After bashing our fingers with the hammer a few times, we had found the work quite easy and it had gone along at a spanking pace. What had taken most time was plugging the chinks between the logs; the normal local procedure was daubing, namely stuffing the spaces between the logs with a mixture of clay and chopped straw. I didn't care for this method; I didn't find it very elegant, and besides, the season wasn't conducive to it. Then one day in Athabasca, as I went by the Hudson's Bay warehouse, I saw near the riverbank, a pile of abandoned cables. They were the leftover ropes the Indians use on the scows and boats plying to and fro on the rivers to the big northern lakes. I asked what was to happen to them and was told by the manager that I could take them if they were of any use to me. I didn't need to be asked twice, because the sight of these cables had given me a sudden illumination: why not unwind the cables and stuff the floss obtained from them into the chinks, hammering it in with wooden caulks? So that is how we achieved successful weather-stripping, which was almost invisible.

Our first evening seemed very pleasant, in a real house, nice and warm, with real windows through which we could see, when we were working outside, the friendly light of the lamp. And no ordinary old storm lantern from the tent, either, but rather an up-to-the-minute Tito-Landi model![22] From now on we could come and go, read or write at a table, set a table for a proper meal, just like city folk. We knew that our trusty horses were under cover on a good bed of hay, which brought us great peace of mind. We celebrated the move with a hefty splash of our "real cognac" after dinner, accompanied by a royal cigar.

Jean and I started to live like real settlers, looking after the horses, hauling firewood and preparing it for our own stove or for sale in town — the hotel had ordered a load. And there was still work to be done finishing the house and the stable. Out of unused planks, I'd made a kind of sideboard with doors at the bottom where we could store kitchen utensils and dishes; and above it I'd built shelves where we put the few French books we'd been able to find, together with the reports of experimental farms in Canada. These reports, which were huge volumes, were extremely interesting, especially for newcomers like ourselves. Another favourite occupation when the weather was bad was the perusal of the big Eaton's catalogue from Winnipeg; a tome as heavy as a dictionary, it offered everything one could desire or imagine and could be found in the home of every settler right up to the most remote corners of the far North.

I'd also built, along the outside wall of our room, on the part that was still unfinished, a big wardrobe where we could finally store our clothes and various other things we'd brought from France and had remained in trunks until now. We had a real home at last, and this was a source of moral strength for me as I saw in it the first root attaching my destiny to this new land. I enjoyed playing the handyman, which was a useful occupation when the weather kept us from working outside, but which still improved our living conditions by imposing some order upon them and adding a personal note to them. I might say, without self-congratulation, that there was always perfect order in our house, unlike what was often the case in bachelor quarters.

One black mark in all this euphoria was the question of water. We had to take the horses three times a day to drink at our little lake, which was a dreadful chore. For our own needs, the problem didn't arise for the time being, as the snow, of which we kept a kettleful on the fire, was more than sufficient. We'd discussed this problem with our Canadiens, but they couldn't stay any longer. They'd taken stock of our surroundings and had pointed out a good spot in a slight dip near the house.

So one day, when we were particularly tired and fed up, we decided to take the bull by the horns. Our neighbour Menut had made a spontaneous offer of his services the first time we'd met, so we went to his house to lay out the problem and to ask his help with a task that was quite beyond us. He and his sons-in-law, on the other hand, were ex-miners and had a working knowledge of picks, shovels, and props. Also, it was the period of calm before the snow melted, when there was little work to be done on the soil. So he and one of his sons-in-law turned up most willingly and we began work the following day. It was already April when we started; the days were drawing out gradually and there was an almost imperceptible promise of the coming spring.

With our partners contributing experience and muscle power and we ourselves doing our utmost to help, the digging advanced quite fast as soon as we'd got past the layer of frozen ground. The soil was good, with a few round stones here and there, but one way or another it wasn't too difficult. From time to time, we put in a prop of small logs as a cautionary measure until the real one would be installed at the end. About five metres down we came to some slight dripping, which increased as we went on until the dirt started to come up as mud. But we had to keep on digging another metre and a half or two metres before there was a good supply of water at a steady level. Better to be safe than sorry: I preferred to do another couple of hours' work now rather than to have to start all over again if our livestock increased and our needs with it, and our water supply proved insufficient. Towards the end of the fourth day we decided to stop and see whether the basin was filled the next day.

Indeed, as soon as we got up, we were able to tell that the bottom of the well was full already, and by noon, the water had reached the first oozing. So now we had to put in the wooden sides, which was child's play for our team of miners. To keep it clean, I spread a layer of pebbles at the bottom: at the opening, a solid wooden tripod, a pulley and rope, and the well was ready. When the water had settled, it turned out to be cool and fresh, although there was a slight pine taste at first, which lessened little by little over the next few months and finally disappeared altogether. This well must have been fed by water that drained from land to the south of us and that flowed towards the riverbank: wherever it came from, it never ran out. The Menuts very kindly refused to take anything for their work, saying that they'd get their payment some day when they needed a helping hand, either to haul goods or to borrow our horses for a day.

First Spring and First Furrow

Our first spring

It came in mid-April, as it does in this country, almost in a single moment. One morning, the wind came up, moving over the snowy wastes like a breath of warm air. It was the famous Chinook, blowing from the Pacific through gaps in the Rocky Mountains, the wind of resurrection, the magician, who, like Prince Charming, comes to awaken slumbering nature. The snow melted before our very eyes; water, freed from its icy corset, ran everywhere, clear and singing down the frozen roofs, along paths and trails, cascading towards the streams, where it soon wore away the wintry carapace.

Migrating birds began to fill the skies — empty till then — in their flight northward: geese in their triangular formation, teal and canvasback ducks in tightly packed flights, quacking their hearts out as if to announce the new spring and landing with a great flapping of wings on stretches of newly opened water.

Life, as if frozen in the winter ice, started up again almost without transition. Red- or orange-breasted robins began flying in the thickets around the lakes on which appeared the round-topped muskrat nests. At the tops of the tall pines squirrels once more emerged as cheeky little urchins chasing each other from branch to branch and scolding with their high-pitched chattering, and in the still damp undergrowth, spruce partridges were starting their mating ritual, already aware of the love season to come. Within a few days the whole of winter's symphonic whiteness was about to disappear beneath the warm breezes that were bringing the kiss of Pacific islands to the frozen continent, and it wouldn't be long now before the first buds appeared along the willow branches like fluffy pompoms. The rivers groaned and broke up into enormous chunks their armour of ice and there was an infernal collapse of the mighty Athabasca, which, after being shackled by the cold, like a joyful prisoner delivered from his chains suddenly started again its everlasting journey towards the lands above and the Polar Ocean.

I was irresistibly caught up, body and soul, in the powerful atmosphere of the season that was sounding the call in all these different ways to nature's great creation. It was nothing like our gentle spring in France, which, like a child just waking up, opens up its closed windows to the young sun. The Canadian spring was violent: it rapped at your door to urge you to get out to work, for the season is short and you have to live a speeded-up double life. And the earth, like a mistress, offered itself to the plough to fructify the seeds of the next sowing.

Now we could become better acquainted with our concessions, which, free of snow, revealed themselves in their nakedness through the scrub, the woods, or the coppices. We had a fine plateau almost completely cleared of trees up to the old trail that wound up from the cabin on Baptiste Creek where an old Métis came to spend the summer. We probably wouldn't encounter any real difficulty in our first round of clearing, which we decided to begin close to the buildings. This was a precaution usually recommended in case of possible fires. It was relatively easy work, as there must have been fires at some time, so all that was left for us to do was to cut down new-growth trees, pull out the burnt-out trunks that were left here and there like black stumps, and after gathering up all this scattered wood, burn it a few days later. What a pleasure it was, and how proud we felt in the evening, at the end of a day of work, when we could look out over the changed land that was becoming humanized little by little. Just as a wild girl with a tangled mane can become a dazzling beauty when her hair is cut and combed, so the old plateau was already revealing, in wide clearings, the promise of future cultivation. The buildings, the well, a sled near the stable, an axe on a block, the whiteness of washing hanging on the line, it all bore witness to the presence of man, king of this little creation.

But when the ground was completely dried out, we had to think of turning the first furrow, true signature of the settler's claim on his land. For the first year, all we wanted to plant on the cleared land was a few potatoes for the following winter and the rest in green oats — green feed for fodder for the horses with a mix of hay. This green feed is oats harvested green, when the grains are still tender, which, harvested and dried, is the best possible feed. The piece we'd cleared was about five acres, nearly two hectares, therefore one acre in potatoes and the rest in feed. We were following Jo Tobaty's advice. For this work, a plough and harrow were essential, because at this time of year we couldn't think of borrowing from neighbours; the same work had to be done by everyone and with the same urgency. A wagon was also indispensable: without it we couldn't transport anything. We had the means to purchase these things; the sale of wood and mink trapped during the winter had brought in a few dollars, but little by little our bank account was being eroded by our investments, which would bring returns in the long run. And soon the moment would arrive when we had to put into practice the new settler's axiom: six months outside to earn, six months on the land to spend.

First furrow

The first furrow was traced. Jean led the horses and I held the handles, for neither of us yet had enough experience to guide both the horses and the plough by himself. The first furrow is the hardest, especially on virgin land where roots and the remains of stumps can knock the ploughshare off the straight. That first one has to be right, as the whole quality of the rest depends on it. So we'd hammered markers (pegs and bits of cloth) in a straight line, and with the intensity of neophytes, we didn't make a bad first attempt. What a wonderful sight is that first furrow! And as we stood before the soil that was seeing for the first time the sun that would fertilize it, how proud we were to be able to say that this was truly the fruit of our effort and our will!

Despite the complete change in my life and the occasional hardships it brought, I felt, as I looked back on my youthful hijinks in Brive, that there was no room for regrets in my heart. Certain memories rose to the surface of my mind like the bubbles in a fountain that trouble the clear mirror of the water; memories and recollections of young love, tender as an opened bud that needs the morning dew and the brightness of the day to make it flower. If I wasn't careful, these thoughts brought a tinge of melancholy to my mind, so I looked at the newly cleared lands, the vast horizon and its undiscovered woods and our roof guarding the border of our young field. And, caught up in the enthusiasm of our new creation, with the murmur of memories joining in the chorus of great hopes, I set off toward the challenge of the next task with new courage.

For each dawn, with relentless regularity, brought its heavy burden of new chores. After going over the newly turned earth with Jo Tobaty's disk harrow, we had to plant our potatoes, which wasn't too hard, and sow the oats, which was. For we were new to the task, and sowing the seeds required a sower's skill to cast them evenly — not too thick and not too thin. Our first steps were hesitant, but after a while we got into the swing of it, and once we had we couldn't break the rhythm. Another go with the ploughshare and, with God's help, Mother Earth had accepted into her bosom for fertilization our seeds and our hopes.

So life settled into a routine with all the daily contributions of our imagination and initiative. Occupied with the manifold tasks dictated by the season or by our building needs, we were obliged, if we wanted our animals to graze, either to leave them hobbled on the plateau or to have them within view, which meant a loss of time. Besides which, the hobbles often injured the horses' hocks, risking putting them out of action. After thinking it over, we decided to put a fence round a large area of the plateau. Close by were a number of young trees that would provide stakes and crossbars, and our Canadiens had already, either when they were preparing logs for the house or stable or when they were waiting for materials to arrive, prepared a certain number of posts. The work, which demanded no particular skill, was soon accomplished: the posts were sharpened and hammered in at regular intervals, so all we had to do was nail in the bars at the required height. This fence, which would still be useful when we decided to cultivate this area, allowed us to leave the horses outside all day.

In addition, being extra careful, I always attached a bell to their reins, and I liked hearing the tinkling of the bells that enlivened the calm of the plateau and gave affirmation of our presence.

May was already coming to an end, and we'd finished the urgent tasks. We could have gone on living on the property and continued clearing the land, but as we didn't need to plant any more immediately, we preferred to try to get paid employment to fatten our wallets and to create a nest egg for the expenses that would come in the fall and winter.

We'd already spoken to Dr. Olivier and Servestre about the possibility of moving into Athabasca, and they'd promised to let us know of any opportunities that turned up. So one Sunday in June, when we'd gone to mass, Armand told us that Dr. Olivier had reserved a place for our horses and ourselves in the teams doing maintenance work on the streets and avenues that hadn't been graded. As we only had one team, one of us had to drive and the other had to guide the plough or the scraper. It was quite hard work, though not unpleasant, as we could trade places if one of us got tired. The salary was very good, and we could earn on average about $8 or $9 a day, depending on the number of hours we put in. We'd rented a small, rickety wooden shack that had enough furniture for our needs, and we ate at the hotel for twenty-five cents, which was not expensive. We kept the horses in a lean-to on the house, so we didn't have to pay stable fees.

We had the job until mid-August, with three days off to dress the potato crop and to harvest the green feed with the help of the Menut family. It was a wonderful crop of fodder; in the virgin soil and with a few heaven-sent showers, it had grown vigorously, with healthy stalks, which was an advantage, given the use we intended to make of it. We put it in bales to wait for the loft we were hoping to build by the end of summer, if we had enough money.

When the work on the roads ended — like everything else, for lack of funds — we had, after deductions for living expenses for animals and men and the days off — between $400 and $500 that we could use in the fall to finish the stable.

We gave ourselves two days of complete rest, which we spent strolling round town as we'd seen others do — settlers, Métis, trappers, lumberjacks — and we could very well understand the mentality of these people, who, after hard work, enjoyed relaxation and indulgence: whisky, card games, bowling. Sprawled in deep armchairs in the hotel, we watched, with a cigar between our lips, the comings and goings of men from the North or newcomers like we had been, young and old; and I remember my first encounter with a massively built old Métis called "Captain Schott." [23] For years he'd been bringing Hudson's Bay barges down the rapids of the Athabasca to Fort McMurray, and although he was only a river boatman, he looked like an old seafarer. For the rapids also held their perils. He had a handsome, noble face ringed with a pepper-and-salt beard, and wore a peaked cap like a real ship's captain. He was about six feet tall and must have had the strength of a colossus. His two sons, aged twenty-five and twenty-eight, were also strapping young men and looked as if they'd stepped out of a Western movie with their cowboy hats, their red or yellow bandanas, and their beaded moccasins. Big hunters and trappers, they had one of the finest teams of horses in the region. For in those parts, a man's pride and joy was his horses and the fine quality of their trappings: leather harnesses with big brasses and gilded nails, fox tails or coloured tresses on their heads, bells on their collar. Two splendid horses that brought in income for their master, if he actually chose to work.

Armand gave us a surprise we could have well done without. He announced that he'd bought two dogs for wolf-hunting — wolfhounds, magnificent beasts built like greyhounds but more powerful, one, the male, Thauser, silvery black, the female, Rex, silver-grey. I'm fond of dogs, but right at that moment, it was an encumbrance for us, an extra burden (care and food), but we tried to put a good face on it.

Vacations go by faster than working days, they say, but I can honestly say that I had only one desire and one aim: to get back to our property, to organize this and that, to get on with the planning, to dream over our fine spaces that were the delight of my eyes.

So we headed back, and when we reached the Bellevue turnoff, its poor state immediately made us realize that urgent repairs were needed for summer wagons. As it had been cut in winter, the trunks and branches that had been trimmed to the level of the snow now made their appearance, causing the wheels to run up on them on one side or the other and jolting the wagon till it was almost dislocated. Besides all that, there were tree trunks that had been lying there rotting for some time. We would need to clear all this away and level the odd bump to make into a proper road the path that would provide permanent access to our property. This was the task that occupied us for the next few days. It wasn't difficult or even hard work with the horses; after being stripped of their roots, the stumps came away with the chains and all the heaps of debris were burned right there and then.

Each day, then, brought its measure of work, but in recompense, the accomplishment of each task signified progress and improvements from which both we and our lands would profit. And the path, now cleaned out and widened, gave us easy and constant access and was christened from then on with the pompous title of "The Avenue."

Little by little we explored our domain and every day brought a new discovery to be added to our list of projects. As we were hunting at the very edge of our property one day, going down into the coulee into Baptiste Creek we came across a magnificent stand of trees, ideal for building, in the woods that had been transformed into muskeg by the runoff water from surrounding land, thanks, no doubt, to the long-ago work of beavers. And in my mind's eye, where I was always planning new things, I could see a ditch that would canalize the water, draining the adjacent land. We'd also have to clean out the creek that flowed out of the lake down a coulee a mile and a half long into the Athabasca, so that we could improve the hay crop there. Between the river and our house the banks descended in a series of little hollows separated by gentle slopes; to turn these lush pastures full of wild peas into grazing land, we'd have to cut paths with a slope of only five or six metres into the banks. The hardest work would be clearing the area of dead wood left by ancient forest fires; here and there were clumps of young shoots, largely aspen and birch, which would give welcome shade in the summer when, counting my chickens before they were hatched, I saw the cattle plodding there to lie down. All this, naturally, was mere daydreaming, but what is life but the ceaseless pursuit of dreams that a combination of will and chance transform into reality?

The Railroad Comes to Athabasca

It was at this time that the railroad arrived in Athabasca. For some days we'd known that the crews laying the ties and the rails were near the village. Some of the workmen had made an appearance in the bars and saloons in the evenings, and their presence hadn't passed unnoticed. So with no telegraph or telephone, from all directions and from over a hundred miles around, people came pouring into the village: *habitants,* Montagnais and Cree Indians, Métis with wives and children, settlers, prospectors, surveyors, all waiting for the big celebration when the locomotive would appear on the horizon. Tents went up along streets that weren't yet built: prospectors' square tents, Indians' bright, multicoloured conical tepees, some the old-fashioned ones with moose-hide patches. Small horses, the cayuses, tied to a stake or hobbled, huskies near the tents, men and women with brightly coloured scarves and clothes embroidered with pretty beads, cowboys in wide stetsons and leather chaps — it all made for a brilliant tableau in the flaming fall sunshine.

Armand had let us know what day it was arriving, and like everyone else, we'd all come to town in our wagon with the whole Menut tribe. The station, built, naturally, of wood, was on the riverbank almost opposite Main Street, and a solid wooden stage had been built where the local band was already sitting waiting. All the local dignitaries were there, all craning their necks towards the cutting at the southwest of the village where the iron monster was about to appear: Dr. Olivier, the Major, Isaïe Gagnon, one of the more senior of the old-timers from Tawatinaw, Father Desmarais, the minister, MacRae from the Hudson's Bay, Létourneau, the Révillon brothers, the postmaster, the managers of the two banks, journalists from the Athabasca and Edmonton newspapers, Sergeant Fraser of the RMP.[24]

Propelled from behind by the locomotive, the train edged forward metre by metre, and it was an amazing sight to watch the work actually going on as it advanced. The ties and the rails, which had been brought by a system of rollers on platforms, were immediately laid on the ground and hammered down with very precise strokes on the iron spikes. The train kept moving forward onto each rail as it was put in place almost without a pause, and the skilled crews made the taxing work look like clockwork.

As soon as the train reached the first street in town, there was an indescribable explosion, just like an attack in the olden days. The Indians on their cayuses, the cowboys on their ranch horses galloped through the streets shouting hunting or roundup yells. Everyone was whooping for joy. For the whole area, it was the last link in the chain that joined it, finally and definitively, to the civilized world. And when the train, with its complement of sweating, unshaven men, came to a standstill under an arch of greenery beside the stage, the band started playing, but for all their puffing and blowing into their brass instruments, they couldn't manage to drown out the cheers of the crowd. The municipality had done a good job of organizing the event: barrels of beer had been set out and there were enough part-time barmen to serve everybody. All day long there was merrymaking, games, singing, and dancing. The Mounted Police, heavily reinforced, had a hard time controlling the people's exuberance, but their mere presence, from which emanated the calm force of the law, restored some kind of order among the most uninhibited.

Yes, it was a great day indeed, perhaps the greatest Athabasca had ever witnessed, since it was the day its future was changed. From now on, there would be no need to take the rough trail to journey south, to the lights of Edmonton and on to old, established Québec and the Saint Lawrence. Now all the supplies for the Great North, headed for the posts on the big lakes and the Arctic Ocean, would have to pass for the foreseeable future through our Athabasca. Hence speculation ran riot; it was what is called in these new countries a "boom." The land in the village and its immediate surroundings had already been staked out and parcelled into lots. The roads we'd worked on were now opened up and were bordered by the usual wooden sidewalks; real estate offices had their agents out everywhere, and in office after office, lots were being sold in other provinces, as far as the East and even in the States. Everything was bought and sold at breakneck speed, like in the stock market with shares in gasoline or new gold mines. A corner lot we could, at the time of our arrival, have bought for $350, was up for sale for $1,000. I saw a man from the train go into a bar to buy a lot for $800, and a minute later sell it on the sidewalk outside for $1,500. Pamphlets that had been sent out on all sides announced the big "boom" at Athabasca Landing, the former Tawatinaw in Indian language, the golden gate towards the riches of the Great North. The literature was epic in scale, and, as it was everywhere else, the bait was swallowed. We could — and should — have gone along with the mood of the place and thrown ourselves into this wild speculation. There were some shady deals, but there were also some valuable lots well situated for building, either for commercial development or for houses. It was a missed opportunity: we were too new to this situation to understand it and too cautious to seize it.

As the season progressed, we had to start thinking about our plans for covering our stable with a real roof with a steep pitch high enough to house a good, large loft. We could have tried to build it ourselves, using our own skills, which, although still tentative, were beginning to give us a bit more self-confidence. On reflection, however, we thought it would be better to hire a professional workman for three or four days; this wouldn't make too big a dent in our finances, but would give us some guarantee of solidity and also of appearance. And I've always thought of a roof in terms of a hat: each of them can make or break the appearance of the whole. We now had the means to bed down visitors or workmen, which should simplify things if the need arose.

So we went down to Athabasca to get the materials we still needed (planks, beams, tarred paper), and also to find a man who was available and able to do the work. Such a man wasn't hard to find, as any Canadian, whether English, French, or Métis, after a life spent going from one job to another, was up to any task involving wood, and could handle a saw or an axe with equal skill. Isaïe Gagnon, who, as I mentioned before, knew his Athabasca well, immediately suggested a Métis who worked every year building and maintaining the Hudson's Bay scows and barges that carried all its merchandise up North. This Métis, William Riverman, didn't speak much French; he spoke a mangled kind of English mixed with twisted French-Canadian or even Indian expressions and was a Montagnais. As he already knew us by reputation — word gets around fast in these parts — he was willing to come and give us a hand for the three or four days it would take to break the back of the work. And indeed, on the fourth day, our stable had a fine-looking roof with an opening on the front to load the hay and with more than ample storage space.

We were very happy to see our little kingdom take shape little by little: we had a welcoming house that sat in the middle of lands that we could cultivate as we pleased. Now, when one of us returned after dark, he could see through the windows the familiar light casting its warm glow on the place of shelter. Although still close in time, that chill December day when we'd pitched our tent in the wild solitude of the snow-filled coulee already seemed far away. If the place still possessed the beauty of pristine wide-open spaces and the severity of secular forests, it was already tamed by the friendly advances of its new masters, like a young animal upon contact with a gently stroking hand.

Monsieur Menut came by one evening to ask us a favour. As he didn't have any horses of his own, he asked if we'd go and help him pull out of the forest some logs they'd cut to build a stable, and haul them to the place they'd chosen. We were only too happy to oblige, and it was almost like a vacation for us to be free of our petty household tasks (cooking and meals, etc.) because we'd be eating at their place. Madame Menut was a good cook, and she made excellent soups, just like the ones we had "at home." He was a really very nice man and very good fun. When he was irked by something, he'd swear, but without any variation, always saying "Nom de zou," so that came to be the nickname we gave him.

So, one way or another, with people helping each other out, work didn't seem too much of a hardship, and although we were living in a harsh new country, we didn't feel lost in a hostile world.

The days went by, very busy, but very pleasant in the calm accomplishment of our tasks. The potatoes were harvested and laid in the cellar in fine sand from the river. We had a good supply for the winter and following spring. The green feed had been stored in the loft above the stable, and we'd also bought, as a security measure, a big load of oats from a settler at Baptiste Lake, where we'd gone at the invitation of a rancher we'd met in Athabasca, Mr. Perry. He was a recent arrival and had come overland from Montana with a herd of three or four hundred horses and about fifty Hereford cows — "White Faces" — that were to be the basis of his cattle ranching. He'd decided to settle near the lake, where he'd bought some land, rented some more from the government, and bought some concessions from the Métis. So he'd got the makings of a fine ranch, especially since, as he'd left his horses to roam free, he had the grazing on all the land that wasn't yet under concession. He spoke fairly good French with a slight accent of the Berry or Morvan provinces.[25]

We'd had an excellent visit with him, and everything he'd shown us was extremely interesting. He had three cowboys to help him, two he'd brought from Montana and the third, a Métis, whom he'd hired on the spot. His horses were largely prairie horses, fine beasts, if a bit on the light side, but at least more solid than the Indian cayuses. He meant to strengthen them by crossing them with heavier French or Irish stallions. We always remained on good terms with him and saw quite a bit of him, either in Athabasca when we were working there or at Bellevue when we were in residence there.

And so, as the months went by, we'd fulfilled the residence requirement for the current year. Now we could think of a job for the winter months that would bring in a few dollars that we could use the following spring to start on new projects that would involve new expense.

We had to make arrangements for the horses and dogs. We didn't want to give up the former, as we knew them well and liked them, and Armand couldn't help us out. Monsieur Menut came to the rescue again. As he didn't yet have his own team, he was happy to have them, so they had the honour of inaugurating the stable he'd recently built. We also lent him the sled, since the season was advanced and the snow wouldn't be long in coming. He was going to cut and haul a load of posts and bars for the spring fences, and in his spare time, he would deliver, near our stable, a load of logs for us to build a hen-house.

If the problem of the horses was solved in the best way possible, the same couldn't be said for the dogs, which, although they were of no use to us whatsoever, had become good companions. Armand couldn't have them at the hotel with him since they were quite demanding animals. We finally managed to get rid of them, after a lot of negotiating: Sergeant Fraser, who'd sold Rex to Armand, took her back, as she adored her Mountie master. Hauser we gave to Fitzgibbon, owner of the livery barn and a great animal lover, and they soon became good friends.

My Sister Arrives

My sister's arrival was scheduled for the end of the fall. October was fast drawing to a close, so there was no question of her and Armand coming to live on the property. To begin with, Armand was still working at the hotel, and secondly, Marguerite was arriving straight from France with its habits and prejudices, so was in no way prepared to play at being the farmer's wife. We were all agreed on this. And as Armand didn't want her to stay at the hotel, where she would have been confined to her room, the best solution was to find a little apartment or house to rent. This wasn't an impossibility, as some of the settlers who'd bought lots had built little bungalows — wooden ones, of course — like most people in that part of the world. Once again it was the trusty Servestre who pointed us in the right direction, since the hotel was where all the news was aired. A little three-roomed house had just become vacant: the bank manager who had been living there with his wife and child had just been transferred and replaced by a bachelor, who, naturally, was staying at the hotel. The little house was even partly furnished, at least with essentials like beds and kitchen equipment.

Marguerite's arrival was much simplified for us since the railroad had come. The journey by road would have been a sore trial for her, and a romantic acquaintance with the heroic age wouldn't have sufficed to conceal the discomfort. So everything worked out for the best, and as soon as we learned of the date of her arrival, Armand went off to meet her on one of the trains that came to Athabasca three times a week. It wasn't exactly an express route, as it took eight or nine hours to cover the 170 kilometres. But there were many, many stops, and I suspect that out of goodness of heart they stopped anywhere that someone was waving on the line. Here, at last, was Margot, arrived at the end of her long journey; hugs and kisses, questions galore, answers, the whole litany of the traveller come from far, the link between two parts of a family separated by distance, but not by thought. She brought a pure waft of the air from the province, the town, the neighbourhood, the scent of the family and the house, with its old cupboards perfumed with lavender and thyme. To me, in private, she was able to talk about a subject dear to my heart, but that did not yet have a definite form, about the dream that was lodged in the hollow of my exile like a flower garden on a summer's night, about a certain blond girl who had remained under the skies of Brive, and in whom, despite the follies of my youth, I placed my hopes for a happy ending in my life.

Armand and Marguerite settled into the little home, which was already beginning to possess a certain air of intimacy and comfort, and a few days later Marguerite was surprised to see her first flakes of Canadian snow. But they had plenty of wood, as we'd brought them a good supply, and the insulation and double glazing were a serious barrier against the cold that was settling in for the next five or six months. Naturally, it would have been better if her first acquaintance with the country hadn't been at this time of year, but she'd been anxious to be reunited with her husband, which was sufficient reason.

Contract for Mail with the Hudson's Bay Company to Slave Lake: First Voyage

Our lives had not changed, neither in general nor with regard to our work outside. The manager of the Hudson's Bay had spoken to us several times about a government contract for Lesser Slave Lake and the whole region to the northwest of it, towards Peace River, Dunvegan towards the Rockies, and north to the Mackenzie basin. The Hudson's Bay Company owned the contract and subcontracted to third parties. The subcontractor for the last few years had left the country and the company was asking us to take on the job, which was due to start in mid-December and run till the snow melted, after which transport would be by boat on the rivers and lakes.

We accepted, but as we'd need two teams of horses and two sleds, we decided to go to Edmonton to get a job before we started. By train there was no problem, and we did in a few hours and relative comfort what had taken us several days and considerable hardship a mere few months previously.

The Cecil Hotel was our destination again, and the day after we arrived we went to visit the French consul with a message from Lessard, who'd also given us a letter of introduction to his brother, P.-E. Lessard, who was a minister in the provincial government at the time.[26] He gave us a warm welcome, and Lessard hired Jean as driver of the personal and family Pontiac. As for myself, he'd given me a letter of recommendation to Révillon Brothers, so I got a temporary job driving a Dodge as a replacement for an employee who was off sick. It was hardly taxing work: for Jean it meant driving around town either the minister or his family, polishing the car, being fed morning and evening and free afterwards with a secure salary of $70. I sometimes travelled outside of Edmonton to villages where Révillon had a branch to drive the managers or accountants. Jean could keep the job till we went back to Athabasca, whereas

I had to start looking for other employment after my temporary job came to an end. The situations vacant notice board only had jobs far out of town, usually in logging camps about 150 to 175 miles to the west, towards the Rocky Mountains. At a different time of year I would have accepted, as the pay was excellent, but as our contract was due to start in mid-December, there simply wasn't enough time.

A young Frenchman came to my rescue — Marius Clément, who was staying at the Cecil and who worked as a teamster for a transport and work company. He told me that a job had just come up as one of the drivers had fallen and broken his leg. He suggested introducing me to the boss in charge; it was a big business with at least fifty teams, each one more handsome than the last, powerful beasts, either Percherons or Clydesdales of about sixteen to eighteen hands. The wages were fair — $3.50 per day — but the work was pretty hard, because I had to be at the stables by seven in the morning and my day didn't finish before seven at night, after tending to the horses and cleaning the harness and especially the inside collar. One of the foremen took me on and I started work the following day; I was given a team of huge Clydesdales, magnificent beasts but like a pair of elephants. I was a midget beside them and had terrible trouble trying to put on their harnesses, which were magnificent but therefore very heavy and covered with the usual nails and brasses.

The second day I found a little box that I used as a mounting block, and later on I came to an arrangement with a stable boy who looked after my stall, a handsome, vigorous Black who dressed them each morning for a weekly packet of Old Chum. In short, I'd transplanted onto Canadian soil the old French system of skiving familiar to officers' batmen. With the result that when I arrived in the morning, everything was ready, and all I had to do was go straight to the office to get the day's instructions.

I had this job for a month and had no complaints about it; my team were sturdy, honest beasts, gentle and without a spiteful bone in their bodies. The work was varied: sometimes we hauled planks from a sawmill, other times sacks of flour or wheat to a flour mill or to the warehouses of big companies. Once we had to move a wooden house from one part of town to another, which was, for me, a novel experience that lasted two days.

The hardest part for me was setting out at 5:30 or 6 a.m. in the frigid air and the dead of the northern night. We had a long way to go, since our company's stables were on the Strathcona side.

At some point we went through an attractive residential neighbourhood with pleasant bungalows in neat rows with porches and terraces overlooking lawns, which were invisible at this time of year under the winter snow. Here and there a light showed in a window, and I thought of intimate familial warmth and the coziness of an enveloping house. And there were we, poor devils that we were, slogging, like hundreds of others, through the wind that stung our faces, towards work that would hold us hostage in the grip of cold throughout the whole day. And I understood the revolt of the wretches, who, without hope, without joy, saw in the unfolding of their past and future life only one long Calvary, a march towards the Cross. Locked in their miserable fate that held them incarcerated like a prison without bars, they had no hope of escape, except, perhaps, through some stroke of good fortune. And this is why, every time a new discovery was made, there was a new gold rush or petroleum rush or pitchblende rush, an almost demented race towards a new golden fleece or hopeful dreams. And this is also why, alongside little-travelled roads already covered by snow, there are sometimes mounds of stones, graves of the unlucky ones and testimony of their pathetic folly.

For me, although I was living their life, it wasn't quite the same thing. I might suffer physically as they did, I might feel rise within me a revolt against a society that was unthinking and stupid rather than evil and wicked, but what I was doing I did of my own free will and to gain experience, and I got from it an education that would one day enrich my mind and my heart. I might curse fate and the wind and the biting cold of swollen fingers on the reins or the tools, but I knew that if I wanted to, I could call a halt to this stage of life and take up again my comfortable, middle-class existence in some town in the Quercy or the Limousin. But in the enthusiasm of my twenty years, I thought, as I worked, of our property where so many projects awaited realization. We already had a roof to welcome us, a chimney whose smoke signalled human presence, and our footprints had marked a path towards the door. In the evening, after my long day, I'd join Jean in the Cecil. He was happy in his job and respected by his employers, since through his brother in Athabasca, P.-E. Lessard knew who he was — who we were — and I myself received a warm welcome when I went to the house with Jean.

Marius Clément was a good pal. His father was a music director in Marseille; his first name gave a clue to his origins, and his character had been formed under the sunshine of Provence and along the Canebière, with its whiff of anisette.[27] He had a cheerful, expansive personality that was inimical to melancholy. Yet sometimes he became very reserved when, involuntarily or otherwise, the topic of the reasons for his presence in these distant climes came up. Four or five years earlier, he'd bought some land near Buck Lake, and like ourselves and so many others, put in six months of outside work so that he could spend the next six on the property investing the money he'd made, for he'd long exhausted what savings he'd brought from France and was completely broke.

But the time soon came when we had to go back to Athabasca to take up our contract with the Hudson's Bay. When we deducted expenses, we had about $120 available for the remaining payment on the second team we'd ordered from Fitzgibbon.

As soon as we got back to Athabasca, we went to see him to conclude the transaction. It was a lighter team than the one we already had, but heavy enough to pull over the ice a sled loaded with mailbags and that we could also use, if the need arose, as saddle horses or for a light carriage. They were both white dappled with brown and were called Jack and Nelly. They were honest, straightforward beasts and we took to them immediately; but for the first heavy work in construction and hauling, Tom and Chief were thought to be more suitable. We could buy them, together with their harnesses, without going into debt. But what we worked out with Fitz for the extra sled (which would do double duty in normal weather with the one we already had) was that we'd buy a light carriage for summer use, which we'd pay for when our contract terminated, and he'd lend us the extra sled for the winter.

When all this was settled, we went back to the property to spend a couple of days there getting Tom and Chief from the Menuts and checking that everything was in order. The horses had obviously not been suffering, and when we'd harnessed them in their stalls, we were already proud of our livestock. The stable was warm, the gaps between the logs well plugged, the loft full of good hay, so everything was just hunky-dory, and we could look forward with confidence to the coming winter.

When we went back down to Athabasca with a big load of firewood for Margot, it was already very cold: at night, the thermometer must have registered twenty-five or thirty degrees below zero. But the snow was fine and smooth and the clear weather during the day very much to our liking.

Departure

Preparations for the departure didn't take long: we already had our camping gear and all we needed was food ("grub," as our Canadiens called it). According to our contract, it was to be supplied by the Hudson's Bay, and, indeed, they organized things very well. Among other things we had a big side of bacon, cans of corned beef, pork and beans, fish, jam, a twenty-pound sack of

powdered sugar, flour, maple syrup, baking powder, salted butter, tea, coffee, tobacco, etc., altogether a regular grocery store,
as well as a hundred pounds of oats for the horses, with hay to
be bought at the stopping places where we'd be camping. We had
ample supplies for the journey and enough to last us for about ten
days after we got back, without our having to buy anything. We
were carrying eighty or ninety bags of assorted mail — letters or
packages — which were divided between the two sleds, and which
weren't an excessive load, especially on the ice on the river, which
is where we'd be for most of the trip. The only possible difficulty
would be the riverbanks, which we'd have to scale to get to the
stopping places; but if the worst came to the worst, we could
always double the teams for a few dozen metres. The terms of the
contract were that we'd get $800 for transporting the mail until
the 1st of April with about one trip per month. On the way back,
we'd be bringing a few mailbags from Lesser Slave Lake, if there
were any, and we were free to transport on our own account goods
or passengers going to Athabasca or Edmonton.

We spent the night before leaving at the ranch and set out
from there the following morning before dawn, heading for the
river down the trail that descended from our plateau to the mouth
of Baptiste Creek. This way, we saved six or eight miles on this
stage. We were quite calm at the prospect of a journey that now
seemed, after our experience of the country and the horses, fairly
simple — apart from the harshness of the climate. We had no
intimation that in a few hours we'd be put to a terrible test that
would destroy, in a matter of a few minutes, the fruit of long
months of hard labour.

The trail on the river was well marked at this time of year,
since there was regular traffic between Lesser Slave Lake and the
whole area towards Peace River in the west and Grande Prairie.
The teams went along at a good trot beneath a clear sky and an
icy sun that was, however, perfectly pleasant. From time to time
we walked ahead of them to warm up, for with the temperature

at twenty-five below, you had to keep up normal circulation and avoid insidious chapping. Sometimes, all you feel is a pain like a needle going in your cheek or nose and nothing more. Then the chapping gets wider and starts to suppurate. Those are superficial cuts and do no harm, except to your appearance. But when fingers or toes become frozen, that's a whole other matter, and if the freezing goes any deeper, then amputation might be necessary to avoid gangrene. We'd had the tips of our noses frozen a few times, so we'd cobbled together a remedy. We'd made a little nosebag out of a square of an old wool blanket that we attached to the end of our noses with a piece of elastic. As the blanket was red, the Métis and Indians all around nicknamed us "Nikookook," which means Red Nose in Cree and Montagnais. And so mile followed mile accompanied by the jingling of the harness bells, the only sound that broke the silence in the white symphony. From time to time, however, there was a crack like a gunshot: it was the ice reforming, but we'd been reassured about this, since the old hands had told us it was perfectly normal.

Night was falling already (the sun drops suddenly to the horizon on winter days) when we halted at a stopping place, Moose Head Place, which the people from the Hudson's Bay had told us about and which was about thirty miles from Athabasca. It had good, solid buildings that were comfortable for that part of the world, the comfort consisting mainly of a well-heated room, a well-insulated stable, good hay in the mangers for the animals, and, for those people who wanted it, a slice of elk or caribou. The tot of whisky we treated the old Irish manager to put us in his good books. So all in all, apart from the intense cold on the trail, the unpleasant moments unharnessing the horses at night, when the knots and our fingers were frozen, and the same thing in the morning when we had to reharness them and rub them down beneath the boreal sky where stars were shining like burning torches, our journey didn't cause us any problems. As soon as the horses were comfortably installed, rubbed down, and covered with their blankets — they

73   PIERRE MATURIÉ

were, after all, our first priority — it was our turn and we could relax: a good dinner, which in France we would have thought of as a beggar's poor meal but up there in the forest, beside the great frozen river, seemed delicious, boiling hot tea or coffee, a good pipeful of Old Chum and our hands to the fire, when outside the cold was making the trees crack, all that had the feel of a cozy home and a friendly atmosphere. For we were not alone; one after another various other freighters arrived for the night, all characters with plenty to say for themselves who always had a fund of good stories. Thus we spent the evening, albeit a short one, for we were all thinking of the next stage.

An Accident and Drowning

So the next day we got underway at dawn: a Ukrainian settler from Grande Prairie had already set out on the trail about an hour ahead of us. He moved slowly with a heavy load and a team of oxen yoked in the way he was used to, with a yoke and reins and guiding ropes attached to their nostrils and ears. When we reached the river, dawn was barely beginning to colour the sky in the east. Even the great horned owls hadn't yet returned to their nests, and we could hear their deep "whoo-hoos" as they called to each other, sometimes nearby, sometimes farther away. I know that some people find their hooting eerie, but I've heard them often, either in a cabin in one of the camps or in the forest beneath a silver moon, and I've never found it a frightening experience. On the contrary, I've always thought that the worst, most depressing thing is the heavy silence beneath snow-covered trees when everything seems dead and part of another planet. And when one of those huge birds flapped away, it seemed like an immaterial flight, like something out of a silent film.

On the frozen trail that squeaked beneath the iron skis, the horses, well fed and rested, tossed their heads, signalling their eagerness to be on the move. It was cold, twenty-five below zero at the door of the stopping place, and would certainly go lower during the day. Luckily, the air was still and windless. For a few hundred metres we followed the trail along the shore, because on the river itself, the ice that had been broken up in the first freeze was piled up on a curve in the Athabasca, forming heaps of ice chunks that were difficult to navigate.

Then we went out onto the ice, where our team moved along at a spanking pace and we, perched on our load, let our minds wander over the prospect of the coming spring. However, despite raised collars on our lumberjackets, hands thrust into muffs, and legs wrapped in horse blankets, we soon became painfully aware of the cold of the river where we'd lost the shelter of the forest and where the air blew as if down a vast corridor. By now a winter's day had dawned and before us stretched the immense petrified ribbon of the river, beneath which flowed ceaselessly the waters draining from the glaciers of the Rockies.

The morning was already far advanced in the monotony of a never-ending journey. We had no need to worry about directions or landmarks because we knew that the course of the Athabasca was the guiding line towards the mouth of Lesser Slave River, which we were to follow to the lake of the same name. It was near this mouth that we would camp that evening in a stopping place beside the Hudson's Bay. And the following day should see the end of the trip when we delivered the mail at the mouth of Slave Lake, where other teams would be waiting to take over the next stage.

Jean was leading, since he had the heavier team, and it made sense for him to set the pace for the other team, which ought to be faster. I was just thinking about stopping for the midday meal and the usual break, and I was keeping a lookout for a dry tree on the riverbank that would make a good fire. What are the imponderables that often accompany the important moments of our lives?

Suddenly, as when we start out of sleep with a bad dream, I saw Jean's team sway as if on a swing whilst at the same time there was a cracking noise like a bomb exploding and a spout of water shooting over the ice; Jean gave a great leap and landed onto the running-board, which was still intact, helped by his long legs. It took me only a few seconds to realize the nature of the catastrophe: it was that very rare but much-feared phenomenon, a crack in the ice. I heaved the reins with all my might towards the right, trying to pull my horses towards the bank, but my load slipped and I felt myself plunging into the icy water, whilst our poor beasts thrashed frantically with their legs to try to stay on the surface. With the help of Jean, who tore off his lumberjacket to throw it out to me like a lifeline, I, too, managed to climb on to the running board. It was a complete nightmare for us to watch the death throes of our brave horses who were whinnying to us and as if responding to our shouts of encouragement were trying desperately to climb on to the edges of the crack, which kept getting bigger and bigger. There was nothing we could do to try to save them. We would have needed poles to reach them, and then at great risk we'd have had to try to cut the reins that were holding them to the sleds; and cables to haul them; but everything was in the sleds, and in these conditions it was dangerous and almost impossible to approach the great yawning hole, which was at least twelve or fourteen metres in diameter. And we were alone, absolutely alone with our tragedy, and in ten minutes, everything had been swallowed up, our horses had disappeared in a final roiling and all that remained on the surface were a few sacks of mail floating on the surface of the water. And complete silence reigned once more over indifferent, hostile nature.

We stood thunderstruck and speechless in the face of this disaster. We'd suffered the dreadful emotional shock, not only of narrowly escaping death, but also of watching perish before our very eyes, and without being able to help them, our dear horses, our trusty workmates. And within the space of a few minutes, we'd lost everything we'd been able to acquire though our own labour and at the cost of so much toil and fatigue and that constituted our hopes for the future.

At last, when it was all over and the river had gone back to looking like a dead thing, we had to make a decision. I was at the end of my tether, with my clothes frozen solid onto me. While the drama was unfolding, we could only concentrate on the vision of horror. But now we had to act, as it was a matter of life and death. There was no way to build a fire, as the axes had disappeared. My one, single resource was to walk to keep the blood circulating and to avoid, if possible, having one of my limbs freeze. We simply *had* to reach the Hudson's Bay post to alert the people there and to try to arrange to retrieve whatever could be salvaged. It's impossible for me to relate what it was like for me to walk those two or three miles when my legs, frozen into a cast, could hardly bend. It was only my ferocious will to live that sustained me. Providence, which had kept watch over us during these difficult moments, still kept a benign eye upon us; after a walk, which, although short, had been extremely trying, we saw an unloaded sled coming towards us that stopped beside us. When we told the driver of our accident, he immediately turned around and galloped off with us towards the Sawridge post, after giving us his horse blankets and a hefty shot of whisky. I must have drunk quarter of a litre of it without feeling a thing.

As soon as we got to the post, there was a frantic flurry of attention and kindness: new clothes warmed on the stove, an alcohol rub of my whole body, hot tea, half-rum, etc. There was also a flurry of combat activity: rounding up of all available men at the post and the neighbouring stopping place with axes, planks, hooks, chains, cables, anything that could be used to salvage the sacks and perhaps the sledges, and also to set up a salvage relay team. An hour later we set out towards the accursed spot. The post manager wanted me to stay there, but I insisted on going with them. How on earth did I manage not to get congestion of the lungs or pneumonia? Mystery. Providence was indeed guarding over me. A dunking like that in twenty or thirty degrees below zero should have been fatal, my friends told me.

And it's in circumstances like this that this lost land reveals the comradeship between men. These rough and ready guys could suddenly become true brothers to someone in trouble or in danger. We were fortunate in having the comforting testimony of this sense of fraternity during the whole of our misfortune.

In a word, when we got to the scene of the accident, we met with other teams who'd left the stopping place after us and had stopped there. The men got down to the task immediately: they placed rods and planks right up to the edge of the crack to distribute the weight, and with each of them roped with a cable, they began, with the aid of hooks, to salvage the mailbags that were still floating on the surface and by dragging below the water, to heave up those that hadn't been pulled away. About twenty were recovered. Of the sledges and the horses, there was no sign under the ice, as they had been carried away by the currents or by the death thrashings of the poor beasts. What has become of you, my trusty Tom and Chief, my brave little Jack, my dear little Nellie, so affectionate, and yet sometimes so headstrong? When the spring thaw frees the river from its icy armour, perhaps we'll find on a stony beach, where the current has carried you, your already-bleached bones.

We left this sad place at nightfall, as we'd had to stake out a temporary trail on the bank and the forest and make a barrier with branches and tree trunks on the hazardous part of the route. We were well looked after and even spoilt by our hosts, and a freighter going down to Athabasca offered to take us home the day after next.

Around the stove that evening, the talk was naturally about our accident. What had caused it? The ice, which was always thinner because of some rapids at that bend in the river, must have cracked that morning under the weight of the Ukrainian's heavy load that was just ahead of us.

We were told later that the salvaged mail had been delivered insofar as it was possible when the addresses could be deciphered, with an explanation of its state. Three years earlier, the mail service between our sector and Grande Prairie had been caught in a terrible blizzard and the driver and one of his horses had frozen to death. Such, obviously, were the risks, not only of the trade but also of life itself in these new lands where nature's whims have always to be taken into account.

Two days later, we set out for home on our sad journey after thanking our hosts most profusely for their hospitality and their help. But to them, it was perfectly natural, so strong is the notion of hospitality in these lands that treat men so harshly.

A Sad Return to Athabasca

We made the return journey over the forest trail, which was a bit shorter and a bit harder, especially for heavy loads, but since we were not carrying anything, this didn't matter. And also, according to our driver, a man from Slave Lake, it wasn't as cold under the shelter of the trees as on the river, which was always exposed to the wind.

At night, we camped at a stopping place that wasn't much frequented at that time of year, since most traffic moved over the river trail. But a lot of people stopped there in the summer and fall, particularly in wagons that for whatever reason had to travel to Peace River, Grande Prairie, or the Mackenzie. The camp was run by an old-timer who lived there with his wife, a half-blood Indian who spent her time hunting and trapping. He had come from Ireland with his parents, had grown up in the South; he had spent at least forty years in this completely wild North-West and had been in the Klondike gold rush. He could remember going up north with his dogs and his snowshoes and travelling by rivers and lakes to reach the gold country. He looked like an old patriarch with long white hair and a long white beard down to his chest, a face straight out of a stained-glass window. He'd had children who'd kept up the ancestral nomadic way of life of their mother, who, despite age and condition of life, had the nobility of features and expression that old Indian chiefs must have had before the arrival of so-called civilization. The children, all boys, as soon as they were old enough had gone even farther north, fleeing before the Whites who had cleared the land of fur-bearing animals, which had decamped to still virgin lands.

When he'd learnt of our accident from our driver, the old man said a few words in Indian to his wife, who went out and returned with partridges and a piece of frozen moose meat in a meat safe. And then, in a spectacle that we found touching and surprising, we watched the old man pull out of a case beneath the bed (or what served as a bed) a few religious pictures that he pinned up on the log wall with a big "Merry Christmas" framed by a few pine branches. Thus did we realize it was Christmas; in the ghastly days we'd been through, all notion of time had disappeared, and we'd completely forgotten that we should have arrived home that day for the family celebration in Athabasca.

Before the meal, standing ramrod-straight in front of the makeshift altar, he said a few prayers and sang a few hymns that we didn't understand very well, but we were spiritually united in the thought of the prayers that must be uttered throughout the world, in cities sparkling with light as well as in the most remote places in all languages and in all latitudes.

The meal was a revelation for us. We were completely amazed to discover how, in this godforsaken place, with the most primitive resources, this old woman could have concocted what was nothing less than a banquet: a milk porridge, partridge sautéed in the pan with bacon, a thin moose steak seared on a grill, beans and pancakes with maple syrup and blueberry jam that she had made herself. Our contribution was the brandy and tobacco that the manager of the Sawridge Hudson's Bay post had given us as we left. And we spent the night in the warm kitchen rolled up in blankets on bearskins that the old Irishman spread out for us on the floor.

When we left in the morning, he refused to take any payment for his hospitality, and his refusal was so noble that we couldn't insist.

"On this Christmas night, Jesus sent you to me!"

I always remember those words, and in the twilight into which my life had entered, I understood that charity is often in the hearts where one least thought to seek it, among the poor and destitute, who, in giving least, give their all.

When we arrived in Athabasca we were overwhelmed. They'd heard that the Frenchies had sunk in the river and the news had spread from the village to all the surrounding area.

Marguerite and Armand were, of course, beside themselves, not knowing whether we'd survived or not. By what path, by what mysterious means does the news spread so fast in this vast country, so empty and so difficult? Perhaps via the Indians and Métis on their way to and from their traplines or on their hunting expeditions? However it happened, a settler at Baptiste Lake had heard from a passing Indian about the disaster that had overtaken us, and this Indian had heard it from another go-between.

So, completely ignorant of what had happened, the RMP was about to send out one of its men to find out. I should take this opportunity to say that I've never seen such a superb force: they were always on top of their form, and in any weather or in any conditions, the RMP constables often went out on a patrol of hundreds of miles as casually as our gendarmes would set off on a night ride. Acting like orphans, they lived off the land as best they could, and their mere presence was enough to inspire respect for the law in the most remote posts.

Our arrival, then, did not pass unnoticed! Everyone we met greeted us with shouts of joy and great thumps on the back. Our first call, naturally, was to Armand's house, where poor Margot gave us a welcome it's not hard to imagine. And all the time people kept coming to see us and shake our hands. From these demonstrations of affection, it was clear that we were part of the community that draws human beings together in a fraternal group.

A further proof of this — and one that we had by no means expected — was about to be given. We were faced with a harsh fact: the destruction of our efforts and our hopes. What we learnt at the Grand Union Hotel the next day, was that Dr. Olivier, the village mayor and a French Canadian, had sent someone on horseback around the entire village and surrounding homesteads to announce that a subscription had been opened for the Frenchmen and that contributions could be made at the town hall and the Grand Union Hotel. Three days later, he was able to bring us a considerable sum that equalled — and even surpassed — the amount of our losses. It still took us several days to get over the psychological shock of the accident; but with a great effort of will, we had to put our noses to the grindstone again. We weren't very keen on going back on our route and buying another team for the winter. But we thought that it was the right thing to offer ourselves to the Hudson's Bay for at least one more trip, and with this thought in mind, we bought another team, medium-sized this time. It would do for working the land, at least: two geldings of about twelve hundred pounds, dark bay, sturdy beasts and used to the harness, Frank and John. Massey-Harris let us have, for part cash and part credit, an almost new sled for a very reasonable price because it was left unused after a buyer had put down a deposit and stopped making the payments.

We came to an arrangement with the Hudson's Bay manager to cancel the contract for the mail delivery, which was given to a Métis from Baptiste Lake. The Bay gave us a load of sacks of flour and sugar, goods that were easy to handle and easy to balance. Our interrupted journey had been mostly paid for and the company had given Dr. Olivier a substantial cheque for the subscription.

I would have preferred to go alone, but Jean insisted on coming with me; we weren't as concerned with our earnings as with our duty towards the Hudson's Bay. This time the journey passed without incident. We left directly from Athabasca without stopping off at our property, as our load was heavier than the mail. We were one of four or five freighters responsible for restocking the Hudson's Bay posts on Lesser Slave Lake. When we got to the spot where we'd had the accident, there was a detour that mounted the riverbank and cut through a few hundred metres of forest before going back down onto the ice. In this way it avoided the dangerous place of the rapids, which we could see — not without a surge of emotion.

The weather was still cold, but bearable, and the snow, which had been well tamped down, didn't tire our team, which behaved perfectly — brave, docile, and with no hint of spite. We got a very kind welcome at the Hudson's Bay post where they had treated us so well after the accident; the manager congratulated us on our new "outfit" and seemed genuinely pleased to see that we had overcome our misfortune. Thanks to him, we were able to find a load for the return trip, with four passengers, three of whom were paying, which meant a considerable increase in income. The fourth was an Oblate priest, Father Pétour, whom Monseigneur Grouard asked us to take to the train station.[28] This was our first encounter with the great missionary of the epic past, apostle to the Great North. Ordained in 1862 by Monseigneur Grandin, he died in 1931 after spending his whole life in western Canada, founding missions, schools, hospitals, and a small town that bears his name on the shores of Lesser Slave Lake.[29] We met him subsequently on several occasions, and also on my second stay with my wife when we settled in Peace River in 1919.

January was now three-quarters over, so we had several months before us for outside work on our property. But before getting down to it, we decided to have a few days of rest in our home on the plateau, where we were now sufficiently well settled to be able to receive visitors or to give ourselves up to complete relaxation. And also Marguerite and Armand would be needing firewood as their supply was running out. We wanted to get it ready and to deliver two loads of dry poplar wood we knew was nearby, just to the east of the plateau. It was an easy task and took only a few hours. It was truly a vacation for us to get back to our very own house where the warmth of the fire and the light of the lamps offered a true haven of rest after the trials we had undergone. We'd brought with us the French newspapers that arrived one by one in Athabasca, and also some from Edmonton, which we now had time to read. A bit of hunting to give variety to our table, a bit of trapping, which was my domain, household and kitchen duties, that were mainly Jean's business, care of the horses, and a few repairs — thus we spent those few days that were a break for us and rest for the horses, which were in good shape. Once again we were able to come to an arrangement for their stabling with old Monsieur Menut, who was happy to have them at his disposal.

Armand was to have enquired about a job for us, and when we went down to Athabasca, we found out that through the good offices of Lessard, owner of the general store, Jean could go back to P.-E. Lessard in Edmonton, which he did gladly. And for me, there was a job at the Grand Union Hotel as cook and wine server at the bar. Board, lodging, warmth, and $40 a month. In addition, the hotel manager suggested that in my spare time I could pack the empty bottles into cases and return them to the suppliers; at the moment they were left in the cellar, since no hauler was willing to take them back to Edmonton because there was no profit in it. There were thousands of them, all stacked up to the ceiling and taking up practically all the space in the vast basement. Now that the train was running, things had changed radically and it had become possible and profitable to transport them. I looked upon it as easy money and a means of making a little on the side.

I digress for a moment to explain one or two things. You might think that taking on supplementary jobs as we were doing might harm our reputation or diminish us in the estimation of the people we mixed with — businessmen, bankers, doctors, or other professionals. Nothing of the sort, and I suspect that it's still the same today. In fact, in this country, work never demeaned men nor created an inferior class on an artificially created social ladder. It wasn't unusual to see the stable boy in the rental shop in his overalls brushing the horses during the day, and coming to dinner in the hotel restaurant impeccably dressed and with patent leather shoes, sitting beside a lawyer or a local dignitary without any sign of embarrassment or surprise on either side. When I'd finished my day's work, I often went and sat in an easy chair in the lobby watching travellers or passersby come and go and was often invited to join one of them at the bar — "Hello! Frenchie, come on!" — or to smoke a fine cigar — "Peter, have a cigar." On one trip to Edmonton I met a French taxi driver whom everyone called Big Charlie, who was actually a Bourbon.[30] Clément often spoke of one of his friends, born into a distinguished French family, holder of a law degree, who worked in the sewers of Vancouver during the day, and in the evening put on a dinner jacket and went out into high society. Later on, when he'd thoroughly mastered the language, he'd married a very rich young heiress and went into his father-in-law's successful iron business. For us, it was a great handicap not knowing the language when we were looking for a job, and manual labour was our only resource. Back home amongst the French bourgeoisie, manual labour would have been a fatal flaw, for neither those going up the social ladder nor those going down were accepted in society — not even if the former were trying to earn an honest living in spite of everything, and if the latter, by dint of personal qualities, were trying to thrust upwards and emerge like a plant towards the light.

We had made the acquaintance, among others, of one of the great northern pioneers, "Colonel" Jim K. Cornwall.[31] He had started when he was extremely young carrying the mail to the North, to Hudson's Bay and trappers' posts, wearing moccasins and snowshoes, using dog teams, sleeping among the Indians or in trappers' cabins. This wasn't like our French postmen's rounds, but real expeditions of two or three hundred miles, or three to five hundred kilometres. Little by little, with a clear vision of this country's future and a spirit of enterprise, he had created various companies (furs or transport), survived overwhelming failures, started up again from scratch, and when we got to know him, had turned everything around and owned a navigation company on the northern lakes and rivers and a splendid house in Edmonton. He was the very image of the Conqueror of the North, and we were very happy to meet him again when we got back after the war.

The winter months passed peacefully, and we were pleased not to have to dig into our savings but to be able to prepare for the work of the coming spring. Life wasn't unpleasant; work filled part of my day, because, as I was the first one up, to me fell the inspection and cleaning out of the wood stove after the night watchman left. My first task was to light the big cooking stove and to prepare the coffee and breakfast, something the cook took over when he arrived, like a colonel entering his headquarters. Then dishwashing, preparation of vegetables for lunch, and a repetition of it all for each sitting. But in theory, I was free from about four o'clock and I could either go out or settle in the lobby in a comfortable armchair and watch a real kaleidoscope file by: prospectors, Métis or Indians buying supplies and trading their furs, travellers on their way to the far North, representatives of businesses, who were never out of pocket when they came to Athabasca, which was a favourite destination, settlers and planters, cowboys from Baptiste Lake and Sunny Flat. I remember seeing one of the most famous northern fur traders, Colin Fraser, come in at the end of the season, with bales of skins that were carried by his Métis.[32] I can still see him opening them and flinging them in a jumbled heap on to the floor of the lobby, black or silver fox, lynx, mink, ermine, and skunk. "Take a look at that, boys. Not bad, are they? Drinks all round, everybody!" Right there on the floor was a fortune that everyone could touch and admire, and then Colin paid a round for everyone at the bar, with a second round for the big drinkers.

But it wasn't always such a happy scene and sometimes there were terrible fights, the kind that can only be fought by rough, powerful men used to a harsh, miserable existence, who work like navvies for weeks without a break and in the most unimaginable physical conditions, often not young anymore but with no hope of improvement in their lives, cherishing the one thought of escape towards people-filled places with all their temptations: their roaring bars and the warmth of their smoke-filled hotels and gambling and women. For no good reason there would be shots fired and swearing and broken glass. But this was all regarded as pretty much normal and a mere spectacle put on for blasé spectators who took it all more or less for granted.

The Second Spring

In the light of the days that were already lengthening, beneath a sun that warmed the atmosphere as it climbed higher in the sky, the snow began to melt timidly, and little candles that were coated in ice at night fringed the eaves of the roofs. On the river, brilliant ice pans bore testimony to the noonday warmth.

Then, one night, a wind began blowing over the softened snows. Little avalanches slid down the roofs and the pine branches, which sprang back like a sleeper awakening and stretching. And once again the Chinook came, as it had for eons, so eagerly awaited by nature desperate for renewal, and the flow of water in all the coulees and creeks so long silent, on the river and the lakes, clear,

limpid water rainbowed with the colours of the sky and the greenery, singing daughter of the immaculate snows.

For in the forest, the thaw isn't the disgusting thing that turns
roads into mud. It's a riot of waterfalls pure as crystal and babbling like bells as if the snow and the ice of the end of winter were
trying to make up for their rigid immobility and their long silence.

In these days of the April spring, travel by sled was no longer
possible, as here and there on the trails great patches of earth
were already appearing, getting larger as the day wore on, and
the snow trails were gradually becoming summer paths. We had
to start thinking about returning to our property to do the necessary upkeep and to fulfill the terms of our residence obligation.

We had a full schedule for the year, as we had to think about
making improvements not only to the quarter section where we'd
done the building, but also on the other homesteads, mine and
Armand's. The latter, with the permission of the Lands Office,
could manage without putting up a building, given his relation-
ship with Jean, and there was no problem about this; but we had
to clear and plough the two concessions, deferring till next year
building a little house on mine.

We started clearing and ploughing five acres on each of the
quarter sections. Jean's and Armand's were contiguous, and as
the first ploughing the previous year had been on the boundary of
the two pieces of land, it was easy to continue on Armand's and
get one continuous field. On my land, we decided to start at the
lakeshore, to clear the hayfield that bordered it and to clear the
five acres going up to the other sections over land that was slightly
bumpy but didn't present any major obstacles.

You cannot imagine the satisfaction I felt in this work of creation. "Proving up," as they say here, meant taking virgin land
covered with brush or with big trees and turning it into fields
where the plough had made straight furrows to bear a harvest.
In the evening when we returned home, how proud we were to
count the piles of wood cut and stacked and to see the clearing

grow bigger and bigger as it ate into the forest. For it wasn't all saplings: there were also big trees that had seen many a season pass over their foliage and that took hard work and extreme care to cut down. We had to cut off the branches, pile up the trunks, saw them lengthwise if they looked right (they would be good for making into planks next season, when we could always do with them on a newly developed property).

But the hardest part was the stumps; we had to loosen the soil around them and yank them out. Once again old Monsieur Menut was a great help, as he understood explosives and dynamite and knew how to use them. This was by far the quickest, least exhausting way of clearing the land. Stump-pullers did indeed exist, but apart from their cost, they took a long time to use and were much harder work.

This work took us nearly two months. As soon as the early sun had dried the piles of wood we'd stacked up, we set fire to it and had a fine bonfire for Saint-Jean-Baptiste Day. The soil was now ready for the first ploughing, or "breaking," as it's known there. As we'd only bought one team, we had to rent another, as it was very hard work in ground that had never before been turned. It sometimes happened that the ploughshare got caught against the remains of a stump that hadn't been completely removed, despite our best efforts. So then we had to harness a team to the back of the plough to get it out. But despite all these problems and the difficulty of the work, the days passed quickly, and all in all pleasantly, at least for me, enthusiastic as I was about nature and about this whole new project of colonization.

But now we had fifteen acres cultivated, five on each concession, and we had to think of sowing. For the time being, we only wanted to plant potatoes and oats for cereal, with some for green feed for our animals. There'd be time to think about wheat later.

As a corollary to this seeding, it became a matter of some urgency to put up a fence around our ploughed fields: not only did we have to think about our obligation to the Lands Office, but we also had to take precautions against livestock that wandered more or less anywhere and often quite a long way from their home property. For example, Perry from Baptiste Lake let his herd of horses roam over an area of twenty-five miles, since he was used to being a rancher in Montana and letting his livestock wander anywhere. Every two or three days two of his cowboys set out to check on where they were and to point them in the right direction if they thought they'd wandered too far.

Perry, who was a rancher through and through, had a simple but radical axiom: "I let my horses wander: enclose your crops!" This always reminded me of a friend of my mother's, whose sons were a pretty wild bunch and who used to say: "I'm letting my roosters out; shut up your hens!" Apart from the inherent antagonism between farmer and cowhand, Perry was a very nice guy and extremely obliging. When we'd had our terrible accident on the river, he immediately offered us one of his best teams and let us have it very cheaply, telling us we could pay him whenever we could.

We didn't want to build the fence around the crops the same way as we had the fence for the horses. To do that, we'd have to cut down masses of logs, which would mean finding a stand of them and then hauling them. Big waste of time! Barbed wire, on the other hand, was much easier and quicker to install as soon as the posts were in, so that was the solution we adopted.

We already had quite a good supply of posts, but we still had to cut some additional ones, which was quite easy, and we bought a drill to get them into the ground. Even so, it took us the better part of two weeks to get the fence built. But we'd killed two birds with one stone: we'd fulfilled the obligation to enclose our property and we had peace of mind about our future crops, which were now protected against four-footed marauders.

The fifteen acres we'd ploughed were now planted: we kept the two acres of potatoes, and for the rest we put in oats where we'd planted before, and green feed on the newly cleared land. So we should have forage for the horses to add to the hay we were cutting in summer from the shores of the little lake — which we'd have to clear — and also oats for the horses and grain for the chickens we planned to get in the fall, if everything went according to plan.

As soon as we'd finished planting, we began clearing the area around the lake, which wasn't difficult, and the first thing was to burn the dry grass before the new crop started to grow. As a precaution, we proceeded in sections so that we'd have better control over the flames, and we chose a calm, windless day. What we didn't want was that the fire should get out of hand and burn all our reserve firewood, which would have been an awful waste. Everything went as we had planned and almost all the old tree trunks and branches were consumed right there. There were just one or two heaps to gather up and the edge of the lake was clear of what was left of our cutting and also of the grass that had been growing for several years.

After a mere few days, the new shoots started to appear on the burnt surfaces, and the green, velvet-like carpet around the water was a very pretty sight. We'd be able to mow by machine in future, and we'd already have a good supply of hay on the spot.

I still had plans to improve the area around the lake: I wanted to drain the marshes that fed it upstream and clear out the exit waters by redirecting the little stream that flowed out of it, and if necessary, to put in a sluice gate. But, as Kipling says, "That's another matter," and something to think about another year.

One day, as I was going down to Athabasca with a load of wood for the sawmill, I witnessed the departure of several scows going up the Athabasca towards the Great Northern Lakes. There were six or seven barges loaded with boxes or bags, supplies for the Hudson's Bay Company posts or for the missionaries lost in their poor boreal missions.

I noticed two Oblate Fathers overseeing their loading operations, one of whom was the one I'd seen celebrating mass at Whitsun. It was a fine, memorable scene, watching all these men leave calmly and even cheerfully; on the one hand were those spurred on by the call of adventure and material gain, and on the other were those motivated by the single desire to guide souls to the life of the spirit.

I Leave with Clément to Work on a Railroad in the Rockies

For some time, Marguerite and Armand had been asked by a group of businessmen to manage the new hotel they'd built opposite the railroad station. The Grand Union had been altered and was now managed by an English Canadian, Mr. Frank, who was a newcomer to the area. So Armand and Marguerite accepted the offer and Jean himself was taken on as cook!

The grand opening of this palace, which was known as the Athabasca Hotel, took place in the presence of a huge crowd, such events being extremely rare here in the back of beyond. The management christened the place in usual fashion, the only way acknowledged in this part of the world, namely free drinks all round at the bar. Everyone, from the highest officials down to the most modest Métis, was present, and the event was recorded in big headlines that trumpeted the vitality of the North in the local paper and reprinted in the Edmonton press.

Armand was to oversee the reception desk and the accounts and Marguerite was housekeeper in charge of the female staff, the linen supply, the rooms, and the dining room.

I'd been contacted by Marius Clément, who had also fulfilled the regulation time on his property and said that he was returning to Edmonton to look for a job. He'd been told that there was a big company offering good wages for work on the railroad line through the Rocky Mountains. He was anxious to see that part of the country and wondered if I was interested in working with him. As I didn't have anything in particular lined up, the hotel offering nothing but kitchen help and general dogsbody, which I'd been in the Grand Hotel, and as I was always on the lookout for adventure, I made an appointment to meet him in the Hotel Cecil, which, since we'd first arrived in the West, had been our favourite meeting place.

Now that the rest of the family was all settled in the new Athabasca Hotel, I didn't have to worry about them. Jean wasn't in fact staying there, but he'd kept the little house that Armand and Marguerite had been living in. The horses we loaned to Fitzgibbon, their former owner and owner of the livery barn, to do some hauling in town in exchange for their stabling and feed, plus an extra fifty cents per day, with the understanding that road work and earth moving were out. In addition, on the weekends, Jean could use the horses to go out to Bellevue to keep an eye on the land and to check the growth of the crops that Jo Tobaty had promised to cut with his mower.

The owners of the hotel were a consortium of rich men, some of them from Athabasca, and had given Armand and Marguerite a very good deal: they had board and lodging, of course, and a salary of $90 a month. The one disadvantage was that it was a temporary position that would come to an end in the fall. An Irish-Canadian couple had been taken on as permanent managers from then on. They'd sold a hotel in Saskatchewan and had invested in the construction of the one in Athabasca, but as they'd wanted to visit family in the East, they'd been given this time off.

This was not something that had worried Armand, because from a few hints that he and Marguerite had let drop, we'd understood that they found life in these parts too harsh, especially in winter, and too rigorous for a young woman who'd only just arrived from the gentle climes of France, where she'd been used to creature comforts and the pleasures of a social life. So they were thinking of going to live in Victoria in British Columbia on Vancouver Island.

The climate there was milder, since it was washed by the warm Pacific currents, making it the Florida or California of Canada, or like the Côte d'Azur in France.

I left Athabasca at the beginning of June to meet Clément, who was waiting impatiently in Edmonton. He'd already made enquiries at the Employment Offices and had signed a contract for both of us. We were to join a crew of labourers working with a company that was laying a railroad line through the Rockies. The section we were assigned to had already reached the foothills. The daily wage was $6.00, with 75 cents taken out for food. So the pay wasn't bad.

Transport for the hired crew (we were about a dozen taking over from men who were leaving or going off sick) was provided by the company's service train, which consisted of simple platform cars and a sleeping car with wooden bunks. It was no use looking for comfort, as we were considered human livestock provided with just enough to keep us going. It was, in fact, the kind of cattle truck we saw in the 1914 war: forty men — eight horses.

There was nothing noteworthy about the first part of the journey, as we were travelling on the part of the line that had already been in use for some time; stops, shunting onto sidetracks for a convoy to pass in the opposite direction, starting up again, re-stopping etc. For us none of this was a problem, as we were being paid from the time we'd been taken on.

But the trip became more eventful when we reached the part of the line that wasn't finished and was barely functional. The rail ran over ties that had been only temporarily nailed down on a bed that hadn't been properly levelled. Obviously this affected the train's speed, and I think we could have kept up with it on foot.

The thing that was the most amazing and made the greatest impression on me was the way the bridges were built across rivers that were sometimes as much as a hundred metres wide, including the banks and the river bed itself. These bridges were constructed of a line of impressive-looking tree trunks, spruce or pines sticking up like a fence and joined together by a lattice of crosspieces also made of tree trunks and held together by iron brackets. There was no guardrail on these bridges, and when you crossed over them, you could see the seething waters of the river below and you felt as if you were suspended on a rope. And the train inched along slowly accompanied by the creaking of all these tree trunks that groaned in their iron brackets. Finally, after a day and a night, we reached the work site where we'd be spending the next few weeks.

After delivery of this human cargo — which put me in mind of nothing so much as convoys of slaves of long ago — we were shown the bunkhouse where we were to sleep, eight or ten of us to a room depending on the size. As soon as we'd set down our kit, we made our way to the hut that was to be our recreation room — to misappropriate the term. We had the impression, despite all our experience with bars and saloons with their roughneck customers of all stripes, that we'd landed among a band of convicts: young fellows and old geezers with bushy, unkempt beards, shouting and punching, checked flannel shirts and bright scarves, all crowded together in the room built of planks with log seats and in the middle of the room at a table of the same material. In addition, to crown the whole atmosphere, a fug of pipe smoke and the smell of tobacco juice that didn't always reach the tin spittoons that were scattered around.

The refectory — or rather the tent that served as one — was fairly large and in a much better state, since it was overseen by the chief cook and his three helpers — all Chinese, of course.

The food was ample, if not varied, since these ruffians didn't demand much else. It was good, considering the wild nature of the territory and the distance from supplies.

The camp consisted of about a hundred workmen: foremen, smiths, loggers, unskilled labourers, teamsters, cooks, and engineers: there were half a dozen teams of good horses to haul the felled logs from the forest around the camp.

The huts and tents were scattered around a kind of esplanade overlooking the river, and cleared for this purpose of the beautiful forest that until recently had run down to the bank.

The river flowed from the Rockies, the peaks of which were visible in the distance, and we were surrounded by the foothills. Its waters were swift and rushing, with green or blue flashes, light or dark according to the depth, and the work we were engaged in was the construction of a wooden bridge like the ones we'd crossed on the way here.

The next morning, at daybreak, we had our first taste of what a work camp was like on the railroad: the wakeup call was an infernal din of ironmongery: one of the cook's helpers banged with an iron rod on a chariot wheel hanging from a log saddle. Quick rinse in a wooden barrel that was filled each morning and evening by a detail from the dormitories, who took turns filling it with buckets of water from the river. It goes without saying that as soon as Clément and I realized what was going on, we made sure we were the first to use it, as after twenty others had taken their turn, the water lost its limpid clarity to take on a coffee-coloured hue. Some of them had no compunction about rinsing out their tobacco-filled mouths and some sloshed about making gargling sounds that sounded like bears growling.

Then there was a mad rush towards the canteen, where, thankfully, everyone had his own place, ever since a bloody scuffle between Ukrainians and Armenians. We were treated to the thunderous roaring of the horde, still half asleep as they threw themselves on the porridge, pancakes, fried bacon, and steaming steaks surrounded by boiled potatoes. There was at that moment a lot more swearing and "Goddam" than grace, let me tell you.

Although Clément and I were no saints, we felt completely overwhelmed by all this, though we tried not to show it.

Apparently — and we later had confirmation of this — there in those godforsaken work camps, apart from one or two settlers like ourselves more interested in good wages than a comfortable job, were the dregs of society, all the scum of Canadian immigration and all the progeny whom life had rejected: Germans, Russians and Armenians, Ukrainians, Italians, Americans, and if there were a few French Canadians, we were the only Frenchmen from the old country. There were also a few Chinese, but they only did the less arduous work around the kitchen and the fire.

As soon as the meal was finished — and it was scrupulously timed by the boss who was always surveying this mass of men — came the call to work. This was another surprise about the conditions in the camp where we were going to live for a while: we heard a shot and we watched all these men rise and form groups according to category: loggers in one group, diggers in another, and so on. Then we realized that the big boss summoned his flock with revolver shots, and a big Colt hung from his belt as from a cowboy's or a sheriff's, as it did from those of his foremen. There were four or five wolfhound-looking dogs either close at their heels or near the hut where the office was.

The first day we were assigned to the crew that was working in a wooden caisson deep in the riverbed where the log piers were to be placed to form the skeleton of the bridge. In the caissons, which were about ten or twelve metres square and about two and a half metres high, the water was sucked out and evacuated by powerful pumps, with the level stabilized at sixty or seventy centimetres. The gravel was removed in trucks and dumped on the bank. We'd been issued with wading boots for this work, but as soon as we started, we realized that this was a mere formality, since as soon as the pump slowed down, the water rose rapidly, and also, as we moved around, our boots soon filled with the icy water from the Rocky Mountains.

After two or three days, we were racked with dry stomach cramps and we had to keep running up the ladder to find an isolated spot in the woods. If the foreman happened along at that moment, there followed a long harangue about workers who were slacking and how they should get back among the "convicts" right away, and I thought of those poor galley slaves forced to row endlessly on the ancient triremes or on the barges of more recent times. At first, I couldn't help replying in kind and I returned his English curses with the best French equivalent I knew, to the delight of Clément and the French Canadian who was in our crew; but it was pointless to resist. We began to understand why they needed replacement crews so often, since the work really was "hard labour." After a few days of this torture, we decided to go and see the big boss. We weren't refusing to work in the caisson, but we were asking that there be a rotation between the navvies and diggers and the others who were either cutting down trees or clearing a path for the next round of tree cutting. And if there were any justice in the world, solving this really shouldn't be a problem.

So when we finished work five or six days after our arrival, the whole crew went to see the boss. He lived in a wooden hut, in temporary but comfortable quarters. When we arrived, he was naked to the waist, washing in front of his door. After listening to the case presented by the French Canadian who could speak English, he answered us right away, still rubbing his face — which looked like that of an old-timer from the historic past.

"Well, boys, I know that caisson is the biggest sonofabitch in the whole camp. And it's always going to be that way, whatever we do, because where there's water in that goddam river, there'll be water in the caisson as well. And if you're going to build a bridge, you're going to need piers, and piers are always in water. But goddam it, boys, I like it when you tell me to my face when the foremen don't. So now I'm telling you straight that the three digging crews will take their turn in the caisson. Off you go to feed, boys, and mind you fill your plates!"

Next morning when the call to work came, we were there making sure we looked innocent when another crew was assigned to slosh around in the caisson, which provoked much cursing among the newly selected. Our team set off for the forest, a mile or two from the camp, to prepare the logs that would be used for the piers.

Work of angels compared to the diabolic stuff! Which just goes to show you should always speak straight to God rather than to his saints. The man in charge turned out to be very understanding, despite being harsh in every sense of the word — towards himself as well as to others — and it was thanks to him that everything turned out alright.

All this, of course, caused a certain amount of friction with the other labourers, who tried to pick a fight with us; and it nearly came to a general punch-up when the French Canadian, who understood the remarks about our crew, and particularly about us "Frenchies" or "tenderfeet," headed for the one who'd made the remarks and punched him in the face. When we thought about our gilded youth, and compared it with the brutish life led by most of the men in this camp, with the thought of payday and the days of big spending that followed as their one ray of hope, we could understand the need for iron discipline to maintain order among such an unlikely amalgam, which had to be forced into a crew. This camp was nothing like the ones in towns, where the men, despite their brutality, were tempered by a well-ordered, civilized life, and the emollient of a certain level of comfort. Here everything was hard: work, bosses, lodging, and nature itself that was a savage environment. As someone who was simply passing through this purgatory, with the key to resurrection in my hands, it was merely a fascinating experience that fulfilled my dreams of adventure. For a few others, it was a means of making a lot of money so that they could settle on the homestead where, perhaps, a wife and children were already living. But for the majority, the same succession of days and work had gone on for years in a never-ending round of exhausting labour, with nights that gave insufficient rest to their tired bodies, with the crude satisfaction of full canteens and at the end of the dark tunnel, escape, with a bulging wallet, to the wild delights of the city and the pleasures that could be bought there.

An iron fist was really needed to control this wild horde, and the Colt hanging from the belt was indeed a symbol. But for the rest of the camp, with the exception of the foremen, possession of firearms was forbidden, and if anyone owned a gun, he had to turn it in to a "timekeeper."

And a good thing, too, not only to try to head off fights, which broke out constantly, but especially to limit the damage they did.

Reasons for fighting were legion: it could be cheating at gambling, when someone had bet a month's or a few weeks' wages and found that he was left without a cent and had to fight again; or simply for a word — a joke about a picture of a woman hanging on someone's wooden partition; or the influence of alcohol, but this was rare and surveillance was strict.

Indeed, alcohol was forbidden in the camp, but the occasional bootlegger, tempted by the thought of profit, would sometimes venture into the forest around the camp. He would sneak in along little-used trails with a few pack ponies loaded with bad whisky made in secret stills — moonshine, as it was called. Much later, a messenger would creep in, using Indian tactics like a thief in the night, and tip off an accomplice. When the go-betweens returned, there'd be a drinking binge of epic proportions, an unimaginable bacchanalia that made the whole camp tremble. Then the foremen would turn up and set the dogs on the trails, while they themselves went after the bootleggers with their Winchesters at the ready. And if the whisky runners were caught, the police didn't exactly treat them with velvet gloves.

I never had the opportunity (I was going to say good luck) to witness such a scene. But what I did see one day was the arrival of a caravan of peddlers, two whites and a Japanese who travelled with their ponies around the camps selling cards, mirrors, needles and thread, scarves, and, the most popular item, postcards of sexy girls or naked women. But these salesmen, who had the knack of winkling out the gold hidden in the pockets of the wild workmen, were tolerated and sometimes even given supplies and food by the camps.

Thus did we spend the month — a month of hard labour, but with variety as soon as the rotation of crews got started. On one shift it would be the ghastly caisson; on another it would be hacking the branches off the trunks and loading them onto wagons, and on yet another making a trail to a new site where there were good trees. One day I was lucky enough to drive one of those superb teams when the teamster was off sick — and all the while in the midst of wild but grandiose nature that made man seem so infinitely small but that he nevertheless managed to dominate and tame.

At the end of the month, we decided to settle up as we had contracted. Clément, who'd been in the country for four years, was always in favour of changing jobs and wanted to go on, as he had for the last years, to work on the harvest on the prairie in Saskatchewan. Any direction was good for me, as long as it gave me a change of scenery and a little income, so that's what we decided. So we took our pay one morning, as agreed, and when a few dollars for cigarettes, tobacco, and other small expenses were subtracted, we had just under $140.

Now we had about eighty miles to travel on foot to get to Lake Wabamun, where we could catch a freight train for Edmonton. We took a few canned goods that we'd bought from the camp stores, and the cook gave us a few pancakes with some slices of cooked bacon and moose, for which we gave him a good tip, as we would after a nice meal in a restaurant in France. We didn't want to overload ourselves: we already had our blankets and we knew from the outward trip that the trail was no city boulevard. According to directions we'd been given in the camp, we had two choices: either we could follow the railway line with its crude tracks where we'd have to keep jumping from one tie to another, or we could take the trail through the forest, which zigzagged back and forth round the railroad track, making it a bit longer, but easier, despite its unmade state, since we could walk at a normal pace.

We decided to start on the railroad track, which was the lazier solution, and we set off with our bags over our shoulders and our minds free of care. It seemed like a little vacation after a month of hard labour, freedom again. The first few miles were relatively easy, but towards midday our legs were giving way as the distances between the ties was wider than our steps. Finally, towards evening, just before we were ready to set up camp for the night, we decided that we'd be better off on the forest trail, which we could see from time to time from the railroad bed. We camped that night beneath a great spruce that must have been a hundred years old and whose branches spread over our heads like a canopy. After a peaceful night of solitude and calm that was sometimes eerie with its pale shadows, we had breakfast and set off again, with two hours of walking behind us before the first rays of the sun smiled on us for the first time.

Just before the noon break, we left the forest as the trail joined the track to cross a pretty little creek about twenty metres wide, and we wondered whether our pleasant nature walk in beautiful scenery was coming to an end. But we were soon reassured when we saw that the line crossed a kind of swamp, land that lay beneath the level of the water where only thick moss will grow, and where you sink up to the knees and where it's impossible to walk. We got back to the forest trail at last, and from then on we stuck to it till evening when we made our second camp without incident. We had certainly covered more ground than on the first day, and were less tired by it, since we'd been walking on a relatively clear path, except for a few tree stumps or fallen trees that blocked our way occasionally. In addition to the easy walk, we could appreciate the various aspects of the country we were going through: sometimes it was forested with different kinds of trees: spruce, pines, red pines, or tamaracks, and sometimes it was clear, with grasslands dotted with silver birch and reeds that were so pretty in the spring with their white pompoms; and wonderful coulees sloping gently towards a curve, where we came upon a clear miniature lake, home to families of ducks and teal. The last foothills of the Rockies had left their mark on the soil, which was still churned up by them;

and I remember, as we descended a rocky spur, the magic of the sudden sight of a dear little lake, crystal clear, set like a mirror in a frame of grasses and young balsam. Its waters, blue or green, light or dark according to the depth or light in the sky, seemed as if suspended above the little valley we reached later by a rock slide of about forty metres down a scree studded with bushes and clumps of blueberries. Never has a Bull Durham cigarette given me such pleasure and relaxation as the one I smoked contemplating this exquisite spectacle of nature and the might of its Creator.

We camped for the night in the shelter of some big overhanging rocks, and got the unpleasant shock of realizing that our supply of food had nearly run out. We had at least two days of walking before reaching our goal. If we'd had our .22 with us, the problem would have been solved, as we could have got ourselves a couple of nice little roasts, courtesy of the ducks or spruce partridges that we often spotted among the reeds or in the underbrush. We finished our meal quickly — with good reason — only holding back a pancake for the following day's breakfast, and putting our trust in Providence, we slipped into the arms of Morpheus.

But the night was disturbed by an unwelcome visitor we could well have done without. After a few hours of deep sleep, we were awakened by a strange noise coming from the scree that was about a hundred metres away. We soon realized that it wasn't a human visitor, but rather one or two bears that were gobbling down the blueberries that grew in profusion there, and of which they were particularly fond. After a wait that seemed long, our unwanted guests made off and we went back to sleep. Wakeup time came with a group of squirrels chasing each other in the trees around us. Our nocturnal adventure hadn't diminished our appetite, unfortunately, and we had to make do with the two pancakes.

After smoking the usual cigarette to finish off our breakfast, we set off again. Our spirits were still high, which was the important thing. If the worst came to the worst, we could always fast for two days, which wasn't a disaster, because at the end there was a little village in Lake Wabamun with bacon and eggs and tasty foods, the mere thought of which made our mouths water. And to ease the pangs of hunger, we did as the bears did and gathered blueberries that were abundant in sheltered places beside the trail.

Then all of a sudden, after we'd been walking for about an hour, we came out onto a little clearing and saw a pond in front of us with a few ducks, most of which flew off, leaving only one in the water. We saw that a brood of ducklings was trying to swim into the reeds to hide there. This was a golden opportunity for us to try to fill our stomachs, which were floating within us like punctured balls.

What we had to do was to use a few stealthy moves to stop the ducklings from getting to the middle of the pond, which, as it was about five or six metres wide, would have meant that we'd be bogged down for quite a long while; so after rolling up our trousers and picking up branches and sticks, we managed to isolate them at the edge of the pond. At that point it was easy to kill the ones that looked as if they had most flesh on them. These ducklings were just starting to sprout pinion feathers and doubtless in another eight or ten days we wouldn't have been able to do it. We weren't particularly happy about this little massacre, but needs must, and there were seven or eight left in the brood, which the mother duck had tried to protect by attracting our attention to her. It wasn't exactly a sumptuous banquet, but it was enough to appease the rumbling of our stomachs. After cleaning them we decided to grill two immediately and to keep the third as a standby for the evening.

We had two choices for cooking them: either we could roast them on the end of a poplar or cottonwood branch, or we could do a Caribbean roast. We chose the first, which was the easier and quicker: for the other we'd have to dig a hole, line it with stones, burn a lot of brushwood to get a hot fire, find the right sort of clay to wrap around the bird, which would then be placed on the burned-out charcoal and kept in a low fire until it was perfectly cooked; we were in a hurry and we were hungry.

I have to admit that this meal, which might be called *caneton sans canapé* on a sophisticated table, wasn't bad, besides which it's not hard to please a famished stomach. The pieces were small, and the flesh, although perfectly edible, wasn't really ready, but it was a blessing to get a bit of our strength back. One cigarette and we took to the trail again, hoping to see signs of settlement and human presence during the course of the afternoon.

Not long after, the trail led suddenly to the railroad. There was a river to be crossed, wide with fairly high banks and very swift-flowing (no doubt a tributary of the Saskatchewan). We had to walk over the bridge, which had been constructed in exactly the same way as the one we'd been working on, so we were put in mind of all the fatigue and suffering in the camp we'd just left behind. And Clément, true to his Canebière roots, joked, "Before we left, we should have put up a marker on one of the piers: 'Bethink you, O passer-by, of the two Frenchmen, one from Marseille, one from the Limousin, who contributed to the building of this bridge.'"

It was, in fact, amazing to observe the technique and skill of the builders, sons of the pioneers who had crossed the immensity of this wonderful Canada to force a passage through the Rocky Mountains to see spread before them the rich valleys of British Columbia. The view of the bridge seen sideways and from below was like a tapestry of wood. We'd crossed over this work of "art" on our way to the camp and felt we were suspended over the void. But crossing it on foot gives a much more powerful impression. We had to jump from one tie to the next with the water boiling below us, foaming against the wood. The slightest false step could have been fatal. And we were very relieved and happy to get back to solid ground and the poor railroad bed, which now seemed like a sidewalk. We weren't on it for long, since about a hundred yards on, we got back onto the forest trail, which we almost missed. We had to keep an eye out for the fork as we weren't sure whether it was on the left or the right.

PIERRE MATURIÉ

Not long after leaving the rail bed we saw some newly cut trees, which gave us hope of soon seeing some kind of settler's or prospector's dwelling, especially as the grass seemed well trodden.

Indeed, we came to a sudden clearing and saw about two acres of cleared land studded with bush and a log shack with the usual sod roof and a small fence. If Christopher Columbus was filled with emotion when he shouted "Land!" at the sight of the shores of the New World, we were similarly filled with delight and nearly shouted "Roof!" It was the first sign of human habitation we'd seen in this vast, wild nature since leaving camp.

We made our way towards it hoping to see the occupant appear at the door, but to our great disappointment, no one answered our shouts. We pushed open the door, which was unlocked (as is usual in the West where hospitality is the golden rule and theft rare) and entered a classic interior that could equally well belong to prospector, trapper, forester, or homesteader: wooden table made right there out of slices of logs, camp bed ditto, small, portable tin stove, wash-bowl on a packing case, and in lieu of chairs, large logs standing upright, and, in a small cupboard nailed to the wall, a few supplies.

A small lean-to was built on to the shack, obviously for a horse, and with the droppings scattered around you didn't need to be Sherlock Holmes to make that deduction. And the owner had left very recently, because the droppings were fresh and the ashes in the fireplace were still warm. As the summer sun was setting we sat for a rest in front of the cabin waiting in case the owner returned. After a while we decided, regretfully, to go on our way, but as we cast a farewell glance inside, we saw a kind of trap door in a corner covering a hole in the ground. We raised it and saw a good supply of potatoes spread on straw. We were delighted with the sight, as we'd have something to go with the remaining duck, which would have been a bit meagre for two starving men. We took a few of the precious potatoes and Clément left a fifty-cent piece on the table together with a note explaining our predicament.

In these immense unpopulated wastes, any traveller who has run out of supplies or who has fallen ill can find a haven of rest: in winter, warmth to cheer him, dry wood ready to light, canned goods, in fact whatever is necessary to save a life; this is the unwritten law of the North, a law inscribed in word of mouth and ingrained in the consciousness of the rough-and-ready westerners.

We left and went on hoping to cover a few more miles before nightfall. The days were long at that time of year, and after the miles we'd gone that day, we imagined that the next day would see the end of the part of the journey we'd have to do on foot and that the rest would be a cakewalk.

After a few more miles, our legs told us that it was time to stop for the evening meal — meal being an inflated term that didn't convey the reality of the thing. However, the scrupulously shared last duck and the potatoes roasted in the ashes, delicious even without butter, made a perfectly acceptable picnic: which all goes to prove that the secret of happiness is in an optimistic view of the present state. We drank the clear water from one of the small streams that rush down from the Rockies, and Clément, jokingly panning for gold, pretended he'd found a few flakes. And the memory of this halt beside the running water moved us to try an experience I'll tell you about later.

We were about to leave, as we still had about an hour of daylight, when we heard the barking of a dog that appeared out of nowhere and, seeing us, came to a sudden halt. Then a horseman appeared, looking for whatever it was that had caused the barking, and rode towards us. After the customary shout of "Hello, boys!" he dismounted and we fell to talking. And soon, after very few words, he knew where we were from and what we were doing and had explained to us why he was in this sector. He was a forest warden responsible for the surrounding dozens of square miles of forest, keeping watch for fires, which could be devastating. He spent six months of the year in the shack we'd just left and moved around on horseback with only his dog for company. We confessed our "filching" and if he was angry, it was only because we hadn't taken more, and that we'd left money. The best news for us was that we were only about ten miles from the terminus for supply trains, which we could certainly ride on if we could come to some arrangement with the engineer. Before we separated, he pointed out that a short distance ahead on the trail, there was an abandoned cabin in reasonably good shape that belonged to a settler who was sick and had gone to Edmonton for treatment; we could camp there without bothering anyone. So we had comfortable shelter for the night, and above all, we could stay up smoking for a while telling old tales of our former life in France. In the morning, we set out towards the longed-for stop that was to be the end of our toils and the return to civilized life, provided that we happened upon a day when the train was leaving.

By a stroke of luck, the train happened to be leaving the following evening, a freight train with only one wagonload of supplies, and the day after, we got off in Edmonton, thirty-four days after leaving it for our expedition. Our Cecil gave us its usual welcome, and what tickled our fancy after dinner was to take in a show in a saloon on Jasper Avenue, the city's main street. I can still see in my mind's eye, with the nostalgia for things gone by, the clapboard facade, just like in Westerns, and on the stage, chorus girls in glittering costumes, mostly pretty girls, who came to sit with us when their number was over and tried to get us to part with some of the money it had taken so much effort to earn.

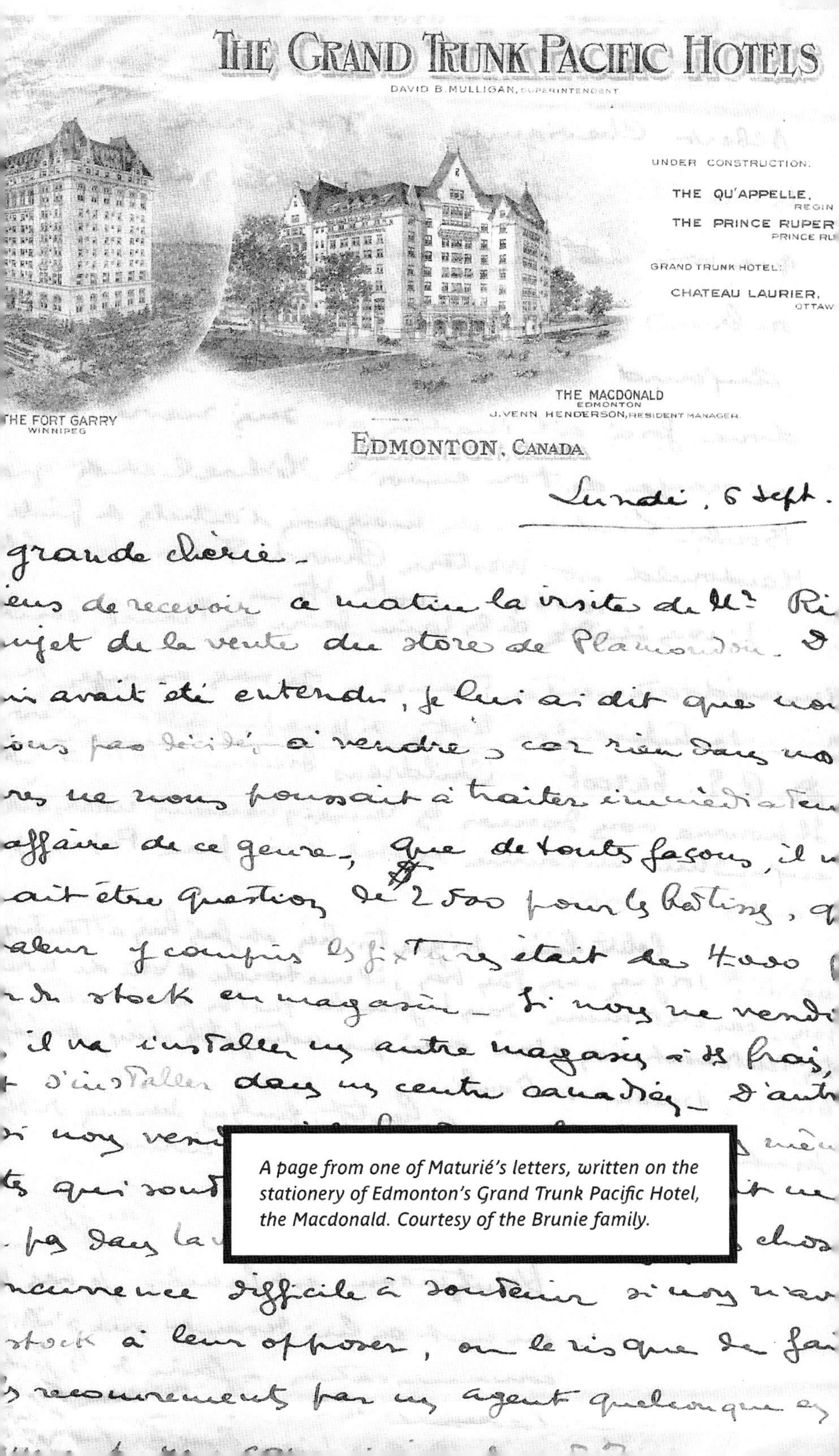
THE GRAND TRUNK PACIFIC HOTELS

DAVID B. MULLIGAN, SUPERINTENDENT

UNDER CONSTRUCTION:

THE QU'APPELLE, REGIN

THE PRINCE RUPER PRINCE RU

GRAND TRUNK HOTEL:

CHATEAU LAURIER, OTTAW

THE FORT GARRY WINNIPEG

THE MACDONALD EDMONTON

J. VENN HENDERSON, RESIDENT MANAGER

EDMONTON, CANADA

Lundi, 6 Sept.

grande chérie –

iens de recevoir ce matin la visite de Mr Ri

ujet de la vente du store de Plamondon. I

i avait été entendu, je lui ai dit que no

ions pas décidés à vendre, car rien dans no

res ne nous poussait à traiter immédiatem

affaire de ce genre, que de toutes façons, il n

ait être question de 2000 $ pour les batisses, q

aleur y compris les fixtures était de 4000

du stock en magasin. Si nous ne vendi

il va installer un autre magasin à ses frais

t d'installer dans un centre canadien – d'autr

i nous vend … même

ts qui sont … ait ne

pas dans la … chos

ncurrence difficile à soutenir si nous n'av

stock à leur opposer, on le risque de fai

s recouvrements par un agent quelconque en

A page from one of Maturié's letters, written on the stationery of Edmonton's Grand Trunk Pacific Hotel, the Macdonald. Courtesy of the Brunie family.

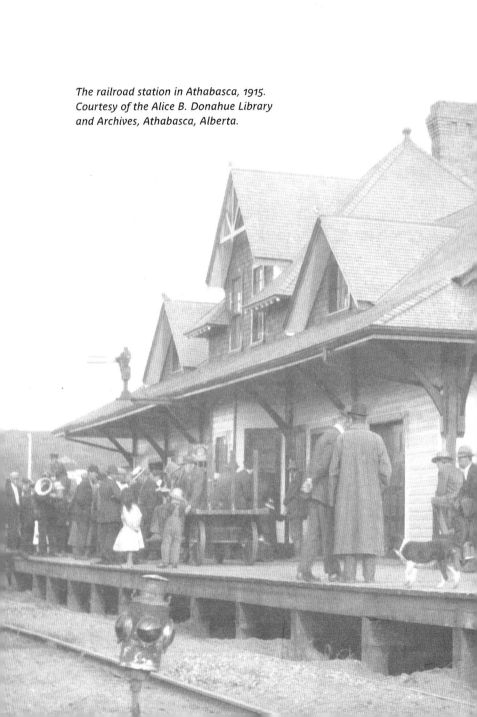

The railroad station in Athabasca, 1915.
Courtesy of the Alice B. Donahue Library
and Archives, Athabasca, Alberta.

Athabasca's ecoonomic boom: prospective homesteaders line up to buy new lots, 1911. Courtesy of the Alice B. Donahue Library and Archives, Athabasca, Alberta.

A horse-drawn wagon, an item Maturié describes as "indispensable."
Courtesy of the Alice B. Donahue Library and Archives, Athabasca, Alberta.

The Grand Union Hotel, one of Athabasca's early landmarks. Courtesy of the Alice B. Donahue Library and Archives, Athabasca, Alberta.

Pierre Maturié in army uniform, ca. 1915. Wounded twice at Verdun, he later resigned from the infantry to join the air force. Courtesy of the Brunie family.

Transport on the Athabasca River. Courtesy of the Alice B. Donahue Library and Archives, Athabasca, Alberta.

Pierre Maturié as a pilot in the French air force, ca. 1917. Courtesy of the Brunie family.

Pierre Maturié's first house, which he describes with enormous pride. The roof, which he designed himself, "was waterproofed with a layer of planks covered by a sheet of tarred, sanded felt" and "allowed us to work sheltered from the elements if the weather was too harsh for outside work." Courtesy of the Brunie family.

The "mess hall" at a railroad camp.
Courtesy of the Alice B. Donahue Library
and Archives, Athabasca, Alberta.

A sketch of Pierre Maturié,
by an unknown artist.
Courtesy of the Brunie family.

Pierre Maturié's sister, Marguerite,
the wife of Armand Brunie.
Courtesy of the Brunie family.

Return to Edmonton and Departure for Saskatchewan, Purchase of a Lot at Palm Beach in Florida, and Harvest in Saskatchewan

As we'd planned to finish up our outside work with the harvest in Saskatchewan, the next day, cigarette between our lips and hands in our pockets, we strolled down to the Employment Offices, a kind of agency of job offers and requests. Two huge two-metre-high boards had all the information about various positions vacant: place of work, hourly or monthly salary, travel paid for almost all of them, etc. The harvest had already begun in Saskatchewan, but work crews were not complete everywhere, and we easily found a job for two weeks with a farmer near Saskatoon with a daily wage of $3, bed, board, and travel included. The pay wasn't bad, but we knew that the days would be long in the broiling sun, for the season commands and man obeys.

We left next day in the late afternoon, and after a change in Saskatoon arrived the following morning at the little station that served the farm, which was about ten miles away. We waited for about an hour, and were beginning to wonder whether we were going have to leave again like hobos when we saw a democrat draw up pulled by two fine trotting horses. It had indeed come for us, and after introductions at the only bar around, we were driven to our new residence. But it was no vacation that was beginning. When we arrived at the farm, the sun was already burning hot. After being shown the bunkhouse where we'd sleep, and which was well maintained, we were put to work, since for the farmer there was no time to waste, time being money for him in all senses of the expression.

The farm, which was magnificent, both from the point of view of the house as well as the stables, was nothing like our pathetic

65-hectare "homesteads." It belonged to a rich Englishman who was practically never there, as he lived in Regina.

Since this Englishman lived in town, where, like all the "old-timers," he took care of his various business interests, he'd given over the management of his land to a young couple employed by the month with all the attendant advantages (bed, board, and in addition a certain percentage of the income from the farm at the end of the year). They were a mixed couple, from different nationalities, he a pure-blood Englishman from the old country and she a French Canadian who brought to the marriage a sociability and spontaneity that was somewhat lacking in her husband. To help with the running of this vast undertaking there were six hired men, each with a specific area of expertise that gave them a certain sense of responsibility.

Besides an impressive herd of beef and milk cattle, the ranch also possessed — in addition to several relatively light horses for the saddle or the carriage (buggy, democrat, sulky) — at least twenty teams of superb horses, mainly handsome, dappled-grey Percherons, with the rest Clydesdales — good, strong beasts, I'm sure, but lacking (all national chauvinism aside) the elegance of dappled greys. And also, they had, in my humble opinion as a mere settler, the fatal flaw of their "horse-guards" fringe around their ankles, which risked causing cuts in damp weather or during the thaw, and could weep and become painful if not treated in time.

The farm grew mainly wheat and oats and covered over 2,500 acres, with a few acres given over to secondary crops like potatoes. We could only dream when we compared these immense fields with the little 65 hectares of our concessions. Still, when I recalled my stay with the Le Galls, I could imagine extending my little realm by the purchase of land from neighbours who became discouraged or indigent.

The work of hired men like ourselves consisted of gathering into stacks the sheaves that fell already tied from the harvester. Six harvesters advanced in a line and the horses were changed at noon. We were a bit like the seasonal workers in northern France working with the beets, or with the grape harvest in the Bordeaux region or with peas in my own Limousin.

At first, it seemed like child's play, but we were soon disabused of that idea. For the teams of horses were very strong and the sheaves fell very fast. We had to work hard to keep up with the general movement. Clément and I had asked to work together as a team, each team being made up of two "servants," so we'd be able to tell each other stories and forget how tired we were. For the whole body ached — arms, legs, and back — and the heat was the crowning pain. For as far as the eye could see, there was nothing but level fields, a despairing plateau, with no shadow except that of our own bodies.

The sun was beginning to warm up, and the break for a meal was greeted by us with great relief, not only because of the moment of rest it would afford, but also to satisfy our curiosity about the atmosphere of our living quarters. The bunkhouse, which was also used as a refectory, was simple but clean, with a long central table, ample food, and friendly co-workers. Among these seasonal workers, there were only settlers, who, like us, had left their concessions to make a few dollars towards the expense of coming winter and the upkeep of their homesteads. They were nothing like the hordes in the camps of big companies like the one we'd just left in the Rockies. Among them there was a French Canadian whose parents lived a comfortable middle-class life in Québec, the father a lawyer and journalist. The table was presided over by the manager himself to make it clear that we weren't just farmhands, but also, and above all, friends.

During the conversation, we learnt that the water in the area was undrinkable; it was brackish, and household water had to be fetched in a large tank from the railroad station where we'd got off. In a time not so long ago, this had been the "vast Prairie" where the immense herds of buffalo had roamed, drinking at the salt-water pools of which traces could still be seen, dried-out depressions white with salt deposits. In some uncleared areas, the trails made by these herds were still visible, deeply marked in the ground where they used to walk in single file to the watering holes, and also, in more remote places, the bones and horns of animals that had died or been shot by hunters.

After the meal there was a half-hour for rest or siesta, then work began again. The afternoons were really difficult, as the sun was literally burning and we had no shade, since from dawn to dusk, the orb of the heavens, glorified and sung by poets, hung pitilessly over our heads. As the French Canadian said: "The only shade in this damn country comes from fence-posts and telegraph poles," which wasn't much use to us. There was also the shade we created when we lifted the sheaves. But when, sometimes, we thought, "To hell with this!" and crouched down for a minute to or two to light a cigarette, the team of horses got ahead of us, and when the foreman realized it, he came down on us, but not in a nasty way, and would shout, for example: "Hey boys! Do you want a rocking chair?" We weren't on vacation, obviously, and work called. But he was so nice about it that it didn't create any ill feeling between us.

About every hour or so, a boy of about fifteen came by with two canteens, one with tea or coffee and the other with water that was supposed to be cold but after five minutes was tepid. Apart from the terrible heat that cooked the skin to the point of leaving burn marks, I liked it there with its almost familial atmosphere. But although I was happy to experience the new horizons of the vast Prairie of adventure stories, I missed the majestic and varied panoramas of the Rockies, the forests with their ancient trees, the rushing waters coming from the glaciers and the little lakes set in their fringe of reeds, and the blueberry bushes. As I thought of the singing brooks and the coolness of the forest shade, it seemed, in the furnace of the harvest, like paradise lost. Yet the days had been long there, too, and the daily toil hard, and above all the atmosphere, so like a gang of convicts, had been hateful. Here, when the work was done, it was like a group of friends meeting around a table that already seemed pleasantly familiar.

One day, it was my turn to go to the station to get the tank of water. It was the only place for miles around where drinking water was available, as the railroad company had dug a well hundreds of metres, as deep as a petroleum well, for the machinery. A windmill pumped water to the surface and filled a huge reservoir like the ones we used to see in our stations before electricity came in.

So instead of leaving at the usual hour, I asked if I could leave very early, so that both I and the horses could take advantage of the cool morning. I set out well before sunrise. The horses trotted along at a spanking pace and it felt good to roll along in the pale half-light before the sun was fully up. From time to time a flight of prairie chickens took off with a loud whirring of wings, and curious gophers started to emerge from their holes and as we passed stood erect as if on sentry duty.

We arrived cool and fresh at the station, where the tank was quickly filled by a big mobile sleeve, and as soon as the thirst of horses and driver had been slaked, together with that of the station master — the former with water and the others with foaming beer of which I'd been deprived for some days — we set out again for the farm, where we arrived before the sun was too high in the sky.

The manager's wife was happy to get water that was cool — for the moment, at least — and invited me to eat another breakfast, telling me to go and rest afterwards, but I preferred to go back to the work crew, which pleased the boss, who thanked me heartily. There was a world of difference between him and the ones we'd had in the Rockies, but even so, no one stinted on work.

To avoid the intense afternoon heat, he decided, after canvassing our opinion, to suspend work from noon till four o'clock and to make up for this pause by starting very early at daybreak and keeping going till the first shadows of night.

Thus were spent in cheerful mutual understanding the days of harvest, which were doubly interesting for me, for in addition to the money earned, I'd taken part in the regular working of a big Canadian farm and had gained valuable experience for the future. Our two-week contract came to an end. The wheat fields had been completely harvested and only about a hundred acres of oats remained to be cut. So we could keep to our original contract without upsetting the work. If departure day is sometimes welcomed because it means good riddance to hard days and the unhealthy atmosphere of the camps, this wasn't the case for our harvesting experience, and I still remember it with great affection. We received our wages at the rate we'd agreed upon and the manager's wife loaded us down with provisions for the return journey — enough for several days! — among them her cakes and pies, which were delicious and always made my mouth water. Our farewell handshakes at the station were truly heartfelt; the foreman had driven us there himself, along with two fellow workers who were going back to their neighbouring homesteads near Saskatoon. The manager had told us that there'd be a place waiting for us the next year if we decided to come back. For, he said, he much preferred to take on men he already knew rather than going to employment offices who sent any kind of livestock walking on two legs.

I spent two days in Edmonton, and Clément went back to his property. During that time I saw a Frenchman called Raoul, whom we'd already met in the hotel lobby. He worked for a realtor for whom he tried to drum up buyers for investment lots. It was the moment of great speculation in the Canadian West and in all the other virgin parts of North America. In particular, he was selling lots in the small town of Palm Beach in Florida (some five or six thousand kilometres away), on credit, of course, and on an unusual system. The platte was divided into two parts: one in the category "city lot," the other farther out designated as "garden lot." These double-numbered lots comprised a city lot with the same number as the garden lot and compensated for each other, so that a well-situated city lot was attached to a garden lot well outside the town and vice versa. You didn't actually buy the lot but rather the right to a lot, and ownership would be granted by a draw supervised by a barrister. The society would then go ahead, if you so desired, with the planting and management of the garden lots, putting in various fruit trees. Cash payment wasn't very important, and the sum due was payable in monthly payments over twelve years, with the vending company as guarantor in the meantime with a mortgage on the land. The initial investment was for $200 and the annual payment during the remainder of the term $120, if I remember correctly.

I had a small sum set aside, so both Clément and I took out an option; we weren't taking any great risk as the future payments were discretionary, so that's how I came to have an interest in property in Florida, at the opposite end of the American continent. But, as I've already mentioned, this was nothing unusual at the time, and maybe there were others like us, living in distant regions, who were involved in speculation on our lands in western Canada.

Return to the Fold and Wintering

But the time had come to return to the fold. Clément and I said goodbye, each of us setting off home and agreeing to meet the following season. I had no complaints because I'd be going back to familiar faces. It wasn't the same for Clément, as there were only strangers around his property — kind strangers, it's true, but who couldn't mitigate his sense of solitude throughout the winter. And my train, although still lurching and swaying, was still delightful compared with the already-forgotten incidents we'd experienced on the trail a few months ago, and set me down on the wooden platform of our little station. It was a real pleasure to see my little village again, and its various sights were like smiles of welcome.

Armand, Marguerite, and Jean still had a few more weeks at the Athabasca Hotel. I took two days of complete vacation and then, having got the horses back from Fitzgibbon, I went back to the ranch, where I settled back in with great pleasure. How satisfying it was to open the door of our house and to see life come back to the yard and the stable! I was alone for the time being as Jean was employed at the Athabasca Hotel until the permanent managers arrived. I had neither the time nor the inclination to become bored, since there was always something to be done: tending the horses, keeping up the area around the house, levelling and enclosing the yard with attractive, well-chosen stakes, which made a neat, solid fence — adding almost a touch of elegance, I might say. So that little by little, our home took on an orderly and tasteful appearance.

When I'd had enough of work, I'd leave the horses in the pasture and, taking my .22, I'd go off in whichever direction took my fancy to reconnoitre the most distant corners of our domain. For if we knew in theory where the boundary was, it took time to inspect it in practical detail. Over an area such as that of the three plots, each 800 metres square, in the woods, valleys, and clearings there was always something that struck me as new and interesting: a hayfield to clean out and develop; a woodlot to tend; in a coulee a little stream to dam to make a miniature pond where the livestock could later come and drink; and also, on the banks below the house, slopes that could later be used to make a path down to the fine beach on the Athabasca River.

I was always on the alert and almost unconsciously my eye took in every corner of the land, and at the same time I started to form vague plans that would come to fruition when the time was ripe or when the situation demanded their realization. What I was doing, in fact, was making a mental list of the resources and possibilities of development for the coming years. But as, here on our poor earth, dreams are a corner of paradise that the unquiet heart of man creates amid the cares of his daily life, I allowed my mind to enjoy them at leisure. And what I saw, spread out in front of the home that stood firm on the soil I had travelled so far to tame, was the whole plateau ploughed up and bearing a fine golden harvest; and grassland around the lake and all the way down the coulee to the river; and on the banks gradually cleared and covered with vetch and wild peas, our herd grazing to the clear tinkling of their bells.

Naturally, there would be a hard row to hoe to make these lovely daydreams come true, but the shimmering image at the end of the row gave me new courage to carry on with the countless tasks. So every day, either with an axe over my shoulder or the horses in my hand, I would cut down wood and brush, tear out stumps and pile them up to create a new land out of this savage wilderness.

The days went by quickly till the end of my sister and Armand's contract and their departure for Victoria.

Their idea was to set up a truly comfortable — even luxurious — family hotel. Indeed, Victoria was a real summer resort for British Columbia and Alberta, a watering place for the rich, just as Nice was for France. Situated as it was on Vancouver Island, it got first-hand the warm Pacific breezes. The young couple had been put off by the unyielding and sometimes harsh life of the first years of homesteading and they were now looking forward to an easier life in a city. So it was with heavy hearts and great sadness that we saw them off at the station. At that moment, a thread was broken and we felt that the break was irrevocable and definitive.

Jean's job was over, so he came back to join me on the concession. He brought with him a cute little six- or seven-month-old black cocker spaniel that had been given him by the manager of the Hudson's Bay. I was very happy, as I've always liked dogs and this one would be a good companion for us. I promised myself that I'd initiate him into the joys of hunting and teach him how to fetch furred and feathered game. We christened him Dianou.

So now we had to organize our winter. We were quite comfortably off financially. We had enough from our summer jobs to amply cover the work we were proposing and also our living expenses until next spring. I had in mind — to satisfy my obligation to the Lands Office — to build a house on my quarter, so I had to think of buying the materials.

We decided to reduce to a minimum our winter expenses by selling eggs, which were a rare commodity in Athabasca, and in great demand by grocery stores. Most of the eggs on sale came from Edmonton and were of dubious freshness. Lessard, who owned one of the general stores, had promised to take our whole production at the best price, or at least better than the price we'd usually get.

To put this plan into execution, we had to buy very young pullets that had only just started laying, or were of good stock. So we had sent from a specialized breeder in Edmonton forty purebred pullets, superb striped grey and black Plymouth Rocks, and two impressive roosters that we put temporarily in the unoccupied stalls in the stable. They had the whole of the right side, separated from the rest by a temporary grille so that they wouldn't soil the forage or cereal for the horses, who were very fussy about their feed. And we started to build — by ourselves, this time — their permanent home.

As they required considerable space to move around, scratch, and keep warm for the winter laying season, we made the henhouse fairly large, following the advice of the experimental farm. The front, which faced south, was all glass, with a small door at the right side with a very small flap so that heat wouldn't be lost.

Although we'd identified reserves of logs on our own property as we walked around making an inventory, I preferred to go farther afield to get them on land that hadn't been claimed, towards the north around Baptiste Creek. The distance didn't matter much, as once the trees had been cut free and pulled by chain onto the plateau, hauling them didn't take us very long. Towards mid-October, the frame was finished and we made do with a flat roof (standard settler or Indian model), poles placed over a central beam (to give a slight pitch), with the whole covered with turf and finally ordinary boards and tarred paper. We were therefore sure that when the first snow came, there would be adequate covering and therefore an acceptable temperature inside for our residents. In a corner, a heater protected by a metal grille, and across the roof an empty fifty-litre gasoline barrel with holes drilled to put a pipe through, which made a sheath to minimize the risk of fire.

To feed our feathered flock we already had some of the oat seed and the green feed, which, mixed with straw, forced the hens to scratch and gave them healthy exercise. We had to fill this out with ground oyster shells and calcium, and, according to the advice of the experimental farm, bran for warm mush (very good for the horses as well) and, according to the always judicious advice of the excellent Tobaty, fish, which should be cooked and mixed with the bran to produce a good stimulant in cold weather.

A Métis from Baptiste Lake, whom we had often met in the Grand Union Hotel, promised to keep us in fish for the whole winter, and as soon as it turned cold, he delivered a good load — a whole cartful — for $5. They were fine, big whitefish that would also enhance our menu. Preserving them was no problem in temperatures between minus fifteen and minus thirty degrees, and they were simply stacked up against the stable wall like a load of firewood.

So before the onset of the bitter cold, we could install our poultry in their permanent residence, and we awaited, calmly and serenely, the arrival of real winter. The chickens we'd acquired looked healthy and would surely bring us some income. We had the potatoes we'd harvested and a stock of flour, lard, bacon, sugar, all the supplies that were the basis of the homesteader's larder, and we had no cause to fear a few months of winter. Snares provided all the rabbits we could eat and our guns yielded partridges and prairie chickens, and from some Métis or other, we'd be able to get a haunch of moose.

Without counting our chickens before they were hatched, we could expect reasonable returns from our poultry. I hoped to make about $50 or $60 from my traps, either ermine from the trapline I'd spread over four or five miles on our own property when I was walking or hunting as far as Baptiste Lake, or, who knows, maybe I'd even find in a trap a fine mink. Then we'd made an agreement with the Hudson's Bay and Royal Bank managers to supply them with a certain number of cords of firewood, which for us, in the forest that surrounded us or beyond our boundary, and using only trees that were already down, either from forest fires or from storms, meant an average of two hours' work per day and two cartloads per week. All of that also provided good exercise for men and horses.

So we settled into the life of established homesteaders. Our house seemed like a haven of peace and was very comfortable in the finished part; the stable was warm and well stocked, with hay and stacks of straw to the side and in the roof itself. Let the long months of the Canadian winter begin!

This period of intense cold is, for the sedentary homesteader, with a good woodpile beside the door, his pipe and a packet of Old Chum on the shelf, a period of rest and reflection; it could, however, for the *coureur des bois* or the isolated trapper, faced with a blizzard or the endless snowfall, become harsh, brutish, and often deadly.

It's a far cry from the poets' sonnets about the great white silence, the jewels and beads that delicately festoon the branches of the pine trees, the immaculate carpet of snow, to a temperature of forty to fifty degrees below zero; an apparently benevolent sun that does nothing to warm; the insidious numbness that suddenly penetrates your limbs and sends to you sleep to kill you more effectively; the frigid air that freezes your lungs; the snow-blindness from the expanses of white. Everything presents a danger for the presumptuous amateur. The initiated must always treasure close to their hearts, like their most precious possession, a dry box of matches. In the immensity of those forests, woe betide the man who for too long puts off doing anything about his frozen fingers and who is at the point of despair when he cannot light a fire.

Knowing how to light a fire is an art: you have to know how to find a place that will act as a screen and reflect the heat towards you. You always have to have dry twigs, and the Indians, with their innate sense of things needful for survival, always carry in their pockets a handful of strips of birch peel, thin as cigarette paper, which they pluck off the trees as they go by. This is why, as part of the coping mechanism that the French are so well endowed with, I always have with me, along with my flask of rum, a canister of gasoline, a few drops of which can start a good fire.

I remember one incident that showed what a terrible grip the cold can exert over a tired body: one morning when I was on my daily — weather permitting — visit to my trapline beyond Baptiste Creek, I was in a forest of red spruce — sometimes called tamarack — when I noticed a mass huddled under the lower branches of a pine tree. As it couldn't be a bear at that time of year, since bears hibernate somewhere warm — a hollow beneath a tree trunk, for example, or beneath a pile of branches hermetically covered by snow — I went up to it and realized that the mass was a sleeping man. I tried to wake him, but I couldn't understand what he was saying. Immediately, I made a bed of young pine branches, laid him on it, and as there was no question of my carrying him to a safe place — an impossibility in two and a half feet of snow, with me on snow shoes, which I wasn't very adept at managing — I made two fires, one on each side of him so that he was surrounded by gentle warmth. Then, making a mental note of the nearest help, I went as fast as the difficult trail allowed to an old Métis who lived in the shack at the mouth of Baptiste Creek. I quickly explained what was the matter, and he returned with me with his sled and dogs, which was the simplest solution for us.

We found him still lying in the same place, surprised to find himself between two fires that had warmed him up; we took him to the old trapper's cabin, where he came to his senses. Nothing was irremediably frozen, only the tips of his toes and his fingers, which were already beginning to freeze. I watched old John get busy, and learnt a useful lesson for the future. You never know. First he took a little snow and rubbed the frozen parts with it, then a bit of gasoline that he added and massaged well; after a while, normal circulation seemed to be restored, and all we had to do was to take our patient to the hospital in Athabasca, which was run by the Grey Nuns who travel to the farthest reaches of the pole to save and succour their fellow men.[33] What saints those women are!

November went by and we fell into the rhythm of the days, which were sometimes cold and brilliant beneath an intensely blue sky with the smoke rising straight up like a white candle in the frozen air; sometimes greyish beneath great snow clouds that fell, occasionally for hours at a stretch. At those times, snug in our well-insulated home, we read and reread the French papers that had come in the most recent mail, or English magazines, or the Eaton's catalogue, which made us yearn for all kinds of things, and we also perused the reports from the experimental farms, which were published by the volume and were free to anyone who applied for them.

When it was fine, we spent the two best hours of the day chopping either the wood we sold to the Hudson's Bay and the bank or, sometimes, fence posts, if we needed new ones. In the morning, when our larder needed replenishing, I went off to hunt and trap whilst Jean took care of the daily chores in the house and stable. And I remember an incident similar to the one I've already recounted, but much less dramatic, obviously, since I was near the house — though in a rather uncomfortable situation, even so. One day after I'd been following a flight of prairie chickens towards Baptiste Creek, I was returning home by the riverbank when I realized that my hands had gone stiff in my mittens and I'd lost the feeling in my fingers. I could see in the distance and far above me the house with its plume of smoke, and I thought of its sweet warmth. I absolutely had to hang on and make it there, but in the thick snow and without snow shoes, which it was impossible to wear on this hilly terrain, walking was very difficult and real torture. One brief invocation and an extreme effort of will gave me the necessary strength. When I arrived at last, absolutely all in, I managed to push open the door with the same joy as if I were opening the door of Paradise after a long voyage; I was incapable of speech and fell into my bed. Jean realized right away what was the matter with me and immediately started a vigorous massage and made me drink a cup of hot coffee, then rubbed me with gasoline exactly as "Old Crow" had done, and gradually, in the warmth of the room, it began to work, but with terrific pain as circulation again reached the extremities where it had ceased. But I was young — twenty-two — and by the afternoon, everything had returned to normal and was forgotten as we both got back down to work.

The winter drifted by with its procession of alternating snow and intense cold, blizzards that made great drifts on the roads and trails.

After the storms everything became calm and still as if nature was ashamed of its rages, and the sky became blue again above this silent whiteness as if to apologize. We had to mark out the trails for the sleds again, and I had to go out into the forest to find my tracks and traps that were buried in the snow but luckily indicated by markers.

We'd heard several times from Armand and Marguerite. They'd rented a large house in Victoria and had made it into a family hotel with a cook — Chinese, naturally — as they'd planned to before they left. They'd spent a very good Christmas and gave us many interesting details about it. We'd decided not to go into Athabasca for midnight mass on Christmas Eve, mainly because of the animals, but also because it was too expensive. So we'd decided to have a French party at our house the following day, after mass, of course, and invited friends from the old country: our good friend Tobaty, old Monsieur Menut and his two sons-in-law and Servestre, who was still at the hotel, and old Monsieur Goyet with his flowing beard.

Morning mass didn't draw as big a crowd as midnight mass, naturally, but there were quite a few people, since many of the homesteaders from twenty or twenty-five miles away couldn't get home during the night, and as both hotels had "No Vacancy" signs, just like the ones in Courchevel or Cannes, they couldn't find anywhere to stay. The Indians and Métis didn't have this problem as hospitality was a given for them, and it was almost unheard-of that their people at the mass couldn't find bed and board, even if was only (as was usually the case) a bearskin on the floor and a blanket near the roaring heater.

The church was nicely decorated: the sisters from the Grey Nuns hospital had done a good job, with little pine trees hung with coloured paper flowers made by the artistic little Métis girls. It's remarkable to see the excellent taste all the Indian tribes — Cree, Montagnais, Dogrib, or Castors — exhibit when they decorate with silk embroidery or coloured beads the moose-hide moccasins or tunics they often wear. Father Desmarais gave the usual sermon in three languages: Cree, English, and French-Canadian, not too long, luckily, as we were anxious to get home to put the finishing touches to the banquet we were preparing for our friends.

When we got back we waited for our guests: Jean, the principal chef, had made the most of what was available. I still have in front of me in my notebook the menu, which wasn't exactly Maxim's but was a true offering of friendship: porridge soup, larded prairie chickens, wild rabbit marinated and stewed the previous evening, Colombian beans, omelette flambée au rhum — with a very large dose of the latter.

In this remote corner of northwestern Canada, we French folk had a real family party, each of us telling tales of his region. Tobaty had brought a flask of French brandy (imported, of course), Servestre some cigarettes from the hotel, old Monsieur Menut, or "Nom de Zou," a superb tart made by his wife, which added a welcome dessert to our banquet. And it was already dark when we separated, some leaving for town by sled and the others on foot with the inevitable lanterns.

But despite it all, the day had left a bitter, nostalgic taste of regret. For far away, across the vast spaces of the New Continent and the immensity of the ocean, in dear old France, lived my cherished, aging parents, and also a secret love that had nestled in my twenty-year-old heart. What were they all doing as I thought of them, and what secret feelings were lodged in a certain child-like heart at this celebration of the Nativity, a moment of such intense emotion?

I received letters regularly from my mother giving news that was always cheerful, optimistic, and full of hope for the future. There was sometimes a subtle hint of regret about my absence, which she would obviously like to see end, but not a single reproach darkened the caress of the words or the fondness of the sentiments. But things were different in the case of my distant princess. As long as Marguerite was in France, I'd been able to get frequent snippets of news, which were a somewhat fragile but nevertheless effective link. Now this link was broken, and I was in total and hopeful ignorance. As she joined boisterous friends in the joyful celebration around the Crèche, what was she dreaming of, what were her thoughts?

January was disturbed by an accident that Jean had as he was chopping down trees: his axe slipped on an icy branch and landed on his right foot, cutting through the moccasin and making a deep gash between his third and fourth toes. We dressed it as best we could with our modest first-aid kit and then went into Athabasca for Dr. Olivier to disinfect the wound and give Jean a shot to prevent a more serious infection, which was always a danger on the land. Jean was laid up for nearly three weeks, able to take care only of household tasks and the cooking. To me, therefore, fell all the outside work: horses, poultry, wood for ourselves and our customers in Athabasca, hunting, and the trapline that I couldn't abandon. We were grateful for our foresight in laying in a stock of wood that would tide us over in case of bad weather or major hindrance. I needed to chop only a few metres when I had a free moment in order to keep up our supply.

Finally, in early February, Jean was able to take on his share of the work without too much effort and things got back to normal. Our poultry barn hadn't been affected by the cold, apart from one or two losses at the beginning. The hens had filled out and were in excellent shape with their little crests starting to turn red. The two roosters were crowing ever more assertively and strutted about looking magnificent. We'd named one the Pasha and the other the Caïd. The hens had begun laying again as they had at first and with greater productivity; the eggs were getting bigger and various neighbours had ordered several dozen from the next hatching. As we'd run out of fish, we decided to go to Baptiste Lake to try to get a new supply to take us through the spring.

We set out on a bright, sunny morning and planned to go on to Perry's ranch, where we'd often been invited, after finishing our business with the Métis. We were fortunate enough to meet at the latter's place (which was an unusual event) Big William, Métis son of a *coureur des bois* and a Montagnais mother. He'd just come back from visiting his trapline, where he'd had the good luck of finding a few muskrats (there were several lodges around the lake) and a superb lynx. It was the first time we'd ever seen a lynx before it was skinned, and it was a magnificent beast, which can be dangerous if attacked or injured. We agreed to bring the price he was asking within a day or two.

After this visit, we went on to our friend Perry's ranch, where it was the day of his annual rodeo for the roundup of the horses that had been broken in and would be up for sale at the auction in Athabasca — or in Edmonton, if he wasn't satisfied locally. Early that morning his boys had rounded up the horses, which were now in a big corral. There was a big crowd there already, as it was a chance to meet people, to make bets, and to play poker, where the losers left their saddle or their Winchester, and some even their horses, which they then had to buy back from the winner, usually on credit.

The entertainment began with a shooting contest; the most popular events were shooting at objects thrown by people in hiding, a bit like trap shooting in France, and shooting at a target on a kind of kite pulled by a rider at full gallop. The carbine used for the contest was, according to my notes, "a Winchester .32 special," and the prize was the gun itself. The distance was about fifty yards, and I was full of admiration for the skill and speed of these men who seemed born to carry a gun and to know how to use it. It goes without saying that there was also a lasso contest, which is relatively simple on a fixed target, but is a whole other matter when a rider has to bring to a halt a charging cow or big calf during the branding roundup.

All these events gave us patience to wait for the meal, after which, like in a circus, would come the main event of the day. The meal was the usual kind at these events, and as everyone present was invited, it was served outside, despite the temperature, around big fires dotted about the place. As for the decor: tables more or less balanced on boxes, barrels, or hay bales, but they were tables groaning with corn kernels, porridge soup, butter, boiled meat and potatoes, loin of elk roasted over fires that reminded me of our Saint-Jean-Baptiste Day, and large quantities of freshly cooked round buns called "banning" locally, and to finish up, gigantic apple pies as big as wagon wheels.

It was no good simply making promises to these cowboys who were in the saddle from dawn till dusk ranging over the countryside keeping an eye on herds of horses or breaking them in for the next sale; you had to actually fill their plates, and that's exactly what our friend Perry did, with a Chinese cook whose talents would have done credit to a deputy minister of Parliament.

The rodeo took place immediately after the meal, which held a double advantage for the contestants: first, it meant that they could eat without bruised limbs, and second — and this was no mean thing — it allowed better food absorption and therefore better digestion. But to get down to serious matters: Perry, decked out in his special costume — chaps with a fringe, tartan shirt, Stetson on his head and Colt in his belt, came into the centre of the corral to announce the names of the five contestants who were going to vie for the prizes he was offering: first prize a splendid saddle, second a bridle, and third Mexican spurs. Appearing on his horse like a god among his subjects, such a man could only inspire admiration. After this announcement, there was general shouting, and then to our total stupefaction, Perry continued and shouted:

"And now, boys, you need to be specially careful because we have an extra contestant that you aren't perhaps familiar with! One of the French gentlemen!"

Jean and I looked at each other, as we had never had the slightest intention of being actors in this drama, but mere spectators. What were we to do? There was no question of Jean getting on a horse for the time being because of the wound to his foot, and for which he must have been secretly giving thanks at this moment; so, unwilling to be a laughingstock among people who were already snickering, I picked up the gauntlet and faced up to the risk, namely a fall on the hard, frozen snow in the ring; hadn't I already faced the same risk playing rugby in Brive at the new athletic field? I had got a fractured shoulder, it's true, but I hadn't been killed!

As I didn't have with me — for obvious reasons — my leather chaps, which I only wore to ride into town or more frequently to inspect our concession in the bush and the forest, I had to ask Perry, who thought this was all a big joke, to lend me whatever I'd need for this absurd performance. As I was an unknown for most of the crowd — some had come from very far away — as well as being a friend of the host, I was to be the last contestant.

The minimum stay on the back of a bronco was eight seconds in order not to be disqualified, with the chance of a second go if the first failed. There was neither saddle nor bridle, but a simple rope that you could hang on to — though only with one hand, which you were allowed to change.

So the only way I could get out of the mess I was in was either to win — pretty remote chance, since I was a mediocre horseman and far from the equal of the centaurs that these men-horses were — or at least to acquit myself with some honour. The whole motley crowd started placing their bets with abandon. As I was seen as a loser, some of them placed their bets on me: "For the Frenchie, just for fun."

And so the game — which was nothing like one for me — began. Eight seconds might seem an infinitesimally short length of time, which it certainly is when one is sipping a cup of tea in a well-upholstered armchair. But I can tell you that it's quite another matter on the back of a bronco: a wild animal doing its utmost to try to rid itself of its unwelcome partner, kicking, bucking, slamming against the barrier, twisting round suddenly, using every possible mean trick, such was the "comfortable" seat — if that's the word I need — we had to remain on for at least eight seconds.

I won't bore you with all the daring deeds of the first five contestants, except to say that only two of them were still in the running, one of them being Jack, Captain Schott's son.

Then it was my turn. Before the gate opened I said a prayer to all the saints above, known and unknown, as I was in a state of panic. And suddenly I was caught in a maelstrom, whirling every which way, plunging into an abyss and hurtling up like an arrow towards the stars, with a giddying vision of the crowd who were cheering me on, then a patch of sky, a square of green grass, a strip of snow onto which I was dying to lie down. That moment came, and I was rolling on the ground like a rabbit hit by a hunter's shot, my dazed eyes still blinking, slightly sore, but not wounded. At that moment I blessed the rugby games when I'd learned to chew on the often hard grass of the old pitch in Brive.

When the bronco had been lassoed by the cowboys perched

on the fence, I emerged from the "playing" field to the applause of the sporting, motley crowd, who were yelling:

"Bravo, Frenchie! You stay nine seconds and you're third!"

Completely knocked out by my adventure, I pretended it was nothing out of the ordinary, and said casually, bluffing like a consummate liar, that it was part of the everyday run of things in France, since we had superb riding schools like the one at Saumur. It wasn't out of simple boastfulness that I told this white lie, but around these macho types, it didn't do to be considered inferior if you wanted to keep their respect. In this case, the important thing wasn't necessarily to win but to try. But ever since that day, distrustful of mad pranksters like Perry, I've carefully avoided every rodeo around Athabasca and Baptiste Lake or Cadotte Lake where we would surely have found friends and acquaintances.

After many handshakes and hearty goodbyes we set off for our "baby ranch," for at that time of year, with an early night-fall, we liked to get home before it was dark to look after our dear hens so that they could enjoy the evening feed and warm themselves for the night by scratching the straw before fluttering up to their roost.

The winter passed in a normal routine succession of days, but which did not seem to us monotonous, as at every hour there was a task to fulfill. And despite the work — or perhaps because of it — I found this life completely satisfying. In our comfortable home, which was almost luxurious for a homestead built with our own hands, we had a view of the stable, the poultry barn, the well, and the fences, a kingdom for me, all things that the will of man had imposed on nature so recently wild and untouched. And that was a great reward.

But after every task was completed, there was always another that awaited us, for the business of clearing the land seemed incomplete and needed to be constantly renewed. Always on the lookout, I could see a corner of a little dip that needed clearing (a miniature Switzerland); vast grazing grounds sloping down to the river that would need to be cleared as soon as we had a few head of cattle to put in there; the lake would have its sluice gate and the stream its course dug out towards the mighty Athabasca into which it flowed; the hay field would be extended by tearing out the brush and thickets that had gradually overgrown it and were choking it. Like Robinson Crusoe, I was always seeking things out, in love with our land and on the lookout for anything that could make it more fertile and more beautiful.

The season advanced: the poultry barn became noisier and noisier with the triumphant clucking of the hens proud of their newly laid eggs. The sun was higher in the sky and warmed the air and a few gusts from the west announced the imminent arrival of the faithful old Chinook, which would sweep away the snow and bring a lovely spring. Every day brought a fresh sign of the new season: the squirrels left their cozy nests to run chirruping in the high branches; the spruce partridges began their cackling pursuit, and the male spread his tail before the females, who were becoming less disdainful. And as I went out on my traplines, I could see my traps sinking deeper into the softening snow with each trip.

The day came when the first threads of water trickled down the slopes to cover, timidly at first like a light mirror, the surface of the ponds, the creeks, and the still immobile river. And then, almost without transition, the great blast of the Chinook swept in, blowing the warm breath of the Pacific over the featureless carpet of snow. Geese and ducks, eternal migrators and harbingers of summer, passed overhead to return to the great northern lakes. Finally the river, with a cracking of its icy carapace, forced itself free with a loud groaning and mighty fracturing.

A New Spring: I Build My House

After this period of winter when outside projects were of necessity minimized or impossible, apart from chopping in the forest, and as soon as the thaw was over and the ground had dried out, we had to turn our minds to the usual tasks of clearing and planting. For after all, our raison d'être on this land was to create a complete farm that would bring in an income: crops, hay, and forage with corresponding livestock.

The first item on my list of things to do was the building of a house to fulfill the legal requirements and to get title to the land as soon as the statutory three-year period had elapsed. Armand's situation was different; on the quarter section we'd done the most work on as far as "dwelling" was concerned, because he was Jean's brother he could file an act of residence right there, on condition he could show proof of other "improvements," like clearing, fencing, and ploughing.

I limited myself to the plan of a small, one-roomed, siding house with double walls that would satisfy the requirements of the Lands Office, but that, according to my plans, could easily be moved to the main concession near the other buildings as soon as I got the title. It would also be useful as an additional sleeping space for one or two hired men (I was still counting my chickens) or as a small workshop. It was quite easy to transport a building from one place to another, especially the kind I intended to build. Indeed, in winter, two sledges of solid wood and a little skill and patience were the main requirements for this job.

As soon as the gushing spring waters had moderated a bit, we had to think of going to the sawmill in Athabasca to fetch the necessary boards, for which we'd taken logs when we were hauling firewood to the Royal Bank and the Hudson's Bay. In exchange, the sawmill gave us some two-by-fours and some six-by-fours and kept, as payment, a small number of planks. So we spent nothing.

We had five big loads to haul, and in three days I had all the materials ready to start building. I'd taken on a French-Canadian homesteader to help us, Jo Ladouceur, whom I'd met when he was working as a carpenter during the building of the Athabasca Hotel and who, as he was a bachelor, had no other ambition than to make a few extra dollars. He brought his two horses with him, which was no problem. I wanted to get the basic construction finished before we started ploughing the old part of the fields and clearing the acres we were going to cultivate that year.

The three of us got down to it, with Jean coming to lend a hand when he'd finished cooking and looking after the horses and chickens. The house was to have one big room with two windows at the front and one on the side looking towards the little lake, a front door between the two windows, and a back door set at an angle so that later on I could add a separate kitchen if I wanted to.

The site I'd chosen was about thirty metres from where our pathway intersected with the Baptiste Lake trail on a little mound overlooking the lake. I'd always been fond of the spot, as it felt healthy and was surrounded by birch and young aspen I wanted to keep at the entrance to the path; I dreamed that when we'd finished putting up a fence around the whole property I'd be able to build a white gateway with "Bellevue Ranch" on a sign above the entrance. I was still counting my chickens!

Building was much easier and less tiring this time than when we'd built the big house. Dealing with planks seemed like child's play, or a construction toy, compared with cutting and manipulating logs. Ladouceur was the foreman and we the apprentices, and the house went up quickly, as it wasn't difficult to put into place and nail the siding when the frame was ready. We put up the frame with two-by-fours, with two rows of planks, one shiplap over another of unplaned wood, with heavy tarred insulating paper between them. Inside, on similar two-by-fours, a row of planks nailed vertically and made out of good tamarack that we'd found in the forest near Baptiste Creek. Between these two, a layer of heavy wrapping paper as double insulation.

I had to buy some more wood for the floor, as well as the windows and doors that were cut ready to install. Luckily we had a fairly healthy bank balance, what with what we'd earned over the summer as well as earnings from the firewood we'd sold to the Royal Bank and the Hudson's Bay, the eggs we'd sold to Lessard, and the ermine pelts — about a hundred — that I'd trapped over the winter, together with a fox and a mink (the latter no doubt tired of living), all best quality as they'd been trapped in the later part of the winter. So not only had we been able to live comfortably during the bitter cold, but we'd managed to hang on to our summer's earnings and to increase our capital in cash and property into the bargain.

We paid particular attention to the plan of the roof. Should it have one or two slopes? Tarred paper or shingles, a kind of tile made of pine or cedar?

There was obviously a difference in price that, although considerable, wasn't too great; the first solution had the advantage of cheapness, but also the great drawback of being vulnerable to sudden gusts of wind if it was ever torn; the second was more expensive and would take longer to install, but it was also more reliable and would last longer. And I must confess, there was also the question of my pride, for I thought that shingles (and you saw them in town on the better kind of houses) gave a better tone to the building, as if my modest house should have the airs of a château. But in fact, it looked like the typical homestead of someone who was making an honest living and who was making progress. Because at that time, it was indeed progress: compared to the covering of sod or tarred paper that formed the roofs of the less fortunate homesteaders or of those who were used to a hand-to-mouth existence, like the Ukrainians, a shingled roof was already a sign of more refined taste and bestowed a certain standing. It was also more colourful, as it could be painted, which always added something to the scenery. In addition, the little four-paned windows that could be found in every trapper's cabin (when it wasn't coarse oiled paper stretched over a frame) were being replaced by large bay windows, like the ones we had in the big house, or by the sash windows that I put in my house.

In less than a fortnight, the building was finished: the roof, painted brick red, stood out among the green tracery that was beginning to appear on the trees: at the fork in our path, the new building already announced that this was where "the Frenchies' place" began. And I was happy and proud to have imposed on this concession, as we had on Jean and Armand's, our imprint as "proving up."

And now I had to furnish the place with some indispensable items to prove to the homesteads inspector, if necessary, that it was habitable — if not inhabited. With this in mind, I went to the furniture store and bought an iron-and-brass bed, a mahogany table, three chairs, and a little solid tin cook stove, and with the leftover bits of planed planks, I made a kind of low cupboard that looked quite nice when I'd painted it.

Getting this work finished brought me great peace of mind, and to mark the final possession of "my land" I decided to spend the first night it was finished there. It was just a whim, and I only took my blankets, but that didn't prevent me from having a good night's sleep filled with most delightful dreams. The house had a strong smell of pine and resin, and I thought, in the semi-darkness of the spring night, that all the beasts of the forest came on tiptoe to see the new work of man. After the construction of the siding house that from then on would be known as "French Lake's House" (from the name of the nearby little lake), other tasks awaited us, for we were slaves to the demanding cycle of ploughing and sowing. Before beginning the ploughing, we had to have our ploughshares recalibrated by the blacksmith in Athabasca, which gave us an unusual two days' holiday.

Since the thaw, our poultry barn was getting along swimmingly and the eggs were quite splendid. Our whole feathered flock could strut about in the fresh spring air and the exercise did them good. We had cases full of eggs to take to Athabasca. The price had dropped, of course, but it was still an exchange that amply paid for our groceries, so that our life on the property was being paid for by our good hens, which had become quite plump.

We set aside the best and most perfectly shaped eggs for our neighbours' orders and for ourselves, because we were already thinking of next winter, which, all things being equal, we would spend on our property, warm and cozy in our house. We'd spend the six months when outdoor work was possible making money for the next winter and for the next round of expenses on the property, as there was always something to be done and always something to be bought. Among other machines, we'd have to buy a disc-harrow, which had now become indispensable for preparing the soil for new ploughing. Until now, we'd always borrowed one from Tobaty, but as our fields had become more extensive, it became obvious that we'd have to buy our own. We already had quite an array of equipment for beginners. We had a sled for heavy winter hauling, a democrat for trips into town, a wagon for the poor spring roads and for heavy loads, a plough for breaking the soil, a harrow in two sections, and a pair of harnesses. In the near future, we'd have to get a mower because now that we'd cleared around the lake, we could cut the hay with a machine. It was quite easy to find second-hand tools in Athabasca, and even good equipment that shrewd traders picked up in auction sales in Edmonton, Calgary, or other towns to the south.

Through our friend Fitzgibbon, who knew what we were looking for, we heard that there was a Massey-Harris disc available, in good condition and not too heavy for our team, and we got it for $18. The tiller was missing, but we could easily make one out of a young birch tree, a hardwood that we'd find on our own property on the banks of Baptiste Creek.

With the new equipment, we began ploughing our land, with the work already becoming easier as the land was turned over.

The plough could now move ahead without encumbrance, the ploughshare made regular furrows, and the horses were able to work a large area every day without becoming overly tired. With the result that we didn't have to rush to sow the available ground with green oats, or greenfeed, cereal oats, and the usual potatoes, the homesteaders' standby throughout the whole year.

The experimental farms, and especially the one in Lethbridge, kept us up to date in their publications with their experiments, both in crops and livestock or poultry raising. Besides making interesting reading, they were treasure troves of all their experiments and all their results. These farms, run by the government, would even hand out on demand little bags of seeds, selected and improved to give the best yield in our area so that everyone could prepare for the following year a little store of seeds for his own use and sowing. One way or another, these publications — veritable tomes — provided instructive distraction for the spare time imposed by the long winter evenings or bad weather. We already had a small bookcase which I'd made myself above the little cupboard.

The sojourn on our land — and how good it felt to say "our land"! — didn't feel to me like an endless round of toil, but rather a constantly varying succession of days in which every morning brought with it the designation of a task to be done and every evening the satisfaction of fulfillment. Every hour brought its own reward, and if sometimes weariness overcame muscles that were always stretched to the limit, it was tempered by the impression of knowing that one was one's own master living the life one had deliberately chosen. There was no one to order one around, only the will to make and get, and the sacrosanct law of the demands of the seasons; in short, it was a life of liberty beneath God's great sky.

If I wished, I could remain day after day without seeing another soul; I could, in communion with strong, beautiful nature, loll at my ease on a tree trunk, watching squirrels at play, one cheekier than the other; I could let my horses wander at will among a patch of wild peas, fill my pipe and daydream about the ancient times in these lands and forests. As I looked at my calm little lake, I could see the incessant tree-felling labours of the beavers who'd built the dams that have now disintegrated, draining the neighbouring swamps and the coulee towards the big river. But the searing desire for profit by unreasonable men had almost exterminated these intelligent beasts, or at least pushed them towards the solitudes of the Great North. I daydreamed about the not-so-distant life of the "red men" who lived in these parts, Cree or Saulteaux Indians whose presence was still inscribed on their ancestral land on the paths and tracks through the forests that are now only trodden by wild beasts or the occasional settler; ruined cabins beside a lake or creek, stone or earth tumuli that cover in the silence what man, what drama, what despair?

For a young man who had left everything in order to seek adventure — family nest, comfort, calm, gentle monotony of days with one week following another in the routine of over-regulated employment, dreams of love, of sweet youth — this life of liberty had affected me like an aphrodisiac or the intoxicating perfume of a desired woman. I could see that Jean was beginning to feel ever more urgently the attractions of an easier city life and an early return to the paternal home. The fire of the first enthusiasm for a great adventure was being dampened by the breath of epistolary summons and the siren call of the family. He was handsome, agreeable, indolent, and somewhat self-absorbed; he knew he'd inherit a large share of his father's fortune: the châteaux of Bonaigues and Arnac with their surrounding property could offer, in compensation for freedom, less risky and less difficult occupations than clearing our Canadian sections. And above all, an advantageous marriage would add a few more comfortable slippers to his hope chest.

It was with a sense of apprehension, mixed with a certain bitterness, that I foresaw the day when my sister and Armand would go off in one direction and Jean in the other and I would be left alone to face the hard work that each year would bring with the changing seasons. It's not that I thought I couldn't manage it, nor was I afraid of loneliness on our property: a few good horses to share my toil, a few milk cows, some chickens, and a dog would be enough to make a friendly circle around me. Little by little, the produce of our land, together with the outside work I could do without leaving home, either on municipal work sites (highways, new streets, etc.) or for neighbours who weren't sufficiently well equipped, all of this would occupy me during the period of rest when the soil was bringing to fruition the crops that had been sown in it, and would provide me with the essentials of life and enough income to go on expanding the farm.

The main thing was to wait for the much-desired moment when, after we'd satisfied the requirements for all categories (planting, clearing, fencing, dwelling, length of stay), the Lands Office would hand over the title to the property — the patent.

For Jean and me, there should be no difficulty: all we had to do was to finish up the cycle of the three statutory years; the houses were built, the clearing and planting were accomplished and the fences in place. But for Armand, even if the improvements to the land were valid, and the question of the house had been settled through common residence with his brother, the Lands Office could, if they wanted to be difficult, invoke against him his permanent absence from the property.

However, to reassure ourselves on this subject, we knew that the important thing was to show off the maximum amount of work visible on the soil when we were inspected. For the actual presence, it was difficult to contest the declarations of the one making the application, especially if, as in this case, cohabitation had been sanctioned.

June had just begun and the essential tasks finished, so we were preparing to go off on our annual absence from the property. The oats were already showing a fine green carpet, and the potatoes were already coming up in good straight lines, testifying to the careful work that had gone into their planting. For a few weeks the farm could do without us, and it was only the hens that demanded human presence to be fed, to have their eggs collected, and to be watched over. All day long, as soon as they'd had their feed, they ranged at will over the plateau, sometimes quite far from the house, and thus became choice prey for the marauding hawks. We came to an arrangement with the old Métis who, when he wasn't out trapping, had long been living in the shack at the mouth of Baptiste Creek where it flowed into the Athabasca, about a mile and a half from our house. He would live in our house when we were away and look after the chickens, taking half the profits from the sale of the eggs. We'd also supply him with fifty pounds of flour, a twenty-pound sack of sugar, a side of bacon, two wads of pipe tobacco and the same of chewing tobacco, and tea and coffee, of course. He'd sleep in the unfinished part of the house, as we were locking our room, not because I doubted his honesty — it was his hygiene I had doubts about.

We made the same arrangement as the previous year with Fitzgibbon for the horses. We'd let him have the use of the team for light work in town like freight deliveries in a cart for Révillon or the Hudson's Bay; in exchange, he was responsible for their keep and in addition paid us 75 cents per day.

When we'd made all these arrangements, we could leave without any worries. Jean, who wasn't keen on hard manual labour, had a job for several weeks at the Athabasca Hotel, where he was to work as assistant receptionist till the winter or early spring. The wages weren't very good — $30 to $35 per month, but the work wasn't hard, and in addition he had bed and board with unlimited access to the bar and to cigars. For me there was the immense advantage that Jean could go to our property to keep an eye on it.

A Second Trip to the Rockies and the Quest for the Golden Fleece

As the work I had been contracted to do on our road wasn't due to begin till early July, my plan was to go back to the Rockies. My friend Marius Clément had written to tell me that promising gold deposits had been found near the source of the Saskatchewan, and had suggested we go there, not necessarily to discover a big lode, but simply to have an interesting trip with our expenses covered by panning the sand, which, according to the information he'd received, contained gold dust and flakes. That was incentive enough for a journey into unknown territory.

I'd accepted eagerly, as I was anxious to go back to the harsh but rugged beauty of this wonderful country. Our first trip to the foothills of the Rockies had made a profound impression upon me. This time we'd have to go on to the upper reaches of the river towards the streams that fed it.

We weren't imagining we'd make a big discovery like the one made recently by two Métis who, as they were coming back broke from a season of trapping, had fallen quite accidentally upon a real treasure. In a pocket beneath a rock constantly battered by the eddies of a river, and almost on the surface, a pile of flakes had collected. They had been tossed around for many years by the currents and were polished and round like peas. And before we left we were able to admire some of them that were on display in the window of a mineral trading company; some extraordinary ones were as big as hazelnuts.

So I met up with Clément at our hotel and we kitted ourselves out for a journey I looked upon as something of a pleasure trip, since we were going to work independently of any company.

Our equipment was soon ready. Besides the tent Marius had brought with him, we each had our own blankets and two shotguns, my .22 and Clément's Winchester 30/30, two fishing lines, all items that should guarantee our safety as well as a good bit of our subsistence. Finally we bought normal and essential supplies for this kind of trip — a fifty-pound sack of flour, bacon, tea, coffee and sugar, a few canned goods, tobacco (quite a few packages of Old Chum and wads of chew for possible barter or gifts), two bottles of whisky, and the always-essential first-aid kit.

The train would set us down at the end of the line, Mile 176, I believe, near where an old Indian — according to hotel gossip — kept a stopping place. He rented saddle or pack ponies, or cayuses as the Indians called them, extremely hardy and economical horses. His clients were prospectors, government surveyors, Indian Affairs agents, etc.

The trip there took place without incident: in our coach — half goods, half passengers — we chugged along slowly, jolted along rails that were nailed to ties only partially secured to the bed, with frequent stops in the middle of nowhere to unload supplies for the occasional riverside settlers or for surveyors of part of the line or for storage of various goods. Obviously, the "stations" were hardly luxurious buildings; the waiting room was either the station master's log cabin or the great outdoors when it was fine.

The journey took us over twenty hours. In several places we went over bridges that were exact replicas of the one we'd toiled over so strenuously: no guardrail and an uninterrupted view of the foaming waters. Under the weight of the train, the wood creaked and groaned, and sometimes on the banks you could see the remains of huts that were already overgrown by large ferns, fireweed, and the forest's luxuriant vegetation.

An unpleasant surprise awaited us when we arrived. We thought that the Indian Limping Jo's place was about five or six hundred metres from the station, as we'd been told, whereas it turned out that it was four or five miles away. It was, indeed, on the river. From the station hut, the railroad continued snaking towards the west and brought back to our minds memories of the harsh days we'd spent laying a similar track, and a kind of pride rose within us when we mentioned casually to the station master that we'd worked on a big wooden bridge and how we'd been in the caisson. So we were finally greenhorns no more, but had finally become "old-timers."

However, we now had to get to Limping Jo's camp, known to surveyors and prospectors as "Lonely Place." And in order to do that, we had to reconcile ourselves to slogging with our packs and part of our kit on our backs over the few miles on a trail that went through forest, creeks, and muskeg. But we had no choice and we decided to set off in the late afternoon with the bare essentials: blankets and evening meal. After thanking our host for his hospitality, we set off on the trail, which plunged almost immediately into the forest. The Highways Division had certainly not wasted any money in this part of the world, which had not yet been really opened up and where walking was so difficult, but luckily, thanks to the innate good sense of woodsmen, markers had been put up all the way: bushes with branches tied together, a notched post stuck in the ground with a bunch of dried grass or a strip of calico tied around it.

A few short breaks, a couple of cigarettes and it was already dusk by the time we saw more palpable signs of life: a fence around the remains of bales of hay that had probably been cut on the banks of some slough or other or some little lake like the one that appeared out of nowhere on the path, cleared of bush and surrounded by promising-looking grass; horse droppings and after a few minutes the barking of dogs, a true sign of human presence. And behind a stand of willows appeared, in the middle of the wilds, overlooking the banks of a clear, fast-flowing river, Limping Jo's shack. Alerted by the barking of the dogs — mastiffs that looked none too welcoming but that, at a command from him, soon quieted down — there appeared in the doorway a tall figure that looked very impressive in the wooden frame.

After the traditional "Hello" and a "tant-se ketesïan" from us, which was the formulaic Indian greeting meaning, more or less,

"How are you?" he ushered us into the cabin, which contained the strict necessities of daily life. Despite a certain air of untidiness that lent originality to the room, everything seemed clean and well kept: floor of small log sections cut with an axe and well swept, rustic table of the same material. Two small windows lit the place.

The man was probably about seventy, but his hair was still black — the bluish-black of a raven's wing common to Indians. He must have had noble ancestry, for his features and his whole bearing were proud testimony to it. When we'd told him of the purpose of our visit and of our intention to camp — all this in a mixture of French, English, Canadien, and Cree that contained enough vocabulary to make ordinary conversation possible — he rose and with great dignity led us to another cabin, which served as a guest hut: same interior decor and outside stones for a fireplace; and inside, in case of bad weather, another fireplace of large river-stones that had been dug out of the white clay of a swamp. In retrospect, it was a precursor of the kind of barbecue and stoves "à la Courchevel"![34] Which goes to show that men who think they are so civilized return unconsciously to their origins in order to make a show or to impress, and call themselves inventors when in fact they are mere imitators; for they will never have that delicacy and humility that is given by great, divine Nature to her faithful lovers.

Jo was waiting on the threshold. Over his fire in front of the door, a teakettle was already singing, and in the pan slices of bacon were sizzling, mixed with strips of moose meat dried in the sun or in the smoke of the branches of green wood. He made a laconic gesture towards these preparations for a meal, thereby inviting us to share it with him. It was hardly the kind of menu one would recommend for fragile or delicate stomachs, but we were young and in good physical shape, and with an appetite heightened by our walk, we did full justice to this meal, which, although fairly primitive, was impeccably prepared and which we washed down with several mugs of tea. As sugar was a rare commodity in these parts, we urged our host to help himself to our supply.

Shadows had already fallen, the pale, light shadows that in these climes precede moonrise in a firmament like a royal blue satin baldachin. We sat crossed-legged on the ground and smoked slowly, telling Old Jo our projects and our needs. He, using few words, gave us advice on the places we would traverse as we went up the river: paths that followed the banks and that we'd have to leave from time to time to wade through shallows or along beaches; places where we'd have to cross a ford to pick up the trail on the opposite bank. It was important to get these places right; in theory, they were marked by a system of posts and rods. But often poles and rods had fallen or were almost invisible, and custom demanded that the last user put it back to rights: solidarity of men of the forest.

We listened to him with religious attention, for in that night that was both calm and wild, near the glowing fire, his words seemed to come from the far distance of his origins: little by little, and in intimate detail, he told us of the end of his tribe, which had, for centuries, travelled along the trails in the forest and of which he was one of the last survivors. During the smallpox epidemic, the infamous "red plague," nearly all of them had been wiped out. Everywhere red flags were hung, by order of the Health Services, at the doorway of the poor cabins or elk-skin tepees, the mere sight of which was enough to make passersby flee. A few had survived and had emigrated downriver to work for the big fur traders, the Hudson's Bay or the Révillon Brothers.

He alone had remained, anchored in his soil like the great pines or the old tamaracks that bent gradually towards the river that would swallow them up on a day of wrath. He lived there alone, but not far from the cursed spot where, half a century before, his tribe had disappeared. Twenty or so miles to the south near a great curve in the river, he told us that you could still see in the brambles and bush the ruins of the log cabins that had been consumed by the purifying fire lit by the Mounted Police. As for the humans, their remains were buried in their ancestral soil beneath great river-stone tumuli, so long that the shadow of the tallest tamarack could not fall on them at sunset.

He also told us, in his slow words as he pulled on the pipe with the bowl made of an old root, the circumstances of the wound that had left him with the limp that was the reason for his nickname. One day he'd been attacked by a mother grizzly, and after a fierce struggle, in which he'd been helped by his two faithful dogs, he'd managed to kill her with a knife blow to the heart. How had he managed to make his way back to his cabin? He never knew and had no memory of it. No doubt his dogs had helped him, and the two fine animals he had at that moment were descendants of those two companions. He would certainly have died alone, just as lonely old trappers or prospectors often die in the depth of the forest, if the railway employee who'd received a message for him from Indian Affairs and was concerned that he had not collected it hadn't come to bring it to him.

Now he lived without ambition and without care, seeking nothing other than to live on the land loved by his ancestors, in winter trapping big, beautiful mountain lynx and mink and otters and muskrats in the waters and in summer renting to prospectors or hunters the ponies that he stabled a little to the east, towards the colonized lands, with one of his rancher friends.

He could certainly have become rich: his knowledge of the land was such that he could have drawn a detailed map of the area for miles around that would not have put to shame government surveyors. He let it be known that the elders of his tribe knew the places where the Great Manitou had hidden the "gold metal," but if the Whites knew, it would be the end of their race. They had transmitted the secret from father to son, but not one of them had betrayed it. For them in the past and for him now, riches stretched before them as far as the eye could see in the great expanse of forest where there was game in abundance, furs in profusion, meat aplenty to prepare pemmican, moose to provide moccasins and tepees, fish in the rivers and lakes that would sustain them through the long months of winter. It was the immense sky above their heads and the dirt trails under their feet in the forests and verdant prairies. That had been their kingdom until the arrival of the White Man, with his smoking machines and his monstrous engines, his dynamite, too, whose blasts sent the forest creatures fleeing, and his vices and appetites — the fever for gold and the firewater that had killed his race more surely than guns and lead shot.

And so Jo had acquired, not a distaste for alcohol, nor a complete refusal of it, but a prudent attitude towards drinking. It was therefore a big surprise for us when we got out our whisky and offered it to him, as was the custom in these fireside conversations, and rather than thrusting out his mug greedily towards the liquid so avidly sought after by others, he made the calm gesture of a man perfectly in control of himself and his desires. No passion in him, but rather an immense serenity in harmony with the beauty of the night; on the dying fire a few dry branches flared up. Then a glow mounted to the tops of the tall trees and the shadows of the living performed a dance of death over the ground and the old cabin.

Old Jo was silent, perhaps seeing in the leaping flames visions of past years. And I, who, despite the harsh life of the last few years still cherished the dreams of a youthful poet, I was bewitched by the grandeur and the magnificence of the moment; a tawny owl passed silently overhead like a big white snowflake and called mournfully to the dwellers of the night; sometimes in the distance the deep wailing of a great lynx on the prowl made the dogs shiver with impatience as they lay around us. From the nearby river rose the sound of the rapids as they were torn apart by rocks. It was the symphony of hundreds of nocturnal sounds that gently lulled men into silence.

The moon was already high in the sky when we decided to seek shelter; tomorrow would be largely consumed by arrangements for our departure: finding old Jo's cayuses that were roaming

PIERRE MATURIÉ

somewhere in sloughs upstream, then choosing the horses that we were taking with us; and finally last pieces of advice from that handsome old man whose deep, unwavering voice seemed to bear within it the wisdom of ancient chiefs. The rest of the night passed calmly in that corner of the forest so far removed from the mad throbbing of civilization.

At first light of dawn, the cheeky squirrels were already tearing around on the sod roof of the cabin and in the branches of over-hanging trees, chasing each other with shrill cries. In the nearby swamps, which a creek of heart-wrenching beauty drained down to the river, wild ducks and coots called to each other among the reeds. And Jo was already standing at his door looking as if he were taking possession of the new day.

After breakfast, we had to find the horses; we were expecting difficult, tiring work, getting lost on the criss-crossing trails. Although we knew that the lead horse had a big bell around his neck like the cowbells in the Alpine regions of France, we still thought we'd have to spend an unrewarding morning in the forest and bush. But canny old Jo had his own method of bringing in his horses with minimal effort; he'd trained his dogs and used to send them out from time to time to get the horses back to camp so that he could check on them.

So now, after we'd waited barely half an hour, we could hear in the distance, muffled by the mass of undergrowth, the sound of the bells — one low, one high — that the leader and one of the other horses were wearing around their necks. And shortly after, the herd appeared and came calmly into the clearing, trotting of their own accord towards the central shelter that was their summer stable. There were about a dozen animals, a rustic breed descended from the wild horses that were the mounts of the ancient prairie tribes. The pack pony isn't a large horse; through cross-breeding, it's given birth to the Indian cayuses, which are stalwart and easy to feed and have an instinctive knowledge of the area and its potential dangers; they're also sure-footed, both in the forest with its fallen trees and over rocky or marshy terrain. Their fodder would consist of the green grass around the lakes and sloughs that we'd pass or some good pasture where there would be a profusion of wild peas. That would be ample to give them healthy and comfortable feed; but in addition, for the two weeks we thought we'd be gone, we had supplies of oats in the form of fifty kilos of grain. For we planned to keep our travel companions in perfect condition, since it was upon their vigour and health that our safety and peace of mind depended.

What we still had to do, after picking out the animals Jo recommended, was to go back to Mile 176 to get the stuff we'd left there when we arrived. We set out in the early afternoon with the three horses on what would be a kind of rehearsal for us and a trial run for them. They were dependable beasts, not very tall, but sturdy, two white and the other piebald: one for the sleeping gear, medicine chest, and guns; one for our supplies; and the third for the oats and washing items, this being the lighter load we'd rotate to rest the others. We also had hobbles and a bell for each of them provided by Jo.

Following his advice, we made the pinto the leader, a position he seemed made for. He was a proud horse, a real Indian cayuse who knew how to forge a path through the forest, and as he had a very regular gait, he wasn't hard on the followers. The trip was fast and uneventful, both coming and going, which gave us confidence for our real expedition.

Our departure was fixed for the following day at dawn, as we were limited by the weather and we had about eighty miles to go to our destination, near the mouth of a little tributary of the river that wasn't marked on the survey maps but that the Indians called White Rock River because it was bordered by a rampart of brilliant white rocks. We took with us a surveyor's information map that we'd managed to get in the Lands Office in Edmonton; it gave an idea of the approximate course of the big river, with marshes and relief.

So early in the morning, one of those magnificent mornings when the rising sun on the horizon seemed to give a fresh coat of paint to the greenery still wet from the night's dew, we left Jo and his welcoming home and took the path down to the water that for about four or five miles would take us alongside the river to the first crossing. The walk through bush and forest, almost beside the river, seemed like a pleasant jaunt. The trail, although scarcely visible from time to time, was fairly easy to follow, without many fallen logs, as the proximity of old Jo was still in evidence. The ponies followed without difficulty and the pinto was an excellent leader, neither rushing nor lagging. So that when we reached the first crossing, we decided to walk together at the head, without making a single file, which was more pleasant for both of us.

After a well-deserved rest beside the river, we had to find the crossing. The water didn't look very deep, but rushed foaming over a bed of pebbles and rocks, some of which showed above the water like the backs of big turtles. The river must have been about fifty metres wide and didn't look hard to cross. Jo had given us very precise instructions about the various shallows, their extent and their orientation. This latter point was very important because some could be crossed in a straight line, whereas others had to be forded diagonally, either facing upstream or downstream, and there was always the danger of falling into a hole, which, though not totally disastrous, wouldn't be very good, either for us or for our supplies.

So, after stripping down to the most basic garments, shorts being enough in this land, somewhat less crowded than the Paris boulevards, and watched by the curious whisky jacks, Marius entered the water, which, despite the season, was very cold and, carrying a pole to sound the depths, crossed over easily. When he'd crossed, it was the turn of our little caravan, and a few minutes later we set foot on the opposite shore, very satisfied with the docility of our animals, which seemed to even enjoy the exercise, perhaps because it was a moment of relief from the little blackflies that were harassing them on land. We put back on the clothes that we'd spread out on top of the baggage and set off again on the path that still followed the river or the forest that overhung it.

We weren't to start panning for gold before the next camp, which we should be able to make, according to Jo, by about nightfall, near a little creek about fifteen kilometres further on. We'd slowed down somewhat since the crossing, as the trail was non-existent, with very few markers. There was no problem with this, as the river, which we were meant to follow no farther than a hundred metres away, was an excellent guideline.

However, a short while before our next camp, we had trouble crossing a little bridge over a creek that was quite narrow but looked like the moat around a castle because of its almost vertical banks; it was the only way over, unless we went around the deep cleft — and we didn't know where such a detour would lead us in the dark. The bridge, which consisted of two large trees covered with young pines and poplars to give it a surface, should have been easy to cross, but I took the precaution of testing its solidity. And a good thing, too, since we could see with our own eyes that some of the logs were rotten, though Marius went over safely. But it was quite another matter for a pony, which could easily break a leg, and that would mean the end of the poor beast, and a loss and great handicap for us. So from the surrounding trees we cut down a few solid trunks to replace the rotting ones, and after we'd anchored them in place and put a good layer of pine branches over them, we led the ponies over one by one without a hitch, so it was well worth the time spent. And as Jo had said, with the philosopher's wisdom he was unaware of: "An hour lost is sometimes a life gained."

It was already dusk when we arrived at the mouth of the little river Jo had told us about. He'd said that if we went upstream for about a hundred metres we'd find a fairly large clearing, no doubt the long-ago work of beavers, before those intelligent and attractive but unfortunate beasts had been massacred by Indian or white trappers. And indeed, after walking for a few minutes through a pine forest, we saw a fine meadow spread before us with plenty of good grass for the horses.

We set up camp in no time; the tent was pitched, the horses fed and hobbled with bells around their necks and we laid the table for our meal, which hardly required the services of a master chef: pork and beans, bacon, and the tea can were the staples of the menu. Then cigarettes or a pipe and daydreaming with a host of memories in the dancing flames.

It was during these moments of rest that the mind and the heart, relieved of the cares of the present, brought back sweet memories of bygone years, years of youth in a calm familial atmosphere under the protection of beloved parents; childish love rising to the surface of life like a summer perfume in a sleeping garden; and wild days of adolescence already marked by a search for direction in the great game of adulthood.

Already in the dark night, owls were calling to each other from the tops of the pine trees and the life of nocturnal beasts started up in the forest around the camp: furtive rustling, cracking of branches, velvet flight of night birds, and, as a sonorous background, the music of the water rushing over the pebbles. But the ponies' bells were becoming more muffled, a sign that they were already under the cover of the trees and that they had eaten their fill. We had to bring them back and tie them up near the tent, as among the trees, the hobbles could be dangerous for them. And so we went off to sleep, rolled in our blankets on a bed of fresh pine branches, in the tent that protected us from the palpable chill of the night, and thought of the following days and the difficulties they might bring.

The first light of dawn hadn't yet appeared in the sky when we were up and ready for the next stage, when we would start panning. Marius made breakfast and I fed oats to the cayuses and let them roam in the meadow until we had to load them, and when the first rays of the sun appeared above the mountains, we were already on the riverbank on the trail that would take us another few miles further to the next crossing, after which we'd start test panning up the river till lunchtime.

We came upon the crossing after about an hour's walk at the confluence of a little river where an old cabin that Jo had mentioned stood on the bank. That was all that remained of the residence of an old-timer from Scotland, MacGilloy, who had lived alone there for several years, trapping in winter and prospecting in the nearby mountains in the summer, and who had died alone with no one present during his last days. One winter's day, Jo had gone with a dog train and sled to deliver supplies left for him at Mile 176, as he did every year. His dogs showed signs of anxiety as they approached, sniffing the air and refusing to go any further. No smoke rose from the chimney, the panes of the only window were completely frosted over and there were no footprints near the cabin door. Jo, seeing these signs of absence or abandon, had an intuition of what he would find inside. And as he pushed open the door, half buried in snow, he saw the old trapper lying as if mummified on his bed. His faithful dog had laid down near the stove, trying to get the last bit of heat. But although starved to death, he hadn't touched his master's body. A good example of love and loyalty.

How long had he been dead? Jo hadn't seen him since the Christmas before when he'd camped with him at Lonely Place. He had come in to get a few supplies that Jo had given him, since Jo thought of him as a friend. He'd left, with his kit stowed on his little sled pulled by his husky. Despite his seventy-odd years, he didn't seem to be bowed down in his gait by the weight of years, which hadn't succeeded in diminishing his stature. Apparently, he was a very tall man.

There was nothing out of the ordinary in the cabin: the tea-kettle was still standing on the tin stove, still full of water, but burst by the ice. Cut firewood was stacked near the heater, which contained only ashes. On the wooden shelves there were still ample supplies and the sack of flour had scarcely been started. No mess, unless it was the usual bric-a-brac found in any trapper's cabin: a waterproof shirt had been hung up to dry near the stove and still hung there, stiff on its string; the Winchester at the head of the bed, seeming to stand its last guard over the old hunter. Hanging from a beam in the ceiling, a packet of furs (mink, lynx, a few foxes, and ermine) bore testimony to the skill of the old trapper who had been surprised by death, since a mink still remained to be skinned.

Old Jo, after resting for a short while and nailing up the door with some nails he'd found in an old can, hurried back and had the station guard notify the Mounted Police. When the two Red-coats arrived a few days later for the statutory enquiry, they made an inventory of the poor possessions of the old Scotsman: a few clothes and undergarments, all very clean, no address of relatives or friends either in Canada or in the Old Country. Simply, in an old wallet, his prospector's licence and the registration for an old claim in the Klondike, a photo that showed him as a young man with a young woman and two children about ten years old. Under his bed, in a tin box, some gold dust (probably from his panning in the river), and around his neck on a leather thong, a moose-hide pouch containing seven or eight good-sized nuggets, most likely a souvenir of his stay in the Klondike during the gold rush.

After what arduous journeys, what dramatic and painful wan-derings had he ended up in this desolate corner at the frontier between the forest and the mighty Rockies, to live and die in this solitude? During his last moments, what thoughts had gone through his mind, what tender or joyful memories or what painful regrets or what feelings of revolt or hatred? His secrets were buried with him. After thawing the ground with a big fire, and digging his grave beneath a tall pine a few metres from the cabin, Jo and the policemen lowered him into the ground for him to find the rest he had perhaps been seeking so far from his homeland. A good load of rocks carried up from the river was spread over this poor grave in which his dog, his faithful companion, had been placed at his feet, as if for his last watch beside his beloved master. After the recitation of prayers for the dead by the Redcoats, the great silence of the forest fell over the camp, disturbed now only by the eternal song of the water over the rapids.

As we arrived at this stage, we were reminded of the sad story of Old Mac that our friend Limping Jo had told us one evening around the fire. We had been profoundly moved by it, so after we'd unloaded the horses, and before crossing the river and starting on our panning, we went up to the cabin, which was still standing in this harsh landscape like a witness to the passing of man. The path leading to it was already overgrown with bushes that seemed to be hastening to protect the poor grave. On the sod and moss roof weeds had grown, as had fresh shoots all round the shack as if Life was trying to beautify Death. Inside, nothing except the square frame of the poles that formed his bedstead and the old tin stove in a corner. A rusted old trap, a derisory relic, hung from a nail. Outside, under a great pine that seemed to spread out its branches, the better to protect it, was the little stone tumulus where a blueberry bush had grown marking the spot where Old Mac the trapper lay in the calm of the place to which he had given life. From here, he could see in the eternal dream of his lifetime the rushing of the clear waters of the glaciers. Before going back down to the river, we cut down two young birches, tied them into a cross with our laces, and planted them to replace the other, which had been rotted by the time and weather.

The moment for starting to prospect in the sand had arrived. Jo had given us tips about panning: the best way to hold the pan; very gentle movements of the arm and wrists; the look of gold mixed with sand, etc. He'd told us that bends in the river should be prospected on the inside curve; that it was a good idea to sound the confluence of each tributary, as that could give information about the possibilities of the land it had traversed; that the half-buried rocks on the beaches and the bends should be searched at their base and even dug up, as the heavier pieces like nuggets could have gathered there over the years.

So before crossing the river, we decided to pan in the sand at the confluence of the creek and in the creek itself. Armed, each of us, with our pan and our little shovel, we got down to work with a will, as if we were about to make our fortune. But after a few shakes, we had to acknowledge the evidence: almost all the sand had been washed away, and all that was left was a residue of gravel that unfortunately contained no nuggets. Obviously, if there was any gold in these waters and these sands (sands that existed in over a hundred miles of river), we didn't yet know how to manipulate the pans. And after all the practice panning we'd done at Jo's!

Finally, after many, many attempts, which initial failure hadn't discouraged, Marius, who was working a bit higher up than the mouth of the creek, called out to me; at the bottom of his pan there remained, at the bottom of the water, a pinch of light brown powder. After drying it in low heat in a pan, we saw that it was a composite of brown powder, a residue of fine sand, and another part that, through the magnifying glass, appeared more yellow and was, indeed, gold dust. That was a nice fillip. A more thorough washing would, no doubt, have resulted in cleaner dust; but Jo had advised us against too fine a washing, which is done only by old prospectors, and had warned us to stop at the first appearance of brownish yellow, for we ran the risk, in our inexperience, of losing in the last shales of the pan, the yield of the whole panning. He had volunteered to wash the amalgam we brought back, and to finish off the process of extracting a pure, marketable dust.

The morning was quite advanced when we decided to ford the river. I was the one who went first this time to sound the depths, and although the river had narrowed and the waters were very rapid, our little caravan made it across a few minutes later without incident. And after the ceremonial drying and dressing, we continued on our way, almost by guesswork this time, as the trail was unmarked and almost invisible, but our Ariadne's thread was the river, which we had to follow. We knew that after a few miles, we'd come to an old panning place that had been exploited a long time ago by several prospectors who'd come from the East, and whom Jo had got to know as they went through. Without making a fortune, they'd taken back after four or five months a fairly substantial sum, just reward for their hard labour.

We reached the place about noon: the sun was already at its zenith, as we'd been held back by vegetation that was so dense that we'd sometimes had to hack our way through it when we couldn't walk along the water's edge. There was practically nothing left of the camp the prospectors had used when they were there. A few metres into the bush that was already thickly overgrown, some fallen logs were the only vestiges of the place where these men had lived with their hopes, their desires, their griefs, and their secrets. There was the rusted blade of an old two-handed saw on the fallen logs; near the river, a few stakes and the debris of some planks marked where their panning sluices had been, for they had put up a real prospecting installation. Over the whole floated an air of mystery, as if the ghosts of those former pioneers were going to reawaken at the sound of new caravans. For years and years had gone by, casting a veil of forgetfulness over everything. New discoveries around the Mackenzie had brought to the unknown regions of the Athabasca and the Great Northern Lakes a great flood of men eager for risk and profit, for whom adventure was a necessity and also a grand game.

We decided to camp right there that night and to prospect around the camp as we followed the river upstream, starting with the old panning site. If these places had been profitable once, there was no reason why the same causes wouldn't produce the same effect. So after tending to the ponies, we started to make our way upriver, and after two or three hours of sounding at various places and getting positive, though modest, results, we went back and finished our day at the old prospectors' camp. There the work was more rewarding as there was fine sand in abundance and the work was easy in shallow water.

After doing several pannings, we realized that unless we happened upon a clutch of nuggets, there wouldn't be any fortune. But money wasn't the only thing we were seeking. For me, at least, and also for my partner, the main thing was the desire to plunge into the magic of nature in the great Canadian West. It was nothing like tourism in France, with a nice, welcoming inn every night, redolent with cheese soup or a good loaf of rye bread cut into thick slices; and yet, despite all the dangers inherent in nature itself, with the possibility of accidents, or sickness or drowning, we were happy as larks, for we had true freedom.

However, it looked almost certain that, given the results we'd got so far, panning for gold would give us remuneration equal, if not superior to, labour in a work camp with a team of horses. So we were almost sure of recouping all or part of our expenses as well has having the opportunity to see new places and to experience many new things that would leave us with vivid memories in the years to come.

We stopped work when dusk was already falling on our camp: we had to put up the tent; the mosquitoes — that scourge of the Canadian forests and woodlands — had already made their diabolical presence felt in the afternoon and were giving warning of a night enhanced, if one could put it that way, by their concert and their dance. As we were prospecting that afternoon, I had killed a couple of wood pigeons, which, when we'd cut them up and fried them with a can of beans, made a meal to which we did full justice. There was no lack of game: rabbits and partridges, which both saved us digging into our canned supplies and offered a healthier and more comforting diet; wild peas grew in profusion at the edges of the bush, and in no time at all we'd gathered great armfuls, sufficient fodder for the night for the horses. And the moon hadn't yet risen over the line of the mountaintops before we were asleep under our blankets, well swathed so that we wouldn't be a banquet for those damned mosquitoes, which managed to squeeze through the tiniest crack.

There was scarcely any light in the sky when we were up and about. Tending to the horses was the first task. Then when they'd had their fill of oats, we folded our tent and ate our frugal breakfast. We were hoping to reach before nightfall a place Jo had pointed out to us as a camping spot, because as soon as we'd gone over the river in the afternoon at a place marked by a well-notched cedar, the banks moved closer together, the mountains got closer, and their last valleys disappeared into rivers that now rushed in a rapid tumult.

The trail, if the few paths through the dense woods or on the banks could be called such, wasn't too hard to follow, and offered few major obstacles except for a few small creeks to cross or dried-out swamps where one sank into thick moss about forty to fifty centimetres deep, and in which we saw a lot of "kini-kinik," which was a tobacco grass for the old Indians. But the mosquitoes inflicted on us and on our ponies terrible suffering, with the latter also harassed by little blackflies that got into everything — their eyes, ears, and nostrils — to such an extent that we had to put leafy branches over them to protect them a bit. As we went along we filled sacks with wild vetch that was growing waist-high in some places, so that we could take a meal break on a sheltered beach somewhere on the river. As soon as we left shelter, the air currents prevented those pestilential beasts from persecuting us. Marius, who was walking at the head of the line at that moment, managed, with his faithful .22, to shoot an overly trusting rabbit that was watching us go by, and that we kept for the evening meal.

It was a beautiful day, and the sun shone with brilliant light on all the wildness of nature, making the water tumbling over the rocks sparkle like thousands of diamonds. It wasn't too hot, and the mountains, which were quite close now, brought through their many coulees breezes from the Pacific slopes. We ate our noon meal quickly beside the water in a creek where the high waters from the winter snows had brought down for many years, perhaps, thick layers of sand among the gravel and pebbles rolled by the current. So, taking advantage of the horses' rest period, we panned all the way along the creek, and without making any startling discoveries, we were assured that in the mountains from which the river flowed, there were sufficient deposits of quartz to enrich its waters through erosion. Given the amount that would be left after we'd given a final washing to our crude powder, it seemed to us that our work would be amply rewarded.

That it would not be good to linger too long before getting to the Red Pine Crossing was already heralded by the difficulties of the trail, which often skirted rocky screes. The spurs of the mountains were now riven by gorges, and the river was flowing ever faster and more boisterously. With this crossing began the real danger, namely of the ponies being swept away by the current or falling on submerged rocks. We weren't really worried that they'd drown, but we feared the loss of the supplies or other items that were absolutely necessary for us to go on and for our return journey. As we cut across a bend in the river through a forest of fine birch trees and perfect clearings that looked like golf courses, we suddenly saw standing at the water's edge, like the lord of the manor, the old tamarack that marked the crossing.

As we made the usual reconnaissance of the crossing, we realized straight away that the current was much stronger since the river was much narrower. Marius, being a good Marseillais, could swim like a fish, and was anxious to try the crossing — though attached with lassoes strung together. He had a job keeping a foothold sometimes, and he often had to skirt rocks that created rushing rapids. Because of this, it was difficult to see the bottom and he needed a pole to sound the depth.

After this trial, we decided to lead the ponies over one at a time to keep a better hold on them. Thanks to these precautions, we all made it to the other side an hour later without accident, but chilled to the bone, as the water, coming down from the summits and the ice of the Rockies, was frigid, despite the season. A brief rest, a pipe, a tot of whisky, and our good cheer was restored. As for the horses, they were so delighted to be rid of the beastly blackflies for a moment that they tucked in with good appetites to the grass on the banks and in the nearby wood. It was getting quite late already, and we decided to push ahead for another few miles before setting up camp for the night in the first place where the animals could browse. Their behaviour was exemplary and had given us no trouble at all right from the beginning; they were fearless and docile on the trail, which isn't always the case if the animal isn't really trained to work along the trails. Indeed, very often stubborn ponies either refuse to follow their leader or stop to eat irresistible grass or rub themselves against trees, damaging their packs as they try to alleviate the voracity of mosquitoes and black gnats, detested little flies that drive them mad. It had looked for some hours, however, as if the pinto's back right hoof was tender and seemed a bit sensitive, which caused us some concern.

Just as the sun was disappearing behind the trees, we had to cross an easy little creek that wound around a small valley, a grassy coulee dotted with stands of willows and cottonwood, and an ideal spot to camp. At the mouth of the stream, the river had a kind of beach of fine gravel and sand carried by the currents. We'd made a note of this place, as well as of other possible ones, on the map that Marius, who was a good draughtsman, had drawn following Jo's directions, which was further proof — if any more were needed — of his perfect knowledge of the area to within a mile.

We decided to camp for the night and to rest the following day, first of all to attend to the pinto, and also to prospect in the riverbed. It was a perfect evening, the ideal place for horses to graze and for us to pitch our tent among the clumps of trees, probably what remained of big, long-ago fires. The hobbled ponies gorged on the fine grass of the valley, and after we'd eaten, we listened to the concert of the animals' bells mingling with the various sounds of nature and allowed ourselves to be bewitched by the charm of this harsh but pure life around us: rustling of wind in the topmost branches, deep sound of the water breaking on the rocks, trumpet call of the nightjars diving from the already-dark sky, calls of the beasts in the forests clinging to the slopes of the nearest mountains. And with the ponies tied up, the last of the brands blackening in the fire, the tent closed up, the great night of the Rockies slowly enfolded us.

The next day, when we had untied the ponies for their morning feed, we could see that the pinto was in greater pain in his back leg and was beginning to limp. This was a nasty blow to us, as it meant that we couldn't go on (which wasn't terribly important), but it made our return problematic in the face of his incapacity. We couldn't possibly put him back on the trail in that state, lest the injury become even worse even if we took off his load completely.

When we examined him, we found that his tendons were intact, but as we cleaned his hoof, we discovered that a pointed stone had become embedded near the cleft and must be causing a lot of pain with the weight of every step. Pulling it out was no mean task, as we had no pliers nor tweezers but just our knives. And the beast, although perfectly docile normally, reacted violently at our every attempt. Finally, after a long time, with one of us holding his head and the other his hoof, we managed to extract the stone, and we realized that it had started to become infected and pus was already forming. It was high time. Luckily, we had some disinfectant in our first-aid kit and we gave it a good soaking. And afterwards, after tying around his hoof some canvas well stuffed with leaves, we released him with the other two. Although we were relieved of the fear of a more serious injury, we still had to make a complete revision of our travel plans. Now we wouldn't be able to move for at least several days to give the wound time to heal.

After some discussion, we decided to make this our definitive camp and to continue our search the next day, one of us staying in the camp, the other going off to prospect with a single pony to get an idea of the area upstream. Marius, who was eager to go off on this little excursion, left at dawn, and I was left to look after the horses and also to pan in the sand at the mouth of the creek and along the beaches. Could it be that I'd acquired the knack? It seemed to me that the quantity of yellow was greater than previously and I could pan faster. I had identified, a few metres from our camp, a spot where the waters seemed to have accumulated, over the course of the years and with each melting of the ice, an enormous quantity of sand and fine gravel that looked as if it would give a respectable yield. And during the course of the afternoon, I had the joy of seeing in the bottom of the pan a tiny gold nugget (oh, by no means a fabulous lump!), but still something different from the dirty dust from the first panning. This was surely a sign that the river we were working was indeed gold-bearing, but from there to finding the source lode was a huge step that we had little hope of making. Besides which, it must be somewhere deep in the mountains, and an expedition in that direction was not in our present plans. Our only hope was to come upon a pocket, a nest of nuggets in a bend in the river as the Indian Métis had done, which was what had prompted us to try our luck. But whatever the outcome, we would have had a splendid trip — which was also free, as we could tell that we would certainly cover our expenses.

Late in the evening, when dusk had already started to fall, I heard the rustling of branches and the sound of a voice: it was Clément coming back. And it was amusing to hear him sing in the Marseillais accent of the Canebière, which he'd never lost, "O Magali, ma tant'amado." [35] And even now, in a reflective mood, when memories of that distant past resurface like dreams, I sometimes hum those lines and see again my cheerful companion, now lost and gone forever.

His trip had gone without incident, and about noon he'd reached the crossing that we would have forded had it not been for the pinto's injury. As he told it, the crossing would have caused us serious problems and risks: the water was extremely rapid and broke against the rocks, making great foaming whirlpools that hid the bottom of the river, which was very narrow at this point. He thought that we'd have had to make ourselves secure by stretching a cable between the two banks, and naturally to let the ponies cross first one by one, with us holding their halter. The panning he'd done hadn't yielded any more than our present camp, and in addition, the grazing wasn't as good. So we had no regrets, which was a consolation for our forced stop.

After the meal, as we smoked a last cigarette beside the campfire, after tending to the pony, we decided on our work plan for the following day. The pony was still limping quite badly, but his hock wasn't so hot, which made us think that the infection wasn't spreading, and he hadn't lost his appetite. But as we had no idea how long he'd take to heal, we decided to try to live off the land to try to save our canned goods and various supplies. This was easy, as small game was plentiful and we could add fish to our diet. So with this optimistic thought, we blew out our storm lamp and drifted into the arms of Morpheus, bringer of peaceful dreams.

The following morning, we got warning of a mountain storm that in a few minutes came thundering down from the Rockies and broke over our heads. A black cloud, as if blown from immense coal mines, rolled in the sky, which had been a clear blue a few minutes earlier, bringing almost complete darkness to the forest, where all signs of life disappeared. The terrified birds sought cover, and our ponies, who were grazing in the coulee, paused uneasily, and we just had time to tie them up firmly behind the tent in the shelter of branches we'd made for them. And in the twinkling of an eye lightning flashed and thunderclaps roared down the gorges of the river like rounds of artillery fire, echoing with manifold reverberations. Torrents of rain fell, whirled by a rushing wind. From the shelter of our fragile tent, fortunately well anchored in a cluster of trees, which swayed but did not break, we watched in alarm but also in awe this unleashing of the elements. Our main worry was for the horses, which might run away if their halter broke. But the sound of our voices close by seemed to give them reassurance, and besides, in their past lives wandering free, they must have been used to such wild outbursts of nature.

As quickly as it had started, the storm stopped; the sky went back to its clear morning blue, and all the greenery, washed by the rain, sparkled with the diamonds hanging from its branches. Farther and farther away, the last peals of thunder retreated into the distance with muffled rumbling, and life, which had been suspended for a moment, came back. The birds emerged from their hiding places and the whisky jacks and squirrels reverted to being cheeky, noisy urchins. And our horses wanted to be set free and to wander off to the tempting, delicious grass. There was no major damage: a bit of water had indeed got into our tent, along the ground, as the protecting ditches weren't deep enough, but no harm had come to our supplies.

The next two days passed without incident, taken up with looking after the horses, changing the pinto's dressing, exploring the area around the camp, panning in the river. Life was good for us in our carefree youth, and the sky above our heads provided the perfect shelter.

As I worked my way up the creek, which wound around the coulee in the valley before flowing into the river, I discovered, about a quarter of a mile from our camp, a little lake surrounded by a stand of birch and pine, in the sunshine a diamond set in emeralds. What a wonderful place for a camp! Unfortunately, nothing could replace our proximity to the river and the protecting willows, which, to paraphrase the great La Fontaine, might also say, "We bend but do not break." [36] The creek itself gave no sign of "paying dirt," as it must only have drained the nearby foothills or forest coulees. On the other hand, game was plentiful, and I had the pleasure — or rather the advantage, as killing handsome creatures is always regrettable — of shooting with my .22 a few partridge in the underbrush and a couple of teal in the grass around the lake, which gave us a welcome variation in our diet and helped us save our supplies.

That evening, as we were chatting beside the fire, having tied the horses to a stake to graze at the bottom of the coulee, we suddenly saw them neighing and snorting and giving the appearance of considerable fright. We went up to them and were in time to see a black mass disappear among the trees with a sound of breaking branches. Judging by the shape we'd made out, it was probably a black bear, which was hardly surprising, as the forest was full of wild blackberries and blueberries, which the bears love.

The next day, quite late in the afternoon, we were finishing our daily panning when we heard the sound of voices that seemed to be coming from upstream along the river. Echoes came over the calm air, and in this spot, so remote from human presence, in the midst of the wilds, they presented a significant and unexpected — not to say extremely rare — event. Jo had told us that he'd heard from some Indians from the North-West that some prospectors had left for the Rockies early in the summer for three or four months, but along a trail well to the north of where we were and that would take them much deeper into the mountains.

After a few minutes, we indeed saw emerging from the trees along the river four men, each carrying on his back a frame with a heavy sack. They stopped in astonishment when they saw us, then with a hearty "Hello" came towards us. Introductions didn't take long: they were four beefy, solid guys, two Irishmen and a Métis, all young, and the fourth a French Canadian who was older, but by no means inferior in bearing and energy. They'd been underway for three months already to prospect the area to the north of the river and the streams that came down from the Rockies. On their way back, and for several days, their supplies had run out, and now they seemed, despite their vigour, fairly worn out, as they were surviving uniquely on trapping rabbits and on whatever birds they could shoot with their .22, all of it simply roasted on the campfire.

When we'd put away our panning gear, we invited them into our camp for a meal and to camp, if they liked, an invitation they accepted with enthusiasm. After the traditional tot of whisky, which they savoured like nectar (they hadn't tasted any for ages), they ate the meal as if it were a banquet, though all there was were some slices of bacon with beans, sardines, and jam, but also coffee, which they'd forgotten the taste of, drinking nothing but water from the creeks or the river. But what they enjoyed most were the pancakes that Marius made for them, as we still had a good supply of flour. As they gave a brief account of what they'd seen on their expedition, among other things they confirmed our suspicion that the final crossing would have been very risky, especially for pack ponies. They had had to tie themselves together, as the current was very fast and could carry a man away. Their prospecting had been uneventful; the only handicap was when their supplies ran out during the last week. They were sorry they hadn't taken a couple of pack ponies with them as there was ample grazing in all the places where they'd camped to do some panning, where they'd found only some gold dust and a few grains but no nuggets. The French Canadian, who was more forthcoming with us, showed us a little medicine vial containing some granules of gold ranging in size from a grain of millet to a grain of rice. They seemed quite satisfied, as their gold would fetch, according to the price per ounce, about $750 to $800 apiece. So they had enough money to last them the winter on their land, which wasn't far away, near Calgary. The Canadien would have liked to take a trip "down East," which he hadn't seen for about twenty years. Despite everything they told us about their work, we had the impression that they were keeping something back, but conscious of the rules of hospitality, we didn't ask any more questions.

They left early in the afternoon of the following day, well rested and laden with partridges and rabbits well browned in the frying pan, a dozen large pancakes, coffee, a little tobacco, and a box of .22 shot, the best guarantee against biting the dust on the trial. We also gave them useful hints about the river crossings and the whereabouts of old Jo's cabin. They tried to get us to accept some gold dust as payment for what we'd given them, but we refused adamantly. So it was with warm expressions of thanks and extra-vagant farewell gestures that they disappeared along the river.

We'd been very happy to see them; to begin with, it's always pleasant and sometimes very useful to meet another human being when one is in the forest. And then, from what they'd said about the places where they'd been prospecting, we gathered that they were no richer than the ones where we were. The real gold-bearing veins must be much farther in the mountains, and it would require a large-scale expedition to reach them: supplies for two or three months, extra pack ponies, and an arrangement with someone like Jo who would take the ponies into the back country and come and get them at the camp on a predetermined date. And in that case, as we'd be 170 to 200 miles into the Rockies, we'd be cut off from the rest of the world, completely off the beaten track and subject to all kinds of accident or illness. It was something that was beyond us, at least for the time being, and didn't fit in at all with the life of a settler I'd planned for myself. Our little camping excursion was quite enough for us.

The pinto's wound was starting to heal. His gait had become almost normal and supple; there was no longer any need for dress-ings, and often, overcome with pleasure, he took off with the others, jumping around and kicking up his rear. We decided to make an early departure and planned it for three days hence. I absolutely had to be back in Athabasca with my horses for the work on the road that was due to begin early in July. Our team had been contracted to pull the scraper, and the money we earned would be most useful so that we could spend the winter in the warmth of our nice house, where we planned to make improvements as well as in the stables.

We broke camp early in the morning in order to give the pinto a good rest at noon; his load was much reduced — as were the others', as the supplies were used up (flour, canned goods, oats for the ponies). So we thought that as long as the pinto didn't get worse again, we'd make it back in three days, as we weren't expecting any nasty surprises on the trail since we knew all the marks and had replaced the doubtful ones. So it was an uneventful trip, a cheerful jaunt when our only worry on the first day was our plucky little pinto's hoof, which was a real question mark. But we were reassured by the first camp at noon: he'd had no trouble on the way and wasn't showing any signs of soreness in his leg.

As we crossed the little bridge we'd rebuilt on our way out, we were delighted to see on the opposite bank, standing like a bronze statue and sniffing the air with his great nostrils, a splendid elk at least ten years old by the look of his magnificent antlers. He'd smelt the presence of humans, but hadn't yet placed them, as we were downwind. When he saw us, he ambled away unhurriedly, and disappeared among the branches with his head back over his shoulder.

As we'd hoped, the sun was scarcely setting on the third day when we heard the joyful barking of Jo's dogs welcoming us back. Even if they didn't know the humans, they recognized their friends the ponies. The latter, who had been able to smell their stable and oats since the beginning of the afternoon, would happily have abandoned us if we hadn't taken the precaution of going back to our initial formation, one at the head and the others in single file. And it was with real pleasure — the pleasure one feels on seeing a friendly roof — that we brought up the caravan in front of Jo's cabin. He was doing his washing in the river, but when he heard the chorus of dogs barking, he realized that something was afoot, and came to meet us in his usual tranquil, noble manner. He was the true descendant of the chief of his tribe. When he saw us he gave a deep, friendly "Hello boys." Then, ever the perfect host, he ushered us into his shack and began himself unloading the packs and saddles. Our baggage was considerably lessened, only the tent, the blankets, and the tools remaining as they were. As for the supplies we had left over, we gave them to Jo to fill out the meals and to make our contribution to our keep; he was particularly pleased with the sugar.

The horses were put in the stable and tended to — and they were well deserving of our care, as we had had no trouble with them — and then it was the turn of the humans to sit down to a welcome-back feast. Jo insisted on adding to our beans and bacon some slices of dried moose meat that Marius, as master cook, had enhanced with a tomato sauce that everyone agreed was particularly tasty. Completely sated, we stretched out with our cigarettes in front of the doorway beneath the sky that night was turning dark blue, listening almost religiously to the last sounds of the wild — the call of the nightjar, the quacking of the coots in the reeds along the river. And we gave Jo a simple account of our trip, almost in the form of a monologue, as he never asked any questions. And when we finished, a great silence fell, accompanied by the dull roar of the water over the stones.

Next day, Jo set about the final washing of our gold dust, as he had promised. We were very curious to see how he did this, but also a bit nervous, as it looked to us as if a lot of the yellow powder was being washed away. But how astonishing it was to see him working the pan — his own, which was bigger and shallower than ours. He had several of different shapes and sizes, according to the consistency of the dust and the percentage of light gravel. His movements were so gentle that his arms remained perfectly still, and he used only his wrists to roll the dish around, which spread the dust out towards the edges. And little by little the worthless sand was expelled and in the middle, like a tiny sun, the clean, golden dust appeared. When he finished and the dust was dried in the sun after several shakings, Jo's scale, which was made of a delicately worked moose bone, showed a weight of twenty-two ounces ready to be handed over to the dealer. This was an excellent daily return, after all the expenses had been deducted (supplies, oats, hire of the ponies, train fare). So we were very satisfied, since our little expedition had been a source of pleasure and moral enrichment. We could, therefore, go back to the serious business of our lives with respectable savings, to which I personally would be adding the sum I would make on the road work in Athabasca.

Old Jo smiled a wry, and perhaps slightly disdainful, smile at our ecstatic response as we contemplated this magic dust. And the following evening, during our usual conversation as the moon was rising slowly in the night sky, he felt impelled to tell us about his ancestors who wandered over their hunting grounds right into the Rocky Mountains in times long past. They well knew where the "yellow metal" was to be found and passed on the information from father to son, jealously keeping the secret from the White Man to avoid having their lands invaded by these hordes rapacious for profit. Unfortunately, progress — or what passes as such — had gradually and inexorably pushed westwards. The CPR, CNR, and GTP rails had followed the discovery, and the surveyors with their train of work camps and motley population: traders and their paraphernalia, settlers creating embryonic villages that speculation quickly turned into prosperous towns. The Rockies themselves, although proud mountains, had been violated by dynamite and had been unable to halt the marching colossus. And thus had old Jo's tribe, a branch of the mighty Cree, suffered the onslaught of colonization, only to disappear little by little like burnt-out forests, or to retire to a reserve, accepting the government's Indian Act.

As we listened to Jo, we realized that had he wished, he could himself have found his people's old path to gold. His bear claw and gold nugget necklace were proof that in some hidden spot, he must have visited his ancestors' treasury. But his existence lay in the heart of nature, in which he relived the history of his people and the heady scent of liberty. Rather than the violent, artificial light of the city, with its endless noise, he preferred the gentle splendour of the starry nights and the peace of the great forest amid the rustling of the leaves and the babbling of the waters. Faithful to his promise to his clan, he had never served as guide to prospectors of gold or other minerals.

We were leaving the following day for Edmonton, the day we'd arranged with the factor at Mile 176 for a freight train that was bringing to a camp under construction a few miles farther on supplies and "grub" for the head of the line. Naturally there was no fixed time, so we had to be there early in the morning to wait for the train to come back — which might be late in the evening or even the following day. So we were up and about at dawn, ready to hit the trail after taking our leave of that noble and lovable Jo. We gave him all the supplies we had left, only keeping enough for the day's meal, so we set out with a much-lightened load and much-reduced kit. And we were very sad, as we went around a bend in the trail, to wave farewell to noble old Limping Jo, who stood, impassive, in front of his log cabin like a fine and living image of a wiped-out past. We knew that at that moment we were turning a page that in future could show no more than a clear and gentle reminder of the past, and for me, many regrets.

Almost sixty years have gone by as I write these lines. And on this earth where humans dwell, in this country that used to be called "la douce France" and where now only acts of cowardice and denial are manifest, where, in heedless hearts that are aroused only by self-interest and profit, the shadow of deceit has veiled the light of truth, I can still see, if I close my eyes, on the path of my young days, the figure of old Jo like the ghost of those proud, free, and loyal men Kise-Manitou had placed under his vast sky.

Return to Edmonton and to Athabasca

Uneventful return journey: for fifteen long hours in the goods wagon, in the company of the chief engineer who, in return for $5, had agreed to take us on board, we again experienced the great comfort of the track under construction. And it was with immense pleasure, like the civilized people we had, despite every-thing, remained, that we again saw the boardwalks of Edmonton, its Jasper Avenue, and our dear old Hotel Cecil. By now we had become not simply clients, but also friends of Joseph Bourassa, the establishment's owner. This French Canadian who had knocked around the whole of Canada and the States enjoyed the company of Frenchmen from the old country. For us he was a living book who opened up his pages when, seated in a comfortable easy chair in the evening, he would tell tales of his past life. It wasn't that he was particularly old — only about fifty — but having left Lower Canada at the age of sixteen as cook in a logging camp, and advancing further and further towards the seductive West, like all the emigrants, he had behind him a great store of wander-ings. Powerfully built, he'd been in the Klondike, then in Frisco in California in the Gold Rush, and after a few years on a ranch in Montana, had answered the call of the North-West Territories, just as Edmonton was being built up. Extraordinarily strong (the story ran that in the time of the Klondike claims, in self-defence, he'd killed a troublemaker with one single punch), he was extremely kind and very altruistic, always offering to help out young or old who were hard up during their first days in the "big city."

In the embryonic city of Edmonton, he'd speculated in land and, after making his fortune, had dropped anchor on the solid ground of the Hotel Cecil. It was a period when lots passed from one owner to another several times during a single month. Several trustworthy settlers assured me that they'd bought a building lot in the mor-ning and sold it by evening at a profit of $300 or $400. We liked the Hotel Cecil as it was the meeting place for prospectors from the North, ranchers from the surrounding area, and buyers and sellers of furs, all of whom had travelled in places still unknown.

We were already into the last fortnight of June, and it was time for Clément and me to start thinking of returning home. So we decided to sell our little bag of dust the following day and after splitting the proceeds to spend a day of relaxation before going our separate ways. Bourassa, who was a mine of information, advised us to go to the Smelting and Prospecting Company, which, in addition to its main business of prospecting and mining, bought raw minerals and, in particular, gold. It was not without a certain pride that we saw our dust weighed, like an apothecary's mixture, on highly calibrated scales. And when the cashier told us the weight and value of what we'd brought, namely $380, minus a $20 guarantee for impurities, we saw that Jo's scale, with its little moose-bone rod, so finely carved that it looked like ivory, was more than a match for the scales of civilization.

With our little fortune in our pockets, all we had left to do was loaf around Jasper Avenue, do a bit of shopping, and see the inevitable show, with the girls singing on the stage and mixing with the audience afterwards, like in the saloons at the time of the march towards the West.

I had a meeting with Raoul, who'd sold me the lot in Florida and told me that the draw had taken place and I'd got a "city" lot that was very well situated, being within 600 or 700 metres of the post office according to the survey map. According to the clauses and conditions of the contract, however, my "garden" lot was farther away, which didn't make any difference to me. The Society undertook to plough the soil and turn it into a fruit farm if the owner so desired.

The day of separation arrived: we said farewell to follow each his own destiny, promising to meet again as soon as we could and to visit each other some day. But it was the parting of the ways, and the best-laid plans of mice and men gang aft agley. We could not have known that this goodbye was in fact a final adieu. For since that June day in 1913, our paths have never crossed. I had word from him in September to say he was going off to Alaska via British Columbia to work for a mining company with a promising salary. And from then on there was total silence. What became of him? I could only surmise: in that faraway and harsh country was he stricken by sickness or accident, and is he now, in a forgotten spot in the forest or beside a trail, nothing but a lonely grave and soon to be anonymous? Or did the Great War of 1914, that monstrous devourer of men, chew him up in its bloody maw? He was a good friend to me, cheerful, carefree, loyal, always willing to help and be of service.

Thus are we, poor mankind, like little ants, forever scurrying around filling in our time and believing we are giants.

Armand Returns to France, Work on the Road

When I trod again the wooden sidewalks of my Athabasca, I had the pleasant impression of feeling enveloped in the loving atmosphere of home. Indeed, the former Tawatinaw was dear to me, the place I had known in its earliest years and that, over the past three years, had changed its appearance completely. New roads had been opened up; the CNR had pushed its track up to us; houses and bungalows in their attractive light colours had sprung out of the old slopes, as well as banks, hotels, and stores. The hospital had been enlarged. In short, beneath the skies of the Great North, man had made an indelible mark. But although the coin had a fine, brilliant side, the other side was not so attractive: saloons and sleazy bars had sprung up like poisonous mushrooms; hotels all had bars, and whisky flowed when the end of the harsh winter months saw the arrival of trappers with their rich furs, loggers and camp workers with their hard-earned dollars, boys from the ranches around Baptiste Lake, and all the prospectors who were impatient for the big thaw to descend the Athabasca with the scows and paddleboats towards the unexplored lands on the Big Lakes and the Mackenzie. So the Mounted Police needed reinforcements.

Two additional constables came from the elite branch of the police force, splendid examples of manhood in their scouts' hats, red tunics, blue trousers with the yellow stripe, and leather boots. As soon as a criminal turned up, he was hunted down like game, as far as the shores of the Arctic if necessary, and it was a rare man who escaped the Mounties.

This evolution in Athabasca wasn't necessarily an evil inherent in the country, nor in our own life. As long as man evolves in the heart of unsullied nature, he remains pure despite all its harshness and danger. His soul, even if it is uncultivated, feels intensely all the beauty nature offers to those who dwell in its heart: the peace of a summer's evening beside an unnamed lake, where, at eventide, an elk or wapiti comes to drink; the sun rising in a blaze of light over the tops of the silver birches and the sombre pines; the magic of silvery nights beneath an opaline moon and the splendour of the Northern Lights, their banners flaring with all the colours of the rainbow. But when this nature, in a state of immaculate virginity since its creation, undergoes brutal rape by our civilization, when what is usually known as "human progress" violates this virginity like a marauding army, it is never for the sole good of mankind but always and above all motivated by interest and the thought of profit, with its train of vices, perverse pleasures, and almost always evil consequences.

I found Jean in his hotel, manning the reception desk as expected, work that was interesting for the variety of patrons and the living kaleidoscope they offered; and not very taxing, since pretty much all that was required was his presence. As soon as I arrived, I hired a saddle horse from Fitz and went up to our property. As I had imagined, the green feed was ready to be cut and stored; it was a fine crop that had grown well in the new soil, and with the hay that we'd get from the coulee and the clearings we would probably have enough winter feed for the livestock. The old Métis had looked after the hens, which were in fine fettle and in great laying form. Jo Tobaty was willing, as a favour to us, to come up and help with the harvesting of the oats. One day was enough to bring in our crop, and I felt enormous pleasure at the sight of it safely stored in the hayloft and the barn.

Work on the road had already begun, at least at the south and east exits of town. And by the end of the week, Jean told me that the teams of horses would be summoned to our road the following Monday. So I decided to stay in town, but unfortunately there was nothing available at the time except the hotel, which would have been too expensive for an extended stay. So I decided to leave the horses in Fitz's stable, whilst he lent me a saddle horse so that I could go and spend the night back home, which, after the work, was a pleasant ride at that time of year.

I suggested to John, the old Métis, that he stay on at our place to go on clearing the coulee that ran down to the little lake and that, over a stretch of about half a mile long and forty metres wide, would probably yield good hay once it had been cleared, even — and especially — during a dry spell. It wasn't particularly hard work: just picking up trees that had fallen and been left to rot, a few stumps to be pulled out, gathered, and burnt. At $2 a day and the small amount of food the old man ate, it wouldn't do much harm to our budget, and for him it was a nice little job that allowed him to stay close to home and to survive and put a little money away for the winter.

Elsewhere, I'd made an arrangement with the rancher Perry, who'd suggested we take some of his cattle to graze on our land with one of his men to guard them. I was to get a third of the product of the herd. He'd decided to go on with the horse ranch at Baptiste Lake and to set up a cattle ranch — on other property for the time being, until, either by renting grazing land from the government to the northwest or by buying out some settlers, etc., he could have it exclusively on his property. The winter fodder would be supplied by him, and he would build on the riverbank a small shack for the boy and a shelter for the animals. He started off with thirty Herefords (familiarly called "white faces" because of their white colour). They were good beef and dairy cattle, and I thought he had the right idea, as with the constant arrival of new settlers, he was sure to be able to sell his produce easily. As for me, at the first calving, I found myself with a small herd of young cattle, which, branded with my mark, could very well live side by side with Perry's. The brand I'd been given consisted of my initials and a crescent and was branded on the animals' left thighs.

Anticipating the moment when I'd have the pleasant satisfaction of seeing my Herefords roaming beside the river in a well-fenced pasture, I'd taken the precaution of renting from the government, under the Timber and Grazing Law, the whole of the section on the bank, which, from the point where the stream ran into the coulee with the little lake, went up to the mouth of Baptiste Creek. By doing so, I made sure that some other settler, seeing the quality of the pasture, wouldn't come along and take it, thereby cutting me off from the river, which was the *sine qua non* of cattle raising.

It was reassuring to know that this pasture, spread over 1,803 acres, or 720 hectares, which I rented for the ludicrous sum of $30.40 per year and was unsuitable for cultivation because of the uneven relief, would not slip away from me. So my mind was easy on that score. I owed this useful tip to my friend Perry, who, when we'd made the agreement about my looking after the little herd of Herefords, had warned me about such an unpleasant eventuality.

The work that was being done on our road was no small thing. For one thing, nothing much had been done to it since the trail had been opened by the settlers themselves, so it was very rudimentary. As it left Athabasca there was a very steep slope, as the hill had been broached at its shortest point to avoid the business of cuts and fills, too hard for people with insufficient tools and, for the most part, devoid of funds. And then on the plateau itself, the road had to be trimmed to regulation width, following the line that had been surveyed for this purpose. This demanded digging out with the scraper ditches to drain the water and, if necessary, to dry the road. For all this work the surrounding settlers had priority, with their bare arms or their horses, and it represented for them a source of profit that eventually came back indirectly to the community.

So I began my work with my horses, along with the other settlers who formed a team from our sector. There were about fifteen men — all handy with the spade and shovel, among them old Monsieur Menut's sons-in-law and five or six drivers of teams of horses. The foreman was called Macleod, a big-bellied bon vivant if ever there was one, who was manager of works for the city and very pleasant as overseer. The salary was standard for the area, and I would make $5.50 as driver of a team.

One day I saw Jean coming looking for me with a letter from Armand telling us of his decision to go back to France. In fact, this news didn't come as much of a surprise. For a few months I'd realized that Marguerite and Armand, in their present family situation and with their temperament and habits more suited to the city than the country, were ill adapted to a life that, though it might bring many satisfactions to adventurous, carefree and brave souls, also made heavy demands, like an ardent but jealous mistress who wants to be completely loved. But above all, there was the matter of their child, who, to their great regret, was growing up far away and was a magnet pulling them home.

I knew that Armand had written several times to his friend G., manager of a big insurance company in the rue de Châteaudun, who had the ear of the president, and he'd been assured that a position as inspector awaited him when he got back to France. Obviously I couldn't blame them for their decision, as the perspective of a father or mother is different from that of a bachelor, and although I felt a sense of bitter disillusionment and regret, I couldn't honestly say I blamed them nor did I bear them any grudge. Evidently their decision to leave France had been made on a whim that their present situation could hardly justify.

So during our third year there, we had reached a crossroads when each of us had to decide once and for all what direction his life was to take. Jean, as I well knew, had always considered this journey as a stage, not as a definitive choice. He was constantly reading the summons to return in letters from his family; he was certain that on his return to the fold, he would find, after a suitable marriage, a nice, middle-class position, and as soon as he'd finished his law studies, he would join his father in the society of notaries. And if he were so inclined, he could keep his share of the family inheritance and live the life of a gentleman-farmer. But his somewhat indolent temperament gave him no incentive to complicate things but rather to seek a peaceful existence.

He assured me that he'd stay put until he received the deed of ownership of the concession that was in his name. This was absolutely essential, as that was the concession that was our mother-lot, the one that had taken all our initial efforts and the major part of our expenditure. It was the one on which we'd built the house, which was supposed to be the "family house"; the one on which the outbuildings, stable, shed, hen-house, well, and fences stood; the one where we'd done the most ploughing and clearing; the other lots, as we'd originally conceived it, were seen as a mere extension of the main one in land and cultivation. All of which was only fair, as we'd chosen by drawing straws. A recognition of intention had been settled, with anyone who stayed automatically taking the place of anyone who left, with all the rights attached to it. In addition, it had been agreed that the sale of any one of the lots was subject to the agreement of the co-owners.

So I found myself having to make a quick decision: either follow the others and go back to the Old Country or stay on by myself and take over sole responsibility for the three homesteads. It was this latter that I chose. First of all for my own satisfaction: I'd given myself a specific goal to "prove up" like the settlers around us and to make this virgin soil yield its riches, capable not only of nourishing its own farmer, but also wearing, like an adornment, the mark of work and human effort. Then a kind of human respect towards others: to return to my native land, if not with a fortune, then at least with some accomplishment behind me, the knowledge that I'd managed to create something. That would already be a reward and a success. For the painter, this means projecting onto a white canvas, by a subtle interplay of colours, a landscape or a handsome profile. For the sculptor, it means chiselling, in a formless block of stone, a harmonious body or an impressive capital. For the poet, it means using the music of words to communicate the state of the soul, a fine image, or tender thoughts. And for the pioneer, it means opening up a trail, clearing a plateau, cutting down a forest, thrusting the plough into new soil to make the furrow for the next harvest; it means draining a marsh to make a field; raising towards the heavens the roof of a house. For me, each of these activities was a real joy, pure pleasure. How many times have I turned back at the end of a long day to admire the beginnings of a new field in the midst of wild brush! I have always kept this spirit, this need to create, to make something new, even back in France, when I bought abandoned old houses or fallow land to give them a new appearance or enhance them with new crops.

Jean's departure date wasn't in the immediate offing; there were still some improvements to be made so that the land could be inspected by the Lands Office when it was at its best, as we didn't want to run the risk of having the patent refused or postponed. Certainly if it were cancelled, the land would be seen as desirable and would easily find a buyer, with its proximity and its situation near the main road that would connect Athabasca and Baptiste Lake, the work that had already been done — all of that gave it certain value in the eyes of any settler looking for the Promised Land.

It wasn't until the beginning of the following summer that Jean could think of returning without risk. Until then, he'd keep his job at the hotel and go on saving. And his departure, like Armand's, would be presented to the Settlements Board as simply a visit to the Old Country.

For me, all this made for several days of upset and considerable worry; I went for three days without going home to Bellevue, spending my evenings at the hotel with Jean, trying to get my mind in order and trying to work out, in all its angles and aspects, the problem with which I was faced and which was still to be solved.

Finally I came to a decision, although at my age I wasn't too concerned about going back to France. I would remain alone in charge of the three concessions, paying Jean and Armand their share of the investments we'd made in common over the three properties. This problem was quickly solved in Jean's case: for him the years spent in Canada were a kind of hors d'oeuvre. He'd go back to France and jump with both feet onto the path his parents had mapped out for him. So I wrote to Armand, telling him I agreed, and encouraged him in his venture, which, after all, was simply a counterbalance to the leap in the dark he'd made in coming here. He had more urgent family problems than we did. We were still young and free to move around as we wished. His situation was altogether different: they were newlyweds with the wife completely unprepared for this hard, unexpected life; he was a lover of creature comforts; they had a small child who was growing up far away from them; all this presented a tangled web of relationships difficult to unravel. For him, it was obviously much, much better to take up his life where he had left it and settle down to work in a career he should never have left.

But then again for me it was a heavy burden that I'd have to shoulder all alone. As soon as the titles to the property were delivered, I'd be responsible for nearly 200 hectares: some of it already cleared, some of it virgin land waiting to be cleared, muskegs to be drained, fences to be built around the ploughed land, new buildings to be put up, trails to be created and maintained, wood to be cut, and stumps to be pulled out. But it would be my own kingdom! I was twenty-three years old; in another four or five years, if I felt like it, I'd be able to sell the property as a going concern to a settler with money who didn't want to start from scratch. Already there were whole families turning up, either from the East or from the States, with their wagons, their livestock, and with all the necessary tools, as in the time — not so long ago — of the pioneers, but also now with their bank accounts. This was how Perry arrived from Montana with his herd of horses and settled at Baptiste Lake, temporarily, at least. For in all the settlers was the desire to go ever on into the Unknown in the Great North that people were starting to talk about.

Our property, being close to Athabasca, would surely tempt a buyer with well-lined pockets. The value of the buildings, their size, and their unusual appearance would also give a favourable impression. Jo Tobaty was in the process of liquidating his property (a single lot of 65 hectares) for $10,000, but that was mere speculation. In another few years the time would come for me, too, to think of realizing my profit and going back. My parents, although in excellent health, were getting older, and I could detect in their letters, beneath the transparency of kindly words, all the regrets and perhaps the reproaches involuntarily veiled. The time would come, when I reached twenty-six or twenty-seven, for me to make definite plans for a permanent home, like a ship dropping anchor on a long-dreamed-of shore after stopping at many ports of call. And certain memories, hazy but enduring, would guide my course, like a navigator's star.

Day by day, week by week, July passed and the work went on. As it left the little wooden bridge over the creek at the exit to the town — a bridge now rebuilt and widened — the road now rose in two or three wide loops to join up with the old trail on top of the plateau. The surveyors had staked out a new trail that followed the section line and avoided numerous detours that often infringed on settlers' lands. For Jo Tobaty, nothing had changed, as, shrewd as he was, he'd built his house and outbuildings at the eastern corner of his property, so the route would follow it along an 800-metre slope. As soon as the embankment had been finished on the side of the hill, the scraper and grader went at it on the plateau. There were ditches on either side, which was good for drying and draining the road in spring and fall.

I'd already done twenty-one full days' work, which gave me at least $100 in salary, and I could count on another month at least on the job, which wasn't due to finish till September, when the funding would run out. But it was not written that tranquility would be my lot, as if God wanted to test me to the utmost before the separation and the rupture of our family association.

One evening, I was coming home as usual after work to spend the night on the property, when I saw, just as I was approaching the fork that went to the big house on one side and to Baptiste Lake on the other, smoke coming from that direction. I spurred on the horse, and a vague sense of foreboding gripped me, as no controlled burning was scheduled for our property. What had happened to my house, built a mere four months' ago? A few minutes later I was face to face with disaster. In the place of the dear little house there was now nothing, everything was gone, burnt to the ground. All that remained was the metallic carcase of the bed and the stove. All around, over an area of a few dozen metres, the grass was burnt up and the fire was moving on towards the west, advancing quite gently through the bush, as there was no wind. To the west, on the other hand, the fire seemed to have started from the road that led to Baptiste Lake. I was completely stunned; finally, I got a grip on myself, turned the bridle round and went back to Athabasca to warn the Mounted Police, who came back with me straight away to the horrible scene. No clues were ever found; nobody could give any information, except a settler from Baptiste Lake who'd gone by at about four o'clock and seen nothing unusual. The fire must have started between then and the time when I got back.

There was never any explanation. For us, and especially for me, it was a big loss, as it was essential to have a house on the property to get the patent. Thanks to the RCMP testimony and the petition submitted by the people of Athabasca and the district, the Lands Office supervisor in Edmonton was willing to take the accident into consideration, and to accept, in place of the vanished house, the cultivation of an additional five acres, which would cost me time and labour, but far fewer dollars.

During this difficult time, I once more had personal experience of the spirit of mutual aid and help of the people around. Some of them — businessmen, dealers in materials — offered planks, nails, windows in case I decided to rebuild; others, settlers and other people, and especially the ones who were working with me on the road, offered help, either in hauling materials or in coming to give a hand clearing and ploughing the five new replacement acres.

Despite this harsh blow, my determination to continue on my chosen path was in no way shaken, and I went back to work on the road, first of all from financial necessity, but also because I liked the feel of my horses in my hands, brave beasts I knew well and who, in their turn, seemed to understand and like their master. When I left them in the evening after feeding and watering them, they stopped eating and turned towards the door, whinnying softly with a look of intelligence. Yet quite soon, I would have to leave them. For the fire had caused me to change, if not my decision, at least the way I'd go about it. Given the total financial responsibility I'd have to assume because of Armand and Jean's departure, and the money I'd have to give them to buy their share, I'd have to have some capital on hand to make the first payments. I knew that Jean and Armand weren't going to make immediate demands, but I wasn't happy about being in their debt.

After thinking it over, I decided to return to France to explain to my parents the situation I was now in and to try to get them to lend me 20,000 francs, which, at the current rate of exchange, would be about $4,000. Interest on the loan at 3 percent, or $120, would be easily paid off by my work, which I could certainly get one way or another: in summer I could work with one or two teams on the roads, and in winter, I could take on two or three hired men to help me furnish firewood for shops, banks, and hotels and also for the Hudson's Bay paddleboats that sailed upstream to Slave Lake or downstream to Fort McMurray in the summer. No more would I go off hither and yon; from now on my headquarters throughout the year would be my home in Bellevue Ranch, as it was now known in Athabasca and surrounding area.

I had thought of selling the horses to start paying Jean, but after thinking it over and listening to our friend Fitzgibbon's advice, I decided to keep them. As I would be leaving in mid-January for an absence that would not be longer than five months, it made no sense to give them up now and then have to buy them back again when I got back, not knowing what I'd find at that point; and I knew my good old horses, their strong points and their little quirks. Rather I made an arrangement with old Monsieur Menut, who was more than happy to work with a team and to board mine, only using them for work on the land and promising not to use them for hauling freight. In addition, having complete confidence in the Menut family, I knew that my friends the horses would be treated as well as by me. I did, however, sell the agricultural machinery to newly installed farmers, which was easy. I could buy more when I got back, and the incident with my burnt-down house had made me circumspect.

What I still had to do was arrange for someone to look after the land: as Menut was taking the horses, I suggested that he take over the cultivation of the cleared land. He was grateful to accept an arrangement that was advantageous for them — with three hefty men used to hard work — and for me. They'd keep three-quarters of the profit, and I'd provide the seeds. This was a good arrangement for me, as I'd be able to sell the entire contents of my granary to neighbours who were running short of feed just at the beginning of winter, which was the best time.

Now I had to make money by any means possible. For the time being I had the road work I was already doing and then more that was planned for Athabasca itself. I also hoped to transport goods to Fort McMurray to the northeast, coming back down the river. The winter road went over ice for a way, and it was solid ice up to the falls; these were the falls that in summer were a barrier to the paddleboats but not to the scows belonging to the Hudson's Bay or Révillon or the Oblate Fathers who stocked their posts or missions in the Great North or on the Mackenzie. A winter road had been cut along the riverbanks so that it bypassed the rapids that only froze on the surface.

Once I had made my decision, I turned the already-written page and confronted the white one I was about to begin. I realized I was taking on huge material and moral responsibilities, as well as risks (bad luck, failure, sickness, etc.), since it went without saying that for several years I would remain attached to my land by the very goal I was hoping to achieve, so I would be far from my aging parents and also from the possibility of creating my own family as I was thinking of doing, as do all young people in the illusions of their twenties. In addition, I had before me some very hard work in order to wipe out the debts I owed and the shares I had to repay. But these worries were less onerous in present circumstances, for I knew that in this new country, a man and a good team of horses, if both are willing enough, would be sure to make money, for there would be no shortage of work and opportunity in the near future. The little town was growing rapidly, lots were selling, and not only for speculation; houses and new shops were being built; so new streets would have to be put in, more and more vehicles would be needed, drainage ditches would have to be dug, boardwalks like the ones in Western movies would have to be laid. Settlers were arriving, and as they claimed homesteads in all directions, they would soon be demanding new roads. Neighbours who had no horses were clamouring to have their cleared fields ploughed and cleaned. In short, it was certain that any time left free from the demands of one's own property could be used in gainful labour.

It was with all this in mind that I began to live again: now that I had crossed the Rubicon, all I could do was forge ahead. And in fact, apart from the fact that I'd miss the very pleasant feeling of having near me relatives who created a family atmosphere on foreign soil — and this applied only to my emotional life — as soon as I'd cut the cord, I felt perfectly capable of living in my work, with my eyes fixed solely on the goal ahead. Solitude would not trouble me, as I'd already experienced it during the preceding months when each of us had taken off on his chosen path. And since I like an active life, I didn't feel lonely when I held the reins of my stalwart horses as, furrow by furrow, I ploughed up new earth. Contentedly smoking my pipe in front of the house at dusk, as I took stock of the work already accomplished and what was left to do in the coming days, my thoughts turned to the Old Country, to my dear parents, and also to a certain youthful dream, to a garden near my own, to a fair head passing along a path through the flowers, her sisters. All that was far, far away, not in time or in my heart, but in space, for we couldn't gaze together at the same sky or the same stars.

But I was young; she was young, and I had the future before me. But does not time destroy dreams, as it does autumn leaves at the first blast of winter? The girl I had left still almost a child had grown into a young woman, surrounded by a passel of flatterers, and if absence sometimes exaggerates the beauty of childhood dreams, it also erases their gleam, as tarnish dims the image in a mirror.

All in all, I didn't mind the thought of being the ghost of my youth when I went home and perhaps taking an option on the following years. And then, when I came face to face with all the strutting peacocks who'd never left their narrow sidewalks, wouldn't I be the traveller returned from distant shores and empty spaces, who had trod in the footsteps of the first tillers of the new ground and who added to everyone's sun the splendour of the Northern Lights? Thus, despite the great disappointment I felt at the breakup of our association, I wondered whether the finger of Providence hadn't turned this page in my life with a design in mind.

When the haymaking season came, I borrowed from Jo Tobaty the harvester he no longer used since his land had all been sold; I'd have been happy to buy the machine from him, but I kept thinking of my voyage and various expenses in France. I would have to change my wardrobe, for one thing, since Western wear wasn't exactly the style of Brive. It would be better for me to put off buying a new mower till I got back, since I'd have ample opportunity then.

It was a real pleasure to make the first cut with the harvester in the meadow beside the lake. I needed the sickle only for the edges of the brush and the coulee, where some of the young willows remained uncut. But it was nothing compared to the work of previous years. The old Métis from Baptiste Creek, happy to be earning his $2 and his daily food, did it whilst I worked the machine. With fine weather, it only took us a few days to cut the hay and haul it to the loft above the stable, which was completely filled, not counting the two loads that were sold to old Monsieur Menut for the horses. This was the last big task I'd have to do on the property. Then I went back to my road work, which would last another two weeks; the end of it reached the Menuts' place, about a mile beyond the fork to our property. The work would continue into Athabasca itself to level the riverbank at the boat dock, and also towards the station on the sites where the Hudson's Bay and Révillon warehouses were to be built. There would certainly be enough work for several weeks, which I didn't mind at all, from a financial point of view for one thing, since my savings would be swollen, but also to avoid the inertia before departure. I'd be better off not dwelling on it too much.

When I'd finished with the road work, I made Athabasca my headquarters for a few days to start on the work beside the river. I was able to rent a small house, which was modest in the extreme, but during the summer months there was no need for luxuries. All the essentials were there: one large, clean room with the essential furniture and a little lean-to that provided shelter for the horses. All I had to pay for was meals, which I took at the Athabasca Hotel with Jean.

After two good weeks of work we'd finished the road bed and I went back to the property, where I wanted to spend the time before

I left. Sentimentality, perhaps. It was like the moment before leaving a loved one for a long separation, and you want to take advantage of every moment before the departure; that was how it was with me. I wanted to enjoy right up to the last minute my stay on the land we'd so lovingly cleared. It was all reality for me. So with the horses loose in the pasture, I spent my time visiting every nook and cranny of our concession, as there was still quite a bit that remained unexplored. Indeed, Armand and Jean's concessions were 1,600 metres long by 800 wide, with mine being an 800-square-metre lot, which, in a new land, with no service roads and with everything still to be done, leaves much to be discovered. I made plans for this or that place, deciding to drain completely the slough where we'd pitched our tent that first winter, and which, as you left the plateau, came to an end 400 or 500 metres further on at the coulee that ran out of the lake. Draining at that point would certainly be good for this part of the land, which would become fields or grazing after it had been cleared.

To take a wagon down to the river, you had to take the old trail from the end of the plateau that ended at the mouth of Baptiste Creek near the old Métis' cabin. At the foot of the bank, opposite our house, we had long, wide pebble beaches with a mere two or three feet of water that, later on, would make an excellent summer watering place for my herd, when I had increased it. And I could already see a fence around the good grazing land that descended in steps down to the Athabasca and a cart track leading directly down to the river.

I also weighed the question of the little lake: either to leave it in its present state for our viewing pleasure and also for all the flocks of birds that lived there in summer; or to return it to its original state before the beavers dammed it, to turn it into a meadow by draining the muskeg that fed it.

I stayed there for hours at a time dreaming in one spot or another, fantasizing as I smoked about the projects that drifted through my mind like the faint smell of cigarette smoke on the breeze. And all these dreams could, with time — and above all, effort — become reality. And this was as it should be. For this undertaking, built at the cost of worry, sweat, total fatigue, and even a dose of anguish, seemed like a cherished child fondly tended throughout its early years, whose slightest indisposition gives cause for alarm; so it is with the land that one has found in its primordial state and each day for a long year, and for every hour during that year, one has lovingly fashioned so that it becomes the realization of the image one has dreamed of.

It was this love of personal creation, together with the desire not to give up nor to fail, that impelled me to remain on the path I'd embarked on in the heedlessness of my twenty years.

One morning when I went by the post office, I found a letter from my sister stating that October 3 was their departure date. We were to meet them both at Calgary station to see them before they left — which was like deliverance for my sister: she would see the little child she'd left when he was so young.

It was decided that I wouldn't leave till the following January so that I'd be on the spot to take care of the last few problems left to solve.

Armand didn't stay long in Paris: a few days were enough to settle with G. the business of his re-entry into the Compagnie du Soleil, of which Monsieur M. was CEO at that time. My sister had already rejoined our parents and the little boy, who had grown a lot. And so they were already well on their way back to the success they'd abandoned in a moment of giddiness, when Armand, ever impulsive, had, as in La Fontaine's fable, let go of the prey for its image.[37] However, the money they brought back from Canada was more than enough for them to get settled back very comfortably; they'd made into a flourishing business the family hotel in Victoria, which was known as the best-run and most popular in town. Indeed, Marguerite's elegance and her easy manner in her role as mistress of the establishment, together with Armand's perfect command of English, had impressed the town's upper crust, who recommended "The French House" to their friends. It was the equivalent of the two or three stars awarded to chic hotels and restaurants. They'd been able to sell it for several thousand dollars to another French family, which they were sure would keep up its reputation. It was a vast and impressive house with a Chinese cook, two Chinese valets, and a Finnish chambermaid. The sum they came back with was ample for them to set up their household again.

They spoke reassuringly and with confidence about the future. In addition, I knew that my aging parents were surrounded by family and were less lonely, so that was a great relief to me.

I had decided to leave in mid-January, as I had so many things to organize for a five-month absence. I found the wait very long, but upon reflection, I thought that for emotional reasons, I shouldn't give my parents the impression that this stay was only a dream for them and that as soon as the pleasure of reunion had worn off it would be spoilt by the anguish of another departure.

Life continued calmly for me in Bellevue, interrupted by trips into Athabasca for me to get my payment for my firewood. One day, the manager of the Hudson's Bay suggested I make the trip to Fort McMurray to take supplies for their northern posts. I would be part of a convoy of about fifteen teams, which would be a guarantee against the risks that Jean and I had faced when we were on our first trip to Lesser Slave Lake with the government mail.

We had to wait for the river to ice over completely before we could leave, which in theory wouldn't happen till Christmas. So I accepted the offer, which would add considerably to the sum I already had set aside in the Royal Bank, the bank we'd used since we arrived; it had a branch in Paris, on the rue du 4-Septembre, which would be convenient for me.

In the meantime, I decided to stay on our concession, continuing, with John's help, the work of clearing on the plateau where it was easiest. There were no big trees there; the hardest job was the big old stumps, the already-decayed remains of the forests that had disappeared in long-ago fires. Only sparse bush had started to grow, and this was easy enough to cut down.

The Christmas I spent in Athabasca with Jean was more cheerful than the previous year; now we knew which path we'd both chosen, so everything was clear, which made things easier. The cold had done its job of levelling the rivers and the lakes; thick snow now covered the frozen ground and dormant nature, as it would for some time. The winter convoys were already starting up, and the freighters commandeered by the employers came in to claim the goods they would be transporting. I had known since the beginning of the month that my load would consist of sacks of flour and sugar, things that were easy to handle and, more important, easy to balance on the sleds. I was happy to be making another long trip into a region that was being much talked of on account of the oil deposits that had been discovered there, and also to store up new memories to beguile what I was sure would be the dullness of daily life in the "Old Country."

Fort McMurray at that time was the supply centre for the fur trading posts in the North and the Missions, or rather the hub from which foodstuffs, equipment, trade goods, etc., left for Great Bear Lake, Greater Slave Lake, and also Lake Athabasca in the far north of Saskatchewan, in summer on paddleboats that took over from the ones that stopped at the rapids; and in winter by freighters that took over from the ones that came, like us, from Athabasca and Lac La Biche. McMurray's twin town, called Waterways, which at that time consisted only of a few trappers' or prospectors' cabins, was just starting up, about three miles from the Fort. It was in this region that work had just begun on the tar sands, which have become the richest in the world.

Departure day arrived, and I joined the Hudson's Bay team, about twenty pairs of horses, with one of them carrying a ship's boiler as its load; that was a rotten load if ever there was one; often, in the paths overland that we had to take to avoid jumbled blocks of ice or to cut off a bend in the river, and also on trails through the forest that had been cut specifically so that we wouldn't be in danger of sinking in the rapids as we'd done before, there was considerable unevenness, which might make the load become one-sided and overturn. With my sacks neatly piled and well balanced on the platform of the sled, I had no fear of such an eventuality.

We left on December 28th on a bitterly cold morning. The thermometer on the door of Fitz's livery stable showed twenty-nine degrees below zero; the sky was clear and still sleeping under the care of the stars. But we had a long stretch before us and it was better to walk at a steady pace and give the horses a breather with a long break at lunchtime. There, around a fire where we could have made a crude barbecue of five or six sheep, everyone told his story. Some of them, although natives of the region, might have put to shame a Gascon or a Marseillais.[38] But it all created an atmosphere of friendliness and warmed the heart — even if the limbs remained frigid.

The head of the caravan was a company employee, and in the evening he went on ahead with his saddle horse and made sure that meals were prepared for men and animals at the next stopping place. It was all very well organized and nothing like the "lost boys" enterprise we'd embarked on with the government mail. So we arrived in Fort McMurray without any incident of note, except the sudden death of one of the horses from a colic attack. The load was distributed among the other teams and a collection among us immediately reimbursed the horse's owner for his loss. Although we returned individually, the trip was normal; I remained for a whole day, for the horses' benefit, for one thing, but also to wait for a supplier, Colin Fraser, who was very well known in the region and was bringing his stock of furs to Edmonton and its glittering lights.

On my return, I got from the Hudson's Bay Company the sum we'd agreed on, which was, I believe, $320, to which was added the fare for Colin and his stock. I was very pleased with the whole business that had given such a boost to my bank account.

The moment for my departure was approaching, and I grew nostalgic as I anticipated the day when I would leave for such a long absence this place that was already dear to my heart.

So, during the last fortnight in January, the day of my departure dawned, and it was from the house itself, looking out onto the plateau and the magnificent view of the banks rolling lazily down to the Athabasca, that I looked for the last time on what was, to me, the final goal of the coming years. John, the old Métis, was there holding the saddle horse I'd borrowed from Fitz the day before to came back and sleep on my own property. I'd wanted to leave for France from the very lands that were the stake in the game I was about to play for them. I told the faithful old Métis to do his best to look after the buildings and the house and after shaking his hand and slipping into it a crisp new $5 bill that I'd withdrawn for him from the bank the day before, I jumped into the saddle and left on a return journey that now seemed as full of imponderables and hazards as our arrival in the country "at the end of the world."

I was taking with me enough money for this "uneventful journey" and for the stay of five months I'd be in France, which now seemed so small to me beside my immense Canada. When everything was ready and I'd drunk a farewell round with friends: the Menuts, Jo Tobaty — who had kept their presence a secret — and everybody from Athabasca itself, Fitz, Servestre, old "Papa Goyet," Lessard, Dr. Olivier, mayor of the town, Fraser and McPhee from the RMP, Grimshaw from the Royal Bank, Isaïe Gagnon, the town's rich man, I got on board the railroad coach — which was the only one, as apart from a few government employees, settlers, prospectors, and trappers, there still weren't many passengers, especially at that time of year.

The train started up with the ringing of the little bell that was the distinctive sound of trains in those days, a sound that evoked memories of the early machines that had brought the Prairies to heel at the time of the Indian revolt; the time of Riel, the Métis leader, and of Father Lacombe, who, through his courage and his sway over the rebellious tribes — who, however, were loyal when the promises made to them were kept and the treaties respected — had often managed to avert carnage.

And suddenly, imagine my surprise and emotion when, from the train that was already chugging along (insofar as it was able), I saw Perry, with an escort of three of his cowboys galloping effortlessly alongside our wheezing convoy, and with wild shouts and arm waving, wishing me a good and prosperous voyage, wishes they accompanied with salvoes from their carbines and big Colts.

And so, alone from now on, I was about to make my last pitch, so that my twenty-year-old dreams would have their final flowering.

The Return: Arrival in France, Brive at Last, and the Return of the Prodigal Son to the Family Nest

A journey like this was nothing special, so I have nothing to say about it. There were the same long days, the continuing panorama of the wide-open spaces that we crossed, but it was already more monotonous, as it held none of the excitement of the unknown and the new. The settlers' log cabins, their cleared land, and the dark forests, countless lakes set amidst the greenery in summer or, in the present season, sleeping beneath their white blanket; the wide Prairie, which seemed even more endless covered with snow right up to the grey sky, now all that was nothing but a reminder of my last years and all the things I'd seen and done myself.

But the sight of the shore of one's native land that appears on the horizon and grows bigger as one approaches is always fraught with emotion as the memories of childhood rise to the surface; and the imminent meeting with one's dear parents and certain visions that, in the lonely house, seemed as distant as those left by dreams in the night now suddenly start to take on form and consistency in the heart where they had been so long suppressed.

There was, however, a shadow: the memory of what I was leaving on the new land on which I had so willingly staked my life; all that little creation that had arisen little by little from stubborn but not ungenerous soil, and that finally yielded itself, like a young horse submitting to a rider who has tamed it; and my toil and my sweat and my travails and disappointments, but also and above all the joys and satisfactions of a task accomplished, the contentment of the evenings and the imperious call of the mornings.

I stayed only briefly in Paris; after meeting up in the Latin Quarter with my dear friend Max Gaspéri, who was now studying architecture in the École des Beaux-Arts, I took the train to Brive to bathe once again in the sweet warmth of the family home and also to find the answer to a certain question. What had become of the blond girl I had known when she was a schoolgirl, whom I had accompanied with perfect propriety on the Hôtel de Toulouse omnibus to her class at Jeanne d'Arc school. I'd easily found a pretext to take advantage of the situation: it was a so-called kick on the knee I got during a rugby match at the Brive Football Club, now renamed the Athletic Club of Brive. It was a completely specious reason, for I limped mainly in the house. As she'd now grown up, she'd surely have become part of a lively group from which I would be excluded, mainly though my own fault. Those absent always lose out, especially when the absence is long and far-flung with no date for the return.

Mother and Father were at the station, and it was in their loving embrace that I rediscovered the atmosphere of home. For them it was the return of the prodigal son, but a return that would be only temporary, as they knew from my letters that I'd decided to take over alone everything that Armand and Jean had abandoned. Ever understanding, they didn't try to deter me from my project, but rather promised to lend me the money I needed to carry out my plans.

Armand, with the help of his loyal friend, had immediately been able to get back his position as inspector in the insurance company "Le Soleil" and was already embarked on this interesting work in the Paris region; it was work that suited him much better than life in a tent. He made a good first impression, had a distinguished appearance and ready conversation, and was already a qualified inspector before leaving for Canada.

Unfortunately, the house next door, where the blond girl of my Canadian dreams had lived before I went away, was silent and abandoned. The paths in the little garden had lost their charm, for no shy silhouette flitted there, like a pale wraith.

By means of devious questions, which I tried to ask with all the indifference of unimportant matters, I discovered that the girl of my childhood had had a stupid accident and was being treated, under the grey skies of Berck, for housemaid's knee, which had been botched by a quack and had developed into permanent stiffness.

She was now nearly twenty, that blissful age, when groups of her friends were gathering the rosebuds of their euphoric youth. And I suddenly realized, in a flash of insight, that our youthful attraction was for me something more than a passing fancy or an adolescent flirtation, but had grown, almost without my noticing, like a seed in the hollow of a furrow, into a deep and tender love.

So my days passed calmly and peacefully in the gentle atmosphere of my home, and I was glad to notice that my parents were generously getting used to the idea that I'd be leaving again and that we'd soon be separated once more. They could see that it was possible to return from countries unheard of in France, and I promised that I'd come back every year for what would be a pleasant vacation for me. But for a while it would only be for a month or six weeks, as there was no question of leaving my property without supervision, especially when it was fully productive.

I'd met up again with some of my old classmates and sports pals like the Lacoste brothers, Max Gaspéri, Paul Lachèze from Toulzac Street, Berthy, our feted fullback from the Brive Football Club and the Brive Athletic Club, Gilbert, who was just starting up in banking, Jean Bardon, future surgeon and my good pal from Cabanis school days, both of them seen as rabble-rousers when we went to the principal to demand a fire in classrooms that were unheated. And Jean Margerit, who was already seen by us as a matinee idol; his sister Gabrielle, Lélée Raynal and her brother Albert, who'd just started medical school, the Lamaze family, Milou Lespérut, who looked like a handsome hidalgo, with his swarthy complexion.

But they had all scattered and the circle was broken.

The weeks passed quickly, interspersed with visits to relatives in Martel, where I also rediscovered the sweet impression of a family circle. Armand came home often on the weekends, and one day announced, triumphantly, that he'd found the apartment of their dreams right in Paris, on the Boulevard de Vaugirard, if I remember correctly: a nice apartment raised just above street level in a fairly recent building, so very attractive. My sister left to make another home, which, with the smiles and happy chattering of their little boy, who was now five, would be a place of happiness and hope again.

From time to time I got letters from Jean, which were quite short (letter writing was not his forte) but managed to give me the essential news, which was an echo of my dear Athabasca. Everything was fine, he said, nothing was suffering. The country was peaceful, the neighbours were all good people, busy on their land and not looking for trouble. Naturally there was the black mark of the fire in my house, but I came to think more and more that it must have been due to the carelessness of some smoker.

Jean seemed happy with his job at the hotel: the work wasn't hard and offered plenty of variety; he was well fed, well housed, warm — all of which were the main requirements for a comfortable winter. In his most recent letter, he said that the Lands Inspector would soon be coming to inspect the work that had been done to clear the land and get it under the plough, to put up fences and buildings. The house would certainly be an object of astonishment for him, as we could say without boasting that it would be the first time that a log house of that size and structure would have been seen in that remote region of the West on such a raw concession.

Jean was planning to return to France in mid-June, and all his news provoked great euphoria within me. I already imagined myself on the familiar trail towards the house that I suddenly saw as a dear friend, with its windows shining in the summer sun like astonished, wide-open eyes.

Towards the end of June 1914, Jean wrote to say that the inspector from the Lands Office had been to check on the improvements, and he'd been bowled over by the situation and appearance of our house, that the ploughing and clearing were satisfactory, and that he'd been happy to give the patent, as he realized that it wasn't the work of simple homesteaders, but rather of "people of quality." The title would therefore be issued without delay, both for my quarter section and Armand's, since the work on these latter he deemed sufficient. Indeed, they formed a whole with the concession that the house was on, and for mine, there'd already been an allowance made for the fire in my poor house.

Since all that was settled, Jean planned to come back within a few weeks and I awaited him impatiently, as I naturally had many question for him about many things — how the Menuts were planting the crops, how Perry's herd was coming along.

As soon as Armand was settled in his Parisian home, reunited finally with my sister and their little boy, the normal life that he should never have interrupted could again go on and happiness would be established. Their material needs were almost completely met, and he could look forward, given the results he already had, to being named director in a provincial office. Indeed, his pleasant, unpretentious personality, his perfect manners, and his knowledge of his profession all gave him a big advantage. Despite my disappointment when they left, I was happy for them, and especially for my sister at the sight of the peace and calm that radiated in their home.

Finally, early in July, Jean arrived in Brive, and I can still see him getting off the train as calmly and unconcernedly as if he'd just been on a short holiday. The next day he went off to join his parents, who were living in their chateau in Arnac in Lower Corrèze at the time.

He gave me a letter from our friend Perry, written in the mixture of French, old "Canayen," and English that was his usual language. He announced ceremoniously that Bellevue Ranch now existed, with the birth of two heifers of the first eight calvings from the animals he'd left with me. The dear man took satisfaction in telling me that he had chosen the two best calves to start my herd.

Thus the business of my return, which I'd planned in Athabasca, ran its course just as I had expected. I began to anticipate my departure little by little, and as I talked about it, I prepared my parents for the coming separation.

Now my sister's presence nearby gave me a clearer conscience. Financial questions had easily been solved, as my parents had provided me with the necessary money from their own funds. I would go back to my lands, solitary under the Canadian sun at the moment, and would give them back the master who loved them so intensely — even to the point of giving up everything for them.

I had some business to attend to in Paris with the Canadian High Commission and with some furriers to see whether they were interested in buying directly from the trappers, so I decided to spend a few days there before leaving. I had planned, on my way back home, to stop off at Limoges to ask some breeders of pure Limousin cattle to find out what the possibilities were of getting a sire from that fine breed to cross it with some Herefords, of which there were already quite a few in the West, and especially on Alberta ranches. It was a question that interested Perry, who always had his ear to the ground for something new. I'd already sung the praises of the hardiness of the breed, which, since it was already used to the open spaces of our Limousin province, would surely be able to adapt to the harsh Canadian climate. It would also interest the experimental farms, which already loaned, cost-free to organizations of livestock farmers, Jersey and Holstein sires for milk and Shorthorn and Angus for meat.

I was very interested in it myself, since, not being able to raise a big herd on my property in its present state, I'd have liked to introduce something new when the time came. And Perry's support gave me considerable encouragement.

As I went about my business in Paris — which hadn't yet become the tentacular city of today — I pitied all those people who came rushing out of their places of work with their heads down, like a herd of cows in the ranches of the West, the only difference being that the horizons of the former were limited to blocks of apartments that were often in pockmarked and foul-smelling streets, whereas the latter looked out onto the vast open spaces of the Prairies, with the perfume of pine forests wafting from the Rockies, and the white salt pans where in ancient times the buffalo had come to drink.

And I felt sorry for those poor beggars whose daily toil, never changing, riveted them to the same place, like a convict on his chain, and I considered myself so happy with my daily labour, hard and difficult and sometimes dangerous though it was, but which kept me in the open air of the Canadian forests.

The 1914 War Is Declared: I Sign on as a Volunteer and Depart for the Front

I now had assurance that I could, with no material, not to say moral, disadvantage, take up again my labours where I had left off, and the call of the wide-open spaces became louder and louder, especially after the heavy yoke of city life had been lying on my shoulders for several months.

But man proposes, God disposes. The projects of human beings, however well structured and carefully planned, are as fragile as soap bubbles that burst at the slightest breath of wind. Grave events were developing, and the international sky was darkened by heavy, threatening clouds. Already at the end of July, the assassination in Sarajevo had produced the insanity of war and many homes were haunted by anguish and the thunder of cannon fire boomed from Serbia. The business of war was already launched, and nothing now could stop men's folly.

In light of the uncertainty of this situation, my parents immediately begged me to delay my departure, and I acquiesced to their pleas. There was no imperative about the date of my return, as my business in Athabasca did not require urgent attention. I knew that, as we'd agreed, the hay and green feed would be cut at the right time by the Menuts and stored in the hayloft, which I'd emptied before I left. And then there was in the air a feeling of enthusiasm and bravura to which I could not remain insensible.

In addition, if there was a war, it would be short, as once again it wasn't the horseshoe nail that was wanting but the whole brigade that was lacking.[39]

The wait wasn't long. War was declared on August 3rd, and the very next day the butchery began. Although I was exempt from military service and a naturalized Canadian since 1913, I decided to sign on as a volunteer. But the recruiting offices weren't opening until August 24th, so I had to wait until that date.

Already everything was changed in my little town; my friends who were mobilized had left and scattered. My friend Gaspéri was enrolled in the 138th Infantry at Magnac-Laval; Armand and Jean had joined their regiments, Armand as sublieutenant in the 21st Cavalry in Limoges, his brother in the 109th at Chaumont, with Marguerite and her little boy taking refuge with the family. In the meantime, my far-off princess was still lost in the northern mists.

It was a great upheaval.

On the 24th, when the recruiting office opened, I went to the Brune barracks and signed on, and on August 26th, I left to join the 27th Infantry in Dijon.

After a few days' training, all completely useless, except the firing range, I left with a flower in my rifle and a hundred other men; we were going to replace the gaps in the 95th Infantry, which had been thoroughly routed in Lorraine. I joined the regiment in Mécrin in the Meuse, and for us it was the beginning of that terrible winter of 1914 for which nothing had been prepared, a winter we spent in the trenches of the Bois d'Ailly of sad memory in the forest of Apremont.

Epilogue

It's not my intention to give an account of the war. My aim in writing these modest pages was to give a simple overview of some of the adventures I had in my first years on Canadian soil.

The 1914–1918 war was the main and only determining factor that caused a rupture in the smooth planning of my future years that I'd thought out with such tenacity and hope. But as soon I was caught up in the inexorable machinery of a war that ground up everything, men and materials, I realized the vanity of human decisions, which are as fragile as crystal. Farewell, my Canada, my dear Athabasca, and the log house overlooking the river built with such effort and such love. Farewell my lovely plateau with the ploughed fields and the lake on which I often viewed a flock of young coots swimming like a miniature fleet. Farewell pure sky untroubled by bursting shells. Farewell my calm forests disturbed only by the squirrels' wild dance or the mocking cry of indignant whisky jacks.

Yet despite everything, I had no regrets. As I watched, day after day, my comrades fall beside me, whom yesterday I had not known and were now my brothers, I realized that we were there like a rampart for France, for all its families, for its cradles and its graves.

Everything I had experienced, and also those radiant memories, so recent, but which seemed to rise up from a distant past, seemed to me now like mere dreams in the night that are chased away like the mist by the light of day. I was a soldier; I no longer belonged to myself; I was a tiny entity in a mass of men who had been gathered from everywhere with all their weaknesses, but also their heroism, and were destined for the next hecatomb.

In this state of mind, nothing mattered for us, for me. All that remained was the fragile present; we no longer had the right to believe in a future, and every hour that passed was a moment of survival stolen from the great devourer of men. We were alive and that was good.

So it was not surprising in this atmosphere of abandonment of the self, of pure fatalism for some and submission to the dictates of Providence for others, that I should give up the payments on my Palm Beach property, convinced that if my spirit was still wandering through the wide-open spaces of Canada and my home in Athabasca, my body was already destined to lie on the line along the hill crests and woodland of the hills of the Marne, a line that was forbidden to German brigades.

Carpe diem . . . seize the day. So sing the poets. But for us, every moment of every day was imprinted with the same terror of death. So when we were in the rear, breathing without fear the peaceful air where Death wasn't stalking, we were frantic to seize the day that, for our repose, exhibited its lovely dawn and sweet dusk.

The years went by, years so bitter in the heart, so heavy in the body, that each one seemed like a century. I lived those years like the others did, doing my best, though not perhaps as nobly and courageously as heads of families who, having left wife and children, felt their lives torn asunder.

During my leaves, I had managed, by the subterfuge of an invitation issued by my sister, to see the woman who had always played, perhaps subconsciously, a leading role in my thoughts, like those underground rivers that flow in silence in the depths of the earth, to gush to the surface in a beautiful spring singing in the sunshine.

It was at that moment that I asked the "beautiful blond girl of my youth" whether she would, after the war was over, consent to be united with me for life, for better or for worse. The answer was "Yes." Our common destiny was linked from that moment on.

Providence, in all its might, had led me by the hand to the haven of deliverance. The fact of my return to Canada, the hostilities that had been for many, alas, the destruction of familial or material life, all this concatenation of circumstances had been for me a fulfilment. If, after coming back to France, I'd left again as I had planned, without making a decision about my sentimental life, it's probable that in my absence I would have been banished from the heart of a young woman by the demands of those on the spot, and as I receded into a vague memory, I would have been forgotten.

When I was demobilized, we were married on April 25, 1919. And ever since, through calm or stormy weather, through sunshine and showers, we have lived and cherished each other in a family where the presence of our two beloved children added much joy and happiness.

Unfortunately, before the joyful chiming of the armistice, the death knell had tolled. Léon, my wife's brother, had been killed in battle almost at the end of the awful carnage; Jean was carried off just after the armistice by the terrible epidemic, which took over where the cannon had left off, along with my good friend Max Gaspéri, pilot in the "Guêpes" squadron, who had also survived the holocaust. And so many of my other friends were absent at the roll call of the living.

So my return to Canada, which was scheduled for the end of July 1914, took place in May 1919. I was accompanied by Armand, his wife and young son, and my dear parents. who decided to come along too.

I won't speak now in this modest work about the second stay, which will perhaps be the subject of a second book, if the great Kise-Manitou gives me time. For I have plenty to say about those further years in Canada in the new region that stretched north towards Peace River, and from which we brought back, in addition to precious memories, the best possible present: a darling little girl.

For there was another return, a return that was not of my choosing, and that I regret to this very day. But my wife had given great proof of her love when we married in leaving behind her aging parents, to whom she was very much attached. It was only fair, when she could feel the great weight of solitude weigh on their old shoulders, it was only fair for me to give her the great joy of a reunion.

Thus it was, that by constantly seeking to bring happiness to the other, we've arrived at the rocky path of late life as united as in our earliest days. Now, just as evening brings shadows to the light of the finest day, the sadness of things past descends on my declining years. And when, on nostalgic autumn evenings, my heart sometimes feels too heavy, I see again in my mind's eye the splendour of the Canadian forests and the sweetness of the lakes surrounded by a fringe of leaves, and creeks babbling at the bottom of coulees. But where, now, after half a century, are the trails through the bush and the paths I made? What has happened to my modest dwellings, which, when I opened the door, welcomed me as if to a palace? Probably bent like me beneath the weight of years, tired of waiting for me to return, they have fallen in like the one I found one day in a clearing near the Rockies as I wandered at will. Ah, the dumb pain of poor dead things. . . . And you, my friends, dear, loyal Clément, Perry the rancher, and Fitzgibbon, and you the Menuts, you, old Métis from Baptiste Creek, and you, Limping Jo, beneath what pine along the river did you make your last camp? Where do you all sleep, dear friends of my youth?

Now my life is drawing to an end, corseted by "civilization," where the struggle is as hard, harder, perhaps — since it takes place beneath a mask of hypocrisy and politeness — than in the almost unknown lands called "savage." But where are the "savages"? Over there in our great forests, we could come and go and walk with head held high, since the only thing that made us bend was the whip of the branches we bent back. But here, this debauchery of bowing down before Power of whatever kind, eternal fawners adoring the golden calf.

And should I say, as is carved in the stone of the wonderful sculptures of our jewel of Quercy in Montal, "No more hope"?[40] No more hope in the wisdom of mankind and peoples, no more hope in fraternity and human love, no more hope, in the evening of my life, to see the plough replace the cannon.

And in my memories, I go on dreaming, "in my garden, beneath my broad catalpa tree."

Farewell, My Canada

Farewell, my Canada; when to your shore
I sailed with hope and youthful confidence;
Like, in past days, a brave conquistador,
I sought a new found land's beneficence.

Farewell, my Canada of young fresh days,
For now I feel the weight of passing years.
No more the heady promise of new ways,
Now hope is dead and naught remains but tears.

Farewell you soaring aisles of greenery,
Where every spring all nature's shoots new rise,
Dark, holy, sanctuary of secret mystery
Where wind-blown organ music fills the skies.

No more on far trails lonely graves I'll see,
Mute witnesses of harsh and distant past:
Where some trapper, some prospector blindly
Was lost in Arctic snowstorms chill and vast.

No more will I see from my bright doorway
White pelicans make ripples on my lake.
No more — O! small dead creatures — see at play
The squirrels in the aspens as they quake.

I live in blushing consciousness of shame
At leaving you, a faithless lover, I,
And in my mouth an ashy taste of blame
Will linger through old age and till I die.

Dear land where eagerly in hope I trod
With love and deep regret I think on thee,
As in my garden on my native sod
I dream beneath my broad catalpa tree.

And like a palimpsest of tales retold
Found in an old, forgotten, musty drawer,
I'll read my memories inscribed in goldw
Of all my days in Canada of yore.

AFTERWORD

At the outbreak of World War I, Pierre Maturié enlisted in the French army. He was wounded twice at Verdun and resigned from the infantry to train as a pilot. He remained in the air force until the end of the war. During the war years, Pierre's and Armand's homesteads reverted to the Crown, and, on 15 February 1915, a certain Russell Dawson applied for possession of the former. He farmed it until 1919, when it was again sold. No price for the homestead is listed in the bill of sale, but the added improvements — house, barn, well, and roadways — were worth no more than $345.

Armand's property suffered the same fate. Returned to the Crown, it was claimed in June 1915 by one Jackson Foster. Shortly afterwards, however, on 29 October, Foster signed a declaration of abandonment, giving as the reason: "There is too much muskeg on the land." In their choice of homesteads, Pierre and his brothers-in-law had perhaps been somewhat naïve. Even if the concessions were located on a picturesque site overlooking the Athabasca River, the terrain was too uneven, and the soil was too sandy. Moreover, the land was traversed by streams and dotted with numerous ponds, rendering large areas of it unsuitable for cultivation. Of course, it was winter when they arrived, and they were unfamiliar with the landscape. In addition, they may have been influenced by questionable claims heralding Athabasca's potential as a future big city. At the same time, other areas to the north were opening up vast tracts to colonization and offered an attractive future to anyone determined to succeed. This may explain why, after the war, Pierre Maturié settled further north, in Peace River, where, as a war veteran, he had homesteading rights.

Maturié returned in 1919 with his wife, Marie-Louise Roche, the "blond girl" of the memoir, and brought his parents along as well. His brother-in-law Armand Brunie also returned with his wife and son. Still determined to become a rancher, Maturié settled on a property alongside the Peace River, where he raised cattle and ran a business in partnership with Armand — the Brunie & Maturié Fur Co. Limited, which had offices in Paris, Plamondon, and Peace River. Marguerite Brunie opened a ladies' dress shop, Le Chic Parisien, on Jasper Avenue in Edmonton.

There is, unfortunately, scant record of the second stay, for Maturié never found time to write about that period, as he'd planned. We do know that his first daughter, Jeannine, was born in Peace River in 1920 and that Maturié made friends with the local parish priest, Joseph Le Treste, a friendship documented in their correspondence. The exact date of the family's return to France is not known, but Maturié's second daughter, Francine, was born in Marseille in 1928. Prior to the outbreak of World War II, Maturié was involved in various business enterprises and also worked for an insurance company. During the war, he was active in the French Resistance and distributed their publications in Bordeaux. His work in helping American pilots shot down over France escape to Spain was recognized by General Eisenhower, acting on behalf of the president of the United States.

Gilles Cadrin

PREFACE TO THE ORIGINAL FRENCH EDITION (1972)

The name of Pierre Maturié is associated with the earliest days of my childhood: he was one of my brother's friends. Before I even knew the meaning of the word "adventure" or the name Canada, I learned through my brother that Pierre Maturié and his two young friends had lived a life of adventure in lands far from our native Brive.

Today (and I prefer not to say how many years later), as I read the manuscript of *Athabasca, Terre de ma jeunesse,* I discover with great astonishment the nature of that adventure, and what life was like in the vast spaces of the Canadian West. It all had echoes, if not of the novels by Gustave Aimard, then at least of those by Jack London, or, perhaps better, those of Louis-Frédéric Rouquette.[1] What a novel Pierre Maturié could have written if he hadn't chosen to write a straightforward memoir! Though in fact, his recollections, from the very moment he left France, are no less gripping than the plot of a novel, and there's no lack of suspense — which stretches over several episodes. It could all be resuméd in one sentence: "Will the three young pioneers succeed?"

That's the question we ask ourselves as we turn the pages, and it's a question that would make us race through the book to find out the end if the author's skill hadn't been sufficient to capture our attention with the many details that give us pause for thought and the desire to dream long dreams. How many subjects of reflection he offers! The splendour of untamed nature, man's steadfast industry and patient determination to force this nature into submission, to bring it to life. What we have here is nothing less than the primordial struggle, and we have the impression of being taken back to prehistoric times. Everything had to be made from scratch: not only shelter and a house, but also all the materials to create them: trees felled to build the frame, trunks stripped to raise the walls. Little by little the house rises and is completed, only to be destroyed by fire.

Despite this disaster and many other dramatic or absurd misadventures, Pierre Maturié managed to complete his project. The war of 1914–18 brought it to an abrupt end. Those terrible years still couldn't erase the memories and the fascination of Canada which made our author so nostalgic. In 1919, after his marriage to one of my sister's most charming friends, he returned, as he describes in a brief epilogue. And he adds: "I won't speak now in this modest work about the second stay, which will perhaps be the subject of a second book, if the great Kise-Manitou gives me time."

Let us hope that the time will indeed be granted him, and that a second volume will complete this account so full of life and action, but also of pure poetry; the account where both are so well adapted to the savage grandeur of nature and the nobility of man.

Robert Margerit

NOTES

Preface

1   Janey Canuck [Emily Murphy], *Seeds of Pine* (London, New York, and Toronto: Hodder and Stoughton, 1914), 113.

2   David Gregory, *Athabasca Landing: An Illustrated History* (Athabasca, AB: Athabasca Historical Society, 1986), 96.

3   Louis Lambillotte (1796–1855) was a Belgian Jesuit priest who spent the greater part of his life as an organist in Paris. In addition to being a composer of numerous masses, cantatas, and other religious pieces, he made an intensive study of Gregorian chant and was responsible for bringing obscure manuscripts to the attention of his contemporaries. Lambillotte's own works were thought to be somewhat avant-garde, which suggests that someone at St. Gabriel's Church, possibly the choirmaster, had fairly sophisticated taste in choral church music.

4   Gregory, *Athabasca Landing*, 141.

5   Canuck, *Seeds of Pine*, 116.

Introduction

1   Gerald Friesen, *The Canadian Prairies: A History* (Toronto: University of Toronto Press, 1983), 59.

2   Quoted in David Gregory, *Athabasca Landing: An Illustrated History* (Athabasca, AB: Athabasca Historical Society, 1986), 34.

3   Patricia A. McCormack, *Fort Chipewyan and the Shaping of Canadian History, 1788–1920s: "We like to be free in this country"* (Vancouver: University of British Columbia Press, 2010), 109–10.

4   McCormack, *Fort Chipewyan*, 97, quoting *Fort Saskatchewan Weekly Reports*, 31 May 1897, LAC, RG 18, v. 128; *Edmonton Bulletin*, "Local," 3 June 1897.

5   McCormack, *Fort Chipewyan*, 62.

6   Arthur I. Silver, *The French-Canadian Idea of Confederation, 1864–1900* (Toronto: University of Toronto Press, 1985), 12.

7   Friesen, *The Canadian Prairies*, 260.

8   In 1890, Manitoba passed the Public Schools Act, which terminated public funding for denominational schools (Catholic and Protestant). The same year, the provincial government also ended the use of the French language in the Manitoba courts and legislature. The territorial assembly followed suit in

1892, although the right to French-language schooling was partially restored in 1901. In an effort to solve the Schools Question, Manitoba reinstated the use of French as a language of instruction in the schools in 1897, as part of the Laurier-Greenway Compromise, only to abolish it again in 1916. A similar trend was evident in the other Prairie provinces. Saskatchewan curtailed the use of French in schools in 1918 and eliminated it completely in 1931. As of 1913, Alberta permitted only limited use of French in schools.

9   Friesen, *The Canadian Prairies,* 258–59.

10 Quoted in Friesen, *The Canadian Prairies,* 258–59, citing Arthur I. Silver, "French Canada and the Prairie Frontier, 1870–90," *Canadian Historical Review* 50, no. 1 (March 1969): 11–36.

11 Quoted in Friesen, *The Canadian Prairies,* 258–59, citing Robert Painchaud, "French Canadian Historiography and Franco-Canadian Settlement in Western Canada, 1870–1915," *Canadian Historical Review* 54, no. 4 (1978): 447–66.

12 Friesen, *The Canadian Prairies,* 259–60.

13 McCormack, *Fort Chipewyan,* 159.

14 Quoted in McCormack, *Fort Chipewyan,* 202.

15 Observations on Athabasca in 1908 by Agnes Deans Cameron, quoted in Gregory, *Athabasca Landing,* 152.

16 McCormack, *Fort Chipewyan,* 221.

17 "Agriculture and Settlement, 1909–1914," *Athabasca Landing: Gateway to the North* website, http://athabascalanding.athabascau.ca/html/agriculture/index.htm.

18 David Gregory, "Athabasca Landing," *The Canadian Encyclopedia,* http://www.thecanadianencyclopedia.com/articles/athabasca-landing.

19 Robert Service, *Ploughman of the Moon: An Adventure into Memory* (New York: Dodd, Mead and Company, 1945), 408–9.

20 "Agriculture and Settlement, 1909–1914."

21 Ibid.

22 Ibid.

23 Agnes Deans Cameron, quoted in Gregory, *Athabasca Landing,* 152.

24 Friesen, *The Canadian Prairies,* 303–4.

25 Neil Sutherland, *Children in English Canadian Society: Framing the Twentieth-Century Consensus* (Toronto: University of Toronto Press, 1978 [1976]), xi.

26 Friesen, *The Canadian Prairies,* 319.

27 "The Commercial Boom, 1912–1914," *Athabasca Landing: Gateway to the North* website, http://www.collectionscanada.gc.ca/eppp-archive/100/200/301/ic/can_digital_collections/athabasca/html/commboom/index.htm.

28 Friesen, *The Canadian Prairies,* 311–12.

Man Proposes, God Disposes

Most of the following notes were supplied by Gilles Cadrin, who has conducted extensive research on the history of northern Alberta. The few that are my own are clearly identified.—*Trans.*

1   Henri Giroux (1869–1956) was a priest who served primarily in Saskatchewan and northern Alberta, where he welcomed settlers to Catholic parishes. Donnelly, Girouxville, Guy, and Jean Côté remain francophone parishes in Alberta to this day.

2   Armand Brunie met Philippe Roy (1866–1948) when Roy was still a Senator, representing northern Alberta. Born in Saint-François de Montmagny, Roy studied medicine at Université Laval in Québec and ophthalmology in Paris. He settled in Edmonton in 1898 and immediately became involved in the political struggles of the future Province of Alberta, which entered into Confederation in 1905.

It was in October of the same year that, together with P.-E. Lessard, Roy founded *Le Courrier de l'Ouest*, where he was editor-in-chief. This weekly publication, which openly supported the Liberal Party, sought to establish ties between the francophone communities of the West and to make these communities known in eastern Canada and the French-speaking countries of Europe, with a view to promoting economic development and colonization in Alberta. With the same end in view, Roy helped create the new Société de colonisation de l'Alberta, which in 1907 became the Société de colonisation et de repatriement.

Named Senator by Prime Minister Wilfrid Laurier in 1906, not only in recognition of his social commitment and political gifts but also to give a voice to Western francophones, Roy was a noteworthy presence in the House of Commons as soon as he entered it in November 1906. In response to the Speech from the Throne, he reaffirmed the two poles of his commitment: an energetic policy of economic development for the West and an aggressive policy of immigration, without any misleading publicity.

After founding, in March 1907, the real estate and financial company Jasper's Limited (with, among other shareholders, Léon Bureau, in Versailles), Roy appealed to some of Europe's great capitalists for funds to stimulate development in the West. With this goal in mind, he stayed in Paris from January to April 1909 and again from July to August. He was there once again in December, and in April 1910 he succeeded in setting up the Canadian Mortgage Association, which had its headquarters in Paris and its executive offices in Winnipeg.

In addition to soliciting capital, Roy led an active campaign to recruit immigrants. It was probably in his capacity as a financial inspector for an insurance company that Armand Brunie met Roy at social events in the Canadian High Commission in Paris. In May 1911, Roy was named to the post of Canadian High Commissioner in Paris, replacing Hector Fabre.

3   Baron Edmond de Mandat-Grancey (1842–1911) was a world traveller who, after a military career, wrote articles about his journeys for the French press. His accounts of life on ranches in America and Canada filled disillusioned Europeans with hopes for a better life on the new continent, although with his comment that emigration is "meat to the strong but poison to the weak," he tried to dissuade those whose thoughts turned to such a possibility all too hastily. In speaking of Canada, he mentions the "terrifying cold" and claims that agriculture had been abandoned in certain places because the blackflies drove people mad. His assertion that the Canadian government was more sympathetic to immigrant ranchers than its American counterpart caused our author and his brothers-in-law to describe their ambition as "ranchers" on the passenger list of the *Victorian*.

4   James Fenimore Cooper (1789–1851) was an American writer who, through novels such as *The Pioneers* (1823) and *The Last of the Mohicans* (1826), provided an iconic description of western frontier life to a whole generation of readers on both sides of the Atlantic. Irish writer Mayne Reid (1818–83) travelled to the United States in 1840, where he worked as a businessman in New York City and subsequently fought in the Mexican-American War (1846–48). When he returned to Ireland, he wrote a series of popular novels with titles like *The Rifle Rangers* and *The Scalp Hunters* that were precursors of the western novel.

5   Albert Lacombe was one of the most highly respected of the Oblate Fathers in the Canadian West. Born in Saint-Sulpice, Québec, in 1927 and ordained priest in 1849, he came to Red River in 1852 to serve under Bishop Alexandre Taché. In 1853 he was sent to Lac Ste. Anne and in 1856 joined the congregation of the Oblats de Marie Immaculée. He ministered to the Cree, learning their language and publishing a grammar and a dictionary. In hopes of encouraging them to settle, he urged them to move to the colony of St. Albert, which he founded in 1861. After 1864, he turned his attention to converting the Blackfoot of southern Alberta, where, thanks to his authority, peace was established between them and the Cree. It was also thanks to his intervention that the Blackfoot allowed the Canadian Pacific Railroad to pass through their lands in 1883, and in 1885 it was Father Lacombe who was responsible for the neutrality of the Plains Indians during the Northwest Rebellion.

He was an itinerant missionary for some years and founded several schools throughout the West. His recruitment campaigns in Québec, the United States, and Europe made him a major force in the settling of the Prairies. He died in 1916 in the Foyer Lacombe, Midnapore, a home for the aged that he had founded.

The principal source of information about the Oblate missionaries in western Canada is Gaston Carrière, OMI, *Dictionnaire biographique des Oblats de Marie-Immaculée au Canada,* 3 vols. (Ottawa: Éditions de l'Université d'Ottawa, 1976–79). See also Paul-Émile Breton, OMI, *Le Grand Chef des Prairies* (Edmonton: Éditions de l'Ermitage, 1954), and *The Big Chief of the Prairies* (Montréal: Palm Publishers, [1955]).

6   It was only the whites, of course, who left the carcasses to rot. The Aboriginal population killed the buffalo only when they needed to and used used all parts of the animal, on which they had always depended for food, clothing, housing, domestic implements, and decoration.—*Trans.*

7   The Lac La Biche region was already known in France because of the Notre-Dame-des-Victoires mission established there in 1853 by the Oblates to serve the First Nations peoples and the Métis. Designated as the seat of the apostolic vicariate of Athabasca-Mackenzie in 1869, the mission gained importance as a distribution centre for goods going to the missions in the North, including the wheat produced there in commercial quantities from the beginning of the 1860s. The success of this enterprise demonstrated that northern Alberta was capable of supporting an agricultural economy, despite the risk of early frost. But large-scale cultivation did not begin immediately around the mission until World War I, as settlers preferred to colonize the area west of the mission. Thus was founded the village of Plamondon in 1909, when Joseph and Narcisse Plamondon brought their families and several French Canadians to the region from Provemont, Michigan.

It wasn't until 1912–14 that French Canadians, led by Father J. A. Ouellette, began to settle in Lac La Biche. During these years before the war, settlers continued to arrive from Québec, the United States, and Europe. Several parishes with French names came into being in the region: Grandin, Gourin, Normandeau, Breynat, Berny, Charron, and Donatville, for example. But in 1910, it was Athabasca that profited from a publicity drive, which probably influenced the decision of Maturié and the Brunie brothers.

8   A "democrat" was a kind of simple, light, horse-drawn buggy that, in Canada, was outfitted with runners instead of wheels in the winter. Its name testifies to the vehicle's ubiquity.

9   On November 3, 1757, the French army, under the command of the Prince of Soubise, suffered a crushing defeat against Frederick II of Prussia at the Battle of Rosbach. One of the mocking jingles that Soubise's enemies chortled on his return to France might be translated:

Said the Price of Soubise, his lantern in his hand,
"I've lost my army—where is that gallant band?
But yester morn I saw them fine arrayed
But now today, oh whither have they strayed?
Where did I, absent-minded, leave my men?
Ah, here they are! I've got them back again!
Praise be!—But wait! That's not *my* army that I see.
Oh, no! This is the cursed enemy!"—*Trans.*

10   The arrival of the first paddle steamer, the *Northcote*, in Edmonton in 1877 demonstrated that goods could be transported from St. Boniface via the North Saskatchewan River. No longer dependent on the Churchill River to supply the valleys of the Mackenzie and the Peace rivers, the Hudson's Bay Company was interested in finding a new route, one that would link the North Saskatchewan and Athabasca rivers, thereby allowing them to take advantage of Edmonton's newly acquired importance. This route, known as the Athabasca Trail, was established by the Hudson's Bay Company in 1877.

11   At the beginning of the twentieth century, Révillon Frères was the biggest fur-trading company in the world. Its origins go back to the Maison Givelet, founded in Paris in 1723, which Louis-Victor Révillon acquired in 1829. The company expanded to North America, and Edmonton was its largest centre in Canada. The Révillon Building, built in 1912–13, still stands at the corner of 104th Street and 102nd Avenue in Edmonton, a historic relic of the firm's earlier importance.

12   Ernest Servestre had worked as a miner in France and had come to Canada to work in mines in southwestern Alberta, where some mining companies, like the West Canadian Collieries, were owned by French people. Thanks to the recruiting efforts of these companies in Europe, there was a substantial population of French and Belgians in towns such as Bellevue, Blairmore, Coleman, and Lille. When he arrived in Athabasca, Servestre first worked as a receptionist in the Grand Union Hotel and went on cultivating the land to which he obtained title in 1912. This land was three miles west of Athabasca on the road to Baptiste Lake, a mere four miles from the property where Pierre Maturié and the Brunie brothers settled.

13   Joseph Olivier was originally from Saint-Agapit, Québec. According to *Le Courrier de l'Ouest* of 2 February 1911, he came west as part of a group of people from Saint-Nicholas, Saint-Agapit, and Charny led by a Monsieur and Madame Gagnon. When he set up in practice, he filled the need for a francophone doctor that had been created in 1908 when Dr. Joseph Boulanger left for Lesser Slave Lake.

Keenly interested in agriculture, he settled on a homestead west of Athabasca, where he kept the horses he rode to go to the hospital and to visit his patients. An announcement in the *Northern News* noted that he had opened an office in the I. Gagnon Block (so named for one of the town's prominent citizens). In August 1911, according to *Le Courrier de l'Ouest*, he went to Calgary to sit the exams that would qualify him to practice in the province.

His arrival in Athabasca coincided with the construction of the Sacred Heart Hospital of the Sisters of Providence. He was an enthusiastic promoter of this hospital and contributed to the planning of a modern operating theatre and to the purchase of sterilizing equipment. In April 1913, he married Dorothy Johnson, a nurse at the hospital. *Le Courrier de l'Ouest* reported that the entire population of Athabasca turned out for a celebration in his honour on the eve of the wedding.

When war broke out, he was initially assigned the rank of captain and spent the war years training volunteers for the front. In December 1915 he left the Athabasca region for Coleman, a township near Blairmore that had been founded in 1903 to service a new coal mine. Coleman suffered from strikes and floods in the early part of the century, however, and as the coal industry declined, its importance waned.

14   J. Léonce Lessard was born in Cranbourne, Québec, and came west in 1901. He was a partner in the firm of Gariépy and Lessard in Edmonton and in January 1907 opened the first store in Athabasca Landing, Lessard's Trading Store. The following year, *Le Courrier de l'Ouest* announced on 6 February that Lessard had begun to build a new store. Over time, his commercial activities extended as far as Fort Chipewyan. Deeply involved in public affairs, he was a councillor in the Liberal Club, secretary of the French Academy of Athabasca Landing, and member of the municipal council. He built his last store, the Lessard Department Store, in 1928 just before his death in 1929.

15   Isaïe Gagnon was a businessman who made an enormous contribution to the economic development of Athabasca Landing and was always anxious to promote French-Canadian interests there. He arrived in the 1890s, and upon seeing the numbers of people who were travelling on the Athabasca Trail, either to work for the Hudson's Bay Company or to go on to the North, he realized that there was a need for a hotel. He began with a modest boarding house and a hiring stable.

After a brief stay in St. Albert, where he oversaw the building of a bridge and was elected president of the St. Albert Liberal Association, he returned to Athabasca, where he became owner of extensive lands and a sawmill, as well as the Grand Union Hotel. He took particular satisfaction in the number of French Canadians who arrived in Athabasca and, as one of the directors of the Chamber of Commerce, went to Québec to recruit new citizens and returned with, among other people, Dr. Joseph Olivier.

Most of his property went up in flames in the great fire of 5 August 1913. He still owned the sawmill, but the combination of World War I and the fact that the railroad bypassed Athabasca on the way to Fort McMurray and Peace River put an end to the town's pretensions to expansion (David Gregory, *Athabasca Landing: An Illustrated History* [Athabasca, AB: Athabasca Historical Society, 1986], 41, 125–26, 143).

16   Father Alphonse Desmarais was born in Saint-Damase, Québec, and entered the service of the Athabasca-Mackenzie apostolic mission in 1884 after his ordination in the Oblate order. He served first in Dunvegan and then in Lac La Biche, where he taught for three years and began construction of a convent in 1890. In addition to time spent in Edmonton, the Yukon, and Grouard, he founded missions in Grande Prairie, Saint-Bruno, and

Colinton. When he arrived in Athabasca, he had to call upon his building talents to enlarge St. Gabriel's Church, which had been built in 1906 by Father Beaudry and was no longer big enough for the needs of the 260-odd French Canadians, Irish, and Métis who worshipped there, together with the people from Baptiste Lake and Pine Creek (Carrière, *Dictionnaire biographique des Oblats*, 1:219–21; "Noces d'or du R. P. A. Desmarais, O.M.I. à Athabasca," *La Survivance* [Edmonton], 19 April 1934).

17 Sidore Lafleur was born in St. Albert in the mission founded in 1861 by Father Lacombe to serve the large number of Métis who lived a nomadic life ranging over Manitoba and Alberta. The Oblates hoped to transform the Métis into farmers by grouping them together. With its church, school, and hospital, St. Albert became a centre for francophone Métis, until by 1878 they formed the large majority of the population. In 1890, out of a population of 1,000, 860 were Métis, 120 French or French Canadians, and 20 English. But the massive influx of white people from various places of origin reduced the Métis to a status of inferiority, especially on an economic and social level.

In response to this situation, a new colony was created, which would become Saint-Paul-des-Métis. Sidore Lafleur was one of the independent-minded Métis who moved to the Lac La Biche mission, which had been founded in 1853 to serve the few hundreds of Métis and First Nations people in the area. After his marriage, he moved to Baptiste Lake and made a living trading horses, fishing, and trapping.

18 In the 1880s, a group of Métis from Saskatchewan founded a settlement on Baptiste Lake, which was named after Baptiste Majeau, one of the early settlers in the area (*Atlas of Alberta Lakes*, ed. Patricia Mitchell and Ellie Prepas [Edmonton: University of Alberta Press, 1990], 122). Baptiste Creek, which flowed out of the lake, ran through Maturié's property.

19 Jo Tobaty arrived in Athabasca Landing in the late 1890s. He became part of local folklore on account of the prodigious yield he got from his crops, which allowed him to supply oats to the transport teams arriving from Edmonton or leaving for the North. Reports of his successful farming published in the *Northern News* fuelled propaganda for the Athabasca region. He returned to France in 1914.

20 Joseph Daigneau arrived in Athabasca during the gold rush that, in the space of a single year, increased the population of Athabasca from some forty to fifty souls, in 1897, to about a thousand fortune seekers from the four corners of the earth, in 1898. These men lived in tents before moving on in the spring to Dawson City. Although the town's population dwindled after the end of the gold rush in 1899, Athabasca maintained its importance as a gateway to the Northwest and as a distribution hub for the Mackenzie and Peace rivers. Realizing its potential, Daigneau bought a homestead in 1907. He used his carpentry skills in various building projects (St. Gabriel's

Church, the Sacred Heart Hospital, the Daigneau Block), and as the owner of a hiring stable, a dairy, and a farm implement store, he became a successful businessman. He also farmed on his own homestead.

21 Maturié is mistaken here. These nuns were actually Sisters of Providence, a community founded in Montréal in 1843 by Émilie Tavernier-Gamelin as a teaching and nursing order. (The Grey Nuns were members of the Order of Sisters of Charity of Montréal, founded by Marguerite d'Youville.) It wasn't until 1890 that the first nuns arrived in the West, first in British Columbia, then in Alberta in 1894 in the Grouard mission. Subsequently, they were to be found in the whole province, from Fort Vermilion in the north to Cluny in the south. In 1908, they answered Monseigneur Émile Legal's invitation to work in Athabasca. There they were welcomed by Isaïe Gagnon, who gave over to them the top floor of his boarding house. They began nursing the sick until the construction of a ten-bed hospital in 1911–12. The Sisters of Providence continued tending the sick of Athabasca and the surrounding region in the Sacred Heart Hospital as they went on with their missionary work. When the hospital burned down in 1916, the local economy could not support reconstruction. The Sisters of Providence left Athabasca that year (Hortense Quesnelle, S.P., "Hôpital Sacré-Coeur, Athabasca Landing, Alberta, 18 octobre 1907–8 octobre 1916: Précis des chroniques" [unpublished manuscript]).

22 Auguste Tito-Landi (1873–1947) was born in Italy but became established in France as an inventor and a seller of lamps and various pieces of kitchen equipment, with a large establishment on the Boulevard Henri IV in Paris. The patent for his spirit or petrol lamp (his lamps never used kerosene) was issued in Switzerland in 1898. Among his many inventions was an alloy of metals that allowed for better heat conduction and a long key for regulating the flame of the lamp, which kept the hand at a safe distance from the heat. Had Maturié been writing a little later, he could have enjoyed the benefits of the Tito-Landi camping stove, forerunner of the Coleman stove. The Tito-Landi business survived in Paris for twenty years after the death of its founder. Although the lamps have been dismantled over the years and turned into flower pots and various other domestic ornaments, some are now collectors' items and can even be found on eBay.—*Trans.*

23 Captain Schott was a picturesque person whose real name was Louison Fosseneuve. A Métis, son of a voyageur family, he was popularly believed to have been the first to brave the rapids of the Athabasca River to ferry a group of Grey Nuns from Lac La Biche to Fort Chipewyan. He acquired the nickname in 1883–85 when he demonstrated to the Hudson's Bay Company that goods could be transported by barge between Athabasca and Fort McMurray despite the dangerous rapids. He was famous for his courage, daring, and knowledge of the Athabasca and had become a legend, which made him a much-sought-after guide (Gregory, *Athabasca Landing*, 24, 155).

24   There were, of course, no "Royal Mounted Police." In 1904, the North-West Mounted Police (NWMP) became the Royal Northwest Mounted Police (RNWMP) and then, in 1920, the Royal Canadian Mounted Police (RCMP).—*Trans.*

25   Peter Perry was an Acadian, born in New Brunswick in 1862, which explains why he spoke French with the accent characteristic of Berry, a rich agricultural region in central France. (The province of Berry existed until the time of the French Revolution; today, the area is roughly equivalent to the *départements* of Cher and Indre.) According to Acadian writer and scholar Antonine Maillet, such an accent is typical of the Acadians, who came originally from central France. When Perry was still growing up, his family moved to Providence, Rhode Island, but at the age of eighteen he made his way to Montana, where he raised sheep. In 1909, he returned to Canada with his wife and settled in Athabasca.

26   Prosper-Edmond Lessard, one of the first French Canadians to hold office in the Alberta government, was elected to the legislature in 1909, representing the St. Paul riding. He was named minister without portfolio. In that election, the second in the new province, Lucien Boudreau, from St. Albert, and Jean-Léon Côté, from Athabasca, also won office, and thus began the tradition of always having at least one French Canadian in the Alberta government.

Originally from Cranbourne, Québec, Lessard arrived in Edmonton in 1898 after finishing his studies at the Collège du Mont Saint-Louis in Montréal. His first job was as cashier in a store of which he became the owner three years later. Very active in public life, he was one of the directors of the Board of Trade, commissioner of the Edmonton Separate School Board, and president of the Liberal Association of Alberta. *Le Courrier de l'Ouest* of 28 October 1909 described him as one of the most accomplished citizens, extremely popular both with French and English speakers. He kept up his business interests in Edmonton while in office and continued to represent the riding of St. Paul until 1921. He was named to the Canadian Senate in 1925.

27   Marius is a common name in Marseille—witness the eponymous character in Marcel Pagnol's play. The Canebière is the main street leading down to the port in Marseille. At the many cafés, the drink of choice is pastis, which, like Greek ouzo, is an anise-based apéritif.—*Trans.*

28   Édouard Pétour was born in France in 1877 in Mont-Dol. He was ordained priest in 1902 and in 1903 began a life as Oblate missionary in the Canadian West. He was active for over thirty years in northern Alberta, mainly in Grouard, Desmarais, and Sawridge. In 1912 and 1913 he worked on the construction of the residential school at the Saint-Bruno mission on the south shore of Lesser Slave Lake. The arrival of the railroad in 1914 brought many French Canadians to the region and gave rise to the village

of Joussard, named after Bishop Joussard. Father Pétour founded High Prairie in 1916 and was responsible for the building of several churches in northern Alberta. In death notices in 1935, he was recognized as "a great missionary" (Carrière, *Dictionnaire biographique des Oblats*, 3:70–71).

29 Monseigneur Émile Grouard was a towering figure in the church history of the Northwest on account of his linguistic and artistic endeavours and his social commitment as bishop. He came to Canada from France in 1860 at the suggestion of his cousin, Monseigneur Vital Grandin. Ordained in 1862, he entered the Oblate order in 1863. He served as priest among several northern First Nations and contributed to the expansion of the church in northern Alberta, which was just being opened up to colonization.

In 1890 he became bishop of the diocese of Athabasca-Mackenzie. When the two districts were split in 1901, he moved to the episcopal seat at Grouard, which, because of its site on the route to Grande Prairie, Peace River, and the North, was a place of great promise. In 1923, he published his memoir, *Souvenirs de mes soixante ans d'apostolat dans l'Athabaska-Mackenzie* (Carrière, *Dictionnaire biographique des Oblats,* 2:116–17).

Monseigneur Vital Grandin, by whom Grouard was ordained, was one of the most revered bishops of northwestern Canada. Born in France in 1829, he entered the Oblate order in 1854 and came to St. Boniface the same year. The following year he was sent to the Mission of the Nativity in Fort Chipewyan and in 1857 to Île-à-la-Crosse. In 1861, he made a long reconnaissance journey in the Mackenzie Basin with a view to founding a vicariate in the region. In 1871, he was named bishop of the newly created diocese of St. Albert, where he supported the Métis both before and after the 1885 rebellion. The Canadian government licensed him to create schools and orphanages for the First Nations. He raised funds in Europe and in eastern Canada for his diocese, campaigns that were always accompanied by recruiting attempts for new settlers (Carrière, *Dictionnaire biographique des Oblats,* 2:106–7; Paul-Émile Breton, OMI, *Vital Grandin: La merveilleuse aventure de l'Éveque des Prairies et du Grand Nord* [Paris: Arthème Fayard, 1960]).

30 The House of Bourbon was the last ruling dynasty of France. The first of the Bourbon monarchs was Henri IV (1589–1610), and the family continued to rule until 1793, when Louis XVI was guillotined. Following Napoleon's abdication in 1814, the dynasty was restored to power and survived until the Revolution of 1848, which ended the reign of Louis-Philippe, duke of Orléans, the last of the Bourbon kings.—*Trans.*

31 Jim K. Cornwall came to Athabasca during the gold rush but remained there instead of continuing on to the Klondike. He worked first as pilot and guide on the Athabasca River and then as a fur trader. In 1904, he sold out to Révillon Frères and sank the proceeds into the Northern Transportation Company. Soon his steamships had a monopoly on passenger and freight traffic to and from Fort McMurray. A shrewd businessman, he foresaw

the economic decline of Athabasca and moved his headquarters to Fort McMurray in 1914.

Drawn to politics in 1905, he stood as Liberal candidate in the first general election in Alberta. He lost to the lawyer Lucien Dubuc but in 1909 was elected by acclamation for Peace River. His colourful personality earned him the nickname "Peace River Jim" (*From Out of the Wilderness: A History of Baptiste Lake, Deep Coulee, Forfar, Forfar East, Forfar West, Fraternity, Grosmont, Lahaieville, Larvert, South Athabasca, West Athabasca and Winding Trail School Districts* [Athabasca, AB: Eight Horizons Historical Society, 1986]).

32 Colin Fraser was the son of a Scotsman of the same name who had been a Hudson's Bay employee at posts in Jasper House, Fort Assiniboine, and Lac La Biche. The older Colin Fraser had been personal assistant to the explorer George Simpson and had had twelve children. His son Colin, born in Jasper House in 1849, followed in his father's footsteps as a guide until he moved to Fort Edmonton to work for the factor J. W. Christie. He bought a homestead in Edmonton, but as whites flocked in, he left for the area of Lake Athabasca, where he became a fur trader. He lived in Fort Chipewyan until his death in 1941.

33 The community of Grey Nuns was founded in Montréal in 1737 by Marguerite d'Youville with the aim of providing hospital care and education. The first nuns in the West came to St. Boniface in 1844, summoned by Monseigneur Provencher. Twenty years later, they arrived in St. Albert after spending five years in the Lac Ste. Anne mission. They subsequently opened roughly a dozen schools, orphanages, and hospitals in the Athabasca-Mackenzie vicariate. In Athabasca, however, it was the Sisters of Providence who ran the hospital.

34 Maturié refers here to the luxurious outdoor dining offered at Courchevel, the tony ski resort in the French Alps.—*Trans.*

35 A Provençal song: "O, Magali, My Dear Love." Magali is a common name for women in Provence.—*Trans.*

36 Jean de La Fontaine (1621–1695) is best known for his collection of fables. La Fontaine's line is "Je plie et ne romps pas" ("I bend but do not break"), from *Fables,* Book I, no. 22, "Le chêne et le roseau" ("The Oak and the Reed").—*Trans.*

37 The reference is to La Fontaine, *Fables,* Book VI, no. 17, "Le chien qui lâche sa proie pour l'ombre" ("The Dog Who Dropped His Prey for the Sake of Its Shadow").—*Trans.*

38 Both regions of France are famous for their loquacious boasters.—*Trans.*

39 A reference to the old saying: "For want of a nail, the shoe was lost; for want of a shoe, the horse was lost; for want of a horse, the rider was lost; for want of a rider, the battle was lost; for want of a battle, the war was lost; and all for the want of a horseshoe nail."—*Trans.*

40 The château of Montal, in the Lot, is indeed recognized as one of the glories of the old province of Quercy. Originally a medieval country house, it was transformed early in the sixteenth century (1519 to 1534) into a fashionable Rennaissance-style castle by Jeanne de Balzac. Legend has it that when her husband died and her son fell in the Italian Wars, she had inscribed over the entrance the motto "Plus d'espoir" ("No more hope"). The building fell into ruins, and its treasures were widely dispersed at the end of the nineteenth century. In 1908, it was acquired by a rich industrialist, who bought back all the original appurtenances or had them copied. By the time Maturié was in Canada, restoration was complete, and in 1913 the building was donated to the French state as a national monument. During World War II, Leonardo da Vinci's *Mona Lisa* was secretly stored there.—*Trans.*

Preface to the Original French Edition (1972)

1 Gustave Aimard (1818–1883) was a French writer whose journeys in the American West in the early nineteenth century provided material for some of his ninety or so novels. *Trappeurs de l'Arkansas* (1858) was an immediate success, and many of his other novels that featured Frenchmen and Canadians in the American West were bestsellers in Europe and also in French Canada. Jack London (1876–1916) is best known for *The Call of the Wild* (1903) and *White Fang* (1906), both of which take place in northern Canada and Alaska during the Klondike gold rush. Louis-Frédéric Rouquette (1884–1926) was an author, journalist, and diplomat. His novels of northern Canada focus on the sacrifices and selflessness of the Oblate missionaries, who suffer untold hardships to bring people to God.

A NOTE ON THE TYPE
This book was set in Sabon, designed by Jan Tschichold in the 1960s, and is based on French Renaissance-era typefaces by Claude Garamond and Jacques Sabon. The sans serif is Parisine Plus, created by Jean François Porchez and distributed by Typofonderie in France.